COMMUNITY AND ABBOT
IN
THE RULE OF ST BENEDICT

CISTERCIAN STUDIES SERIES: NUMBER FIVE / ONE

COMMUNITY AND ABBOT

IN

THE RULE OF ST BENEDICT

by

Adalbert de Vogüé
Monk of La Pierre-que-Vire

translated by

Charles Philippi
Monk of New Camaldoli

Cistercian Publications
Kalamazoo, Michigan

1979

Translated from the French *La Communauté et l'Abbé dans la Règle de saint Benoît* (Paris-Brussels: Desclée de Brouwer, 1961).

©English translation, Cistercian Publications, 1978

Edited by Ethel Rae Perkins

Cistercian Publications Inc.
WMU Station
Kalamazoo, Michigan 49008

Available in Great Britain and Europe from

A.R. Mowbray & Co Ltd	*Saint Thomas House*
Becket Street	*Oxford OX1 1SJ*

Library of Congress Cataloging in Publication Data

Vogüé, Adalbert de.
   Community and abbot in the rule of Saint Benedict.

   (Cistercian studies series; no. 5/1)
   Translation of La communauté et l'abbé dans la règle de saint Benoît.
   Bibliography: p
   1. Benedictus, Saint, Abbot of Monte Cassino. Regula.
I. Title. II. Series.
BX3004.Z5V613   255'.12'06   78-18312
ISBN 0-87907-905-3 (v. 1)

TABLE OF CONTENTS

Volume One

AUTHOR'S PREFACE TO THE ENGLISH EDITION

I F EVER A WORK had a chance of being suitably translated, it is certainly the present one. This is due not only to the value of the translator, but also to the close collaboration which has been possible between him and the author.

I thus accept in advance full responsibility for almost all that the reader will find fault with in these pages. Re-reading them at a ten year distance from their first publication, I find the most arresting thing, really, their non-contemporaneous character. Published on the eve of the Council, this study harmonizes little with the tendencies which moved Vatican II or which issued from it. Without having intended a reactionary work, I find that my analysis of the monastic community is not centered on the notion of communion and still less on that of collegiality. The final chapter, to be sure, recognizes in Benedict the merit of having complemented the Master's purely vertical schema with indications of horizontal relations. This chapter, as one might have expected, has been universally well received. But in the perspective traced by the first chapters, which remains the principal one, the abbot appears as the *raison d'être* of the community, pre-existent to it (at least notionally) and engendering it. The desire to submit oneself to his direction is given as the fundamental motive for cenobitic society, which is constituted essentially by the sum-total of personal relationships between the disciples and the one master. The *coenobium* is presented as an endeavor to organize spiritual fatherhood on a social scale.

The author was already conscious when propounding them that these theses savor of 'paternalism' and he has tried to offer opportune explanations. But he could not have reckoned how much more untimely they would seem in the post-conciliar period, when the reality of the people of God came into sharp focus throughout the entire Church. Taking hold in monasteries, this current of thought calls into question the hierarchic vision we believed present in the documents of tradition. It seems that the monastic

5

community, just as the ecclesiastical community, is now the prime reality, having value in itself and for its own sake, and that it ought to be thought of chiefly in terms of fraternal communion. Abbatial authority is only the first of the ministries which should guarantee its life and cohesion. On the practical level, abbots and communities have often modified their relationships. Abbots willingly efface themselves to leave the word to their subjects, either individually or assembled in committees. To grant clearance to the will of the majority seems to be the normal way of government. These democratic methods match a certain disaffection for the heritage of tradition. Docility to a spirit whose origin and purpose one does not know is substituted for fidelity to the norms of the past. Under such conditions, the abbot's role seems to be not so much to impose a rule upon his sons as to help his brethren define it.

To pass judgment on this movement, the amplitude and ambiguity of which escape no one, is not our task. What is important for us here is that it tends to modify profoundly the social and spiritual situation in which our study came to be produced. Certainly, this work did bear on literary data which we intended to analyse objectively. Yet no exegesis is wholly free of the presuppositions and preoccupations of the person who executes it. The present study has its roots in the experience of a young man who desired God. Aspiring to accomplish the divine will in truth and without illusion, he sought a master who could make it known to him. He expected above all, from the monastery he entered, sure guidance in the way of perfection. As sensitive as he was to fraternal communion, which was held in great honor in that monastery and in its novitiate, it was not this that had primarily attracted him, but rather the hope of an encounter with God through the mediation of his superiors and his rule. The community he entered presented itself as a fundamentally hierarchic society in which authority was strong and sure of its mission. To be sure, the observance practised there could not pretend to a strict conformity with the Rule of St Benedict, but reference to the Rule was taken to heart and remained serious. This alloy of spiritual tradition and personal authority, each sustaining the other and both uncontested, gave an impression of solidity. It was upon that more than anything else that the confidence of the postulant in question settled, believing and hoping as he did that God had proposed these means to him for receiving his oblation and imparting guidance to his good will.

Such is the existential setting in which this reflection on the community and the abbot was born. When the opportunity was offered me of preparing a thesis for a doctorate in theology, nothing seemed to me to be of such immediate interest as casting some light on the fundamental charter which ruled both my community and my own life. From the time of my novitiate, I had often asked myself how St Benedict could have grounded the authority of the abbot on the words of Christ: 'Anyone who listens to you listens to me.' This is probably the question which most stimulated the reflections from which these pages have issued. It oriented me from the outset toward the parallel between abbot and bishop, which I came to find in the Rule of the Master. The latter, however, was content to compare the abbot to a bishop, without stating clearly the basis for his office as 'teacher'. In this respect, the present work has not elucidated the Master's thought as much as it might have done. It is not sufficient to have ascertained that the ancient Church, notably through the voice of Gregory the Great, recognized in abbots, even though laymen, the power to preach or to bind and loose.[1] The existence of such charisms, directly imparted by the Holy Spirit to the heads of monastic communities, is doubtless not what serves as the immediate grounds, in the Master's eyes, for the quasi-episcopal authority of the abbot. As I have explained more recently, the immediate ground is rather the rite whereby the bishop 'ordains' the abbot.[2]

This explanation, which to me seems irrefutable on the level of exegesis of the Master's thought, does not entail a complete revision of the theory of the abbacy as set forth in the present volume. It only calls for a modification of certain expressions which present the investiture of abbots as the work of the Holy Spirit acting simply and immediately through the conferring of a charism.[3] In reality, although the abbots of the monasteries of the Master were indeed simple laymen, and although their authority was not based on a *sacerdotal* ordination, they did however receive their abbatial and doctoral power from the bishop in quasi-sacramental fashion. Prior to this 'ordination' it remained true that the nomination of the new by the former abbot, who ought to have perceived in him his best disciple, found its ultimate grounds in the spiritual caliber of the person. Still the Master thought of this quality not as a charism, but as a perfection acquired by effort, a superiority in the exercise of virtues.[4]

I have indicated two of the major sources of this work: a certain

individual and communitarian experience on the one hand, and
on the other the theses of the Master on the abbacy. Their con-
vergent influence had already suggested to me that the monastic
community is first of all a school which one enters to listen to a
master speaking in the name of God. But another current joined
these two, constituting the set of ideas which is developed here. It
is the teaching of Cassian, rediscovered by several modern
authors, on the relationship of cenobitism and eremitism. If the
solitary wages a more difficult battle than the cenobite, one for
which the common life is a necessary preparation (as Cassian says
in his *Conference Eighteen* and, following him, the Master and St
Benedict say in their first chapters) then the community once
again appears as a school, the termination of which may be either
the life hereafter or a life in solitude here below.

Yet this thought, which Cassian presented as traditional, has
been sharply criticized for some time by certain researchers. It has
been said that such a theory cannot lay claim to any authentic
tradition, that Cassian conceived it himself on the basis of his personal experience.[5] In reality, it is said, cenobitism and eremitism
were, in the eyes of the monks of Egypt, two distinct and fully independent ways. The former would have been its own end and
justification, as Cassian acknowledged elsewhere through the
voice of another of his speakers.[6] Likewise contested is the picture
Cassian gave of the observances and spirituality of the cenobites of
Egypt.[7] In effect, it would have been the mores of semi-anchorites
which he described, whereas genuine, pachomian, cenobitism was
altogether different.

From such criticisms as these aimed at Cassian results the conclusion that the Master and St Benedict, to the extent that they
depended on him, did not make contact with the purest
mainstream of primitive monastic tradition. In consequence, the
present work has been censured for having presented as a general
theory of cenobitism, representative of the whole traditional doctrine, what is no more than a single and rather questionable current of thought. This censure, furthermore, envisages not only the
presentation of cenobitism as I have educed it from the *Institutes*
and *Conferences,* but also the thesis, foreign to Cassian, that
cenobitism was born of anchoritism, that the cenobitic abbacy
was only the extension on a communitarian scale of the spiritual
fatherhood of the desert. On this point again, I would be considered guilty of confusing clusters of semi-anchorites with

coenobia. My analysis of the origin of the latter would be an un-justified transportation of the genesis of the former.

The meaning of pachomian cenobitism, the import of Cassian's testimony, the relations between cenobitism and eremitism, the unity and diversity of Egyptian monasticism: these questions which have been raised for discussion cannot receive here the thorough examination they deserve. They shall be studied at length in the final volume of commentaries on the Benedictine rule which I hope to publish in the not too distant future.[8] For the moment I would call attention to just one point: Cassian invented neither the relationship he established between cenobitism and eremitism nor what he presented as the spirit and practice of the Egyptian cenobites. To allege that Cassian had done so would in-dicate ignorance of such authors as Jerome and Sulpicius Severus, who presented the same doctrine and same facts long before Cas-sian.[9] In the light of such information it seems that Cassian is but the witness and theoretician of a form of communitarian monasticism which really did exist, which contemporaries con-sidered cenobitic, and which effectively maintained, with an-choritism, the precise relationships which Cassian defined. That this cenobitism of Lower Egypt at the close of the fourth century was different from that which Pachomius had founded a half-century earlier in Upper Egypt is patent. But one need not exag-gerate this difference to the extent of forgetting the traits common to both scenes.[10] With certain shades of difference peculiar to each, they both communicate the same ideal of communitarian *ascesis,* in which the role of the abbot and the elders is primordial.

In concluding I would descend to some much more modest remarks on the process whereby this work was composed, and on a more convenient reading of it. One reviewer, though an ex-perienced critic of ancient works, imagined I had written this book straight through from beginning to end, simply following the order of the chapters in the Rule. There are few books, I im-agine, which have been composed in so rectilinear a fashion. At any rate, the present volume was not composed in that way. The chronological order of the redaction seldom coincided with the order in which the chapters move in this work. An indication of the original process of redaction may be of some use.[11] I do not, however, recommend that the reader follow this order. I suspect that many will be more interested in perusing this volume accor-ding to a selected program, omitting the arid pages of pure

literary criticism and devoting their effort and attention only to
the doctrinal and historical studies, found generally in the second
part of each chapter.[12]

Easter, 1971   A.V.

NOTES TO THE PREFACE

1. See below p 109, note 80. For a long time the two passages of Gregory cited
there (*Dialogues* 1:4 and 2:23) have drawn the attention of theologians. They are
already found drawn together by Paul Evergetinos, *Synogogè,*4;39, as Irénée
Hausherr has pointed out: 'Paul Evergetinos a-t-il connu Syméon le Nouveau
Théologien?' *Orientalia Christiana Periodica* 23 (1957) 74-79.

2. *The Rule of the Master,* CS6, tr. Luke Eberle (1977) Introduction, pages
reproduced in *Supplément à la Vie Spirituelle* 70 (1964) 321-324.

3. Below pp 100ff. These expressions have been left unaltered in the present
translation.

4. RM 92:72, 77-82; 93:1-5.

5. Julien Leroy, 'Les Préfaces des écrits monastiques de Jean Cassien,' RAM 42
(1966) 157-180; 'Le cénobitisme chez Cassien,' RAM 43 (1967) 121-158. The ideas
of this author ought not be confused with the democratic and innovative tendencies of which there was some discussion above.

6. Cassian, *Conf* 19:8. On these divergent presentations found in Cassian, see our
article 'La Règle de saint Benoît et la vie contemplative,' CC 27 (1965) 89-107.
Note 8 on p. 93 is to be corrected in accordance with the index of J.-C. Guy, *Jean
Cassien, Institutions cénobitiques,* SCh 109 (Paris: Cerf, 1965) p. 513 *(con-
templatio).*

7. Armand Veilleux, 'La théologie de l'abbatiat cénobitique et ses implications
liturgiques,' *Supplément à la Vie Spirituelle* 86 (1968) 367-371; *La liturgie dans le
cénobitisme pachômien au quatrième siècle,* Studia Anselmiana 57 (Rome, 1968)
146-154 and 334-339. See also the interesting remarks of Julien Leroy, 'Le
cénobitisme chez Cassien,' expecially pp. 147-148.

8. The doctrinal commentary will complete the historical and critical commentary already issued in *Sources Chrétiennes* 184-186. See also our paper 'Saint
Pachôme et son oeuvre d'après plusieurs études récentes,' RHE 69 (1974) pp.
425-453.

9. See my article 'Les pièces latines du dossier pachômien, Remarques sur quel-
ques publications récentes,' RHE 65 (1971) 26-67.

10. I touched upon this question in the note 'Points de contact du chapitre xxxii
de l'Histoire Lausiaque avec les écrits d'Horsièse,' *Studia Monastica* 13 (1971)
291-4.

11. Ch. 1; ch. 2 #1-3; ch. 6; ch. 3; ch. 7; ch. 8; ch. 2 #4; ch. 9; ch. 4; ch. 5;
and lastly the Conclusion and the Introduction.

12. See ch. 1 #2; ch. 2 #3-4; ch. 3; ch. 4 #2; ch. 5, Conclusion; ch. 6; ch. 7
#1; ch. 8 #2; ch. 9.

TRANSLATOR'S NOTE

References to the Rule of St Benedict (RB) and the Rule of the Master (RM) are given here according to chapter and verse, rather than chapter and line, as was done in the French edition of this work. The widespread custom of citing the Benedictine Rule in this fashion, plus the appearance in 1964-1965 of a critical edition of the Rule of the Master where, for the first time, this text too is divided into verses, makes a versicular system of references both possible and preferable (see Abbreviations for these editions).

For the convenience of readers, an effort has been made to locate English translations of patristic sources and modern studies referring to this work. Such translations are given in the respective tables and in the notes.

Typographical errors in the French edition of which the author had become aware or which the process of translation brought to light have been corrected. A small number of minor textual revisions have also been incorporated.

The author has been most considerate and helpful both in personal conversation and in reading and correcting the typescript. The editor of the series in which this translation appears, Father M. Basil Pennington OCSO, has also shown himself most thoughtful, allowing me to determine the completion date and otherwise leaving me complete freedom to accomplish the work.

I was prompted to undertake this translation by the conviction that exegetical study of this sort is necessary in order to ground an intelligent return to the original inspiration behind monasticism. Only with the re-acquisition of that inspiration, it seems, shall we be in a position authentically to adjust the monastic life to changed conditions and times, thereby achieving genuine renewal.

C.P.

INTRODUCTION

T HE STUDY which the reader has before him is a commentary on eighteen chapters of the Rule of St Benedict (RB). As the title indicates, these chapters were chosen for the special interest they offer for studying the abbatial function. The abbot is of course present throughout the whole Rule, and a complete treatise on the abbacy would require covering the Rule in its entirety. Our intention, however, is not to treat all aspects of St Benedict's concept of abbot. We propose, more modestly, to meditate on the sense of the relationships which unite him to his monks and on the society he forms with them. In this respect, the chapters studied here are for the most part of obvious interest. Some of them, such as RB Sixty-seven through Seventy-two, may at first sight appear less important, but we hope to show how sharply they elucidate our subject. We do not pretend either that our selection is always made on a basis of necessity. Someone else might no doubt have preferred to draw upon some other choice of texts which in his view would be more characteristic or better documented. Spontaneously our interest has centered upon the chapters which follow. They sufficed to nourish our reflection. The inevitable arbitrary element in giving them preference is balanced by constant recourse to an over-all view of the Rule.

Another criterion contributed to the selection of these chapters: the background which the *Regula Magistri* (RM) provided for them. Adopting the hypothesis that RM was composed before RB, we could not fail to draw comparisons between St Benedict and his predecessor at every stage. As a result, certain passages of RB come into higher relief than we might have imagined. For example RB Sixty-seven through Seventy-two becomes the object of special attention once one has realized that these chapters form an 'appendix' in which St Benedict develops at length some thoughts of his own after setting forth the main body of the Rule in which he follows RM. Again, having ascertained the close ties between the abbatial directory and its adjoining chapters in the Master, one cannot dissociate these sections in RB (Chapters One through Three). For the same reason, Chapters Sixty-three, Sixty-four, and Sixty-five of RB, three texts which derive from a single unit in RM, must not be separated. No more can one ignore the important considerations the Master develops at the end of Chapter One or at the beginning of Chapter Eleven, for of themselves they solicit commentary on the corresponding chapters in RB. The object of our meditation is firstly, as we said, the *sènse* of the relationship which the abbot maintains with his monks. In other words, we are interested in the abbacy not in order to give a detailed account of its duties and tasks, but rather to understand the nature of the abbatial office. At the center of our study lies the question: what is an abbot? Beyond a picturesque description or a juridical definition, an answer to this question is not forthcoming except through an analysis of doctrinal themes. It is a matter of uncovering in the texts the idea of the abbatial power embodied in them: its origin, its model, its essential element and ultimate purpose; how it is related to Christ and his Church, and what relationship it has with the ecclesiastical hierarchy; which scriptural and ecclesial prototypes are proposed for it to imitate; to what extent it conforms to those models, and to what extent it is different, and in this latter case, what are the deepest reasons for its originality, contamination from some type of secular authority or simply the exigencies of its spiritual mission?

Such an inquiry into the theological nature of the abbacy cannot be separated from the concrete situation of the abbot in the monastery. Whatever texts and scriptural themes are employed to describe it, his function ought to be considered from a realistic standpoint. Facts such as the manner in which an abbot is designated, his role in the council of the brethren and his power over the officers of the monastery provide further information about the kind of authority accorded him.

More generally, the abbacy ought to be situated within the whole framework of cenobitic life. It is of some consequence to know whether the abbot is at the head of a more or less numerous community, whether he is assisted by permanent collaborators, whether he lives in contact with the monks and enters into all the details of common life or whether on the contrary he leaves important responsibilities to assistants. It is necessary also to note all indications concerning his influence and prestige. Is he for practical purposes all-powerful or need he reckon with other forces, external or internal? While his rights are clearly defined by the rule, this rule can also reveal some tendencies less evident but no less important, among the monks as well as with the legislator himself. Therefore what the texts have to tell us of the practical behavior of this or that person ought to be carefully noted and investigations made about the meaning of an admonition addressed to the abbot or the punishment levied against a certain fault or a measure taken to reinforce contested authority.

The more or less structured condition of the community is another important factor to be considered by anyone who wants to situate the real place of the abbot in the monastery. According to whether the rule insists more or less strongly on the mutual relations of the brethren, the figure of the abbot stands forth in different degrees of relief. If he has before him simply a group of juxtaposed individuals devoid of mutual relationship and awaiting everything from him or from his representatives, the abbot will be the unique pole of the community, its 'sun' as one of the ancients said.[1] In a more highly structured community, on the contrary, where fraternal relations are taken into greater consideration and regulated with more care, it is inevitable that the abbacy will occupy less exclusive attention, above all if the order established among the brethren rests on bases other than the abbot's will alone.

A theology of the abbacy and the concrete situation of the abbot: these two levels of investigation unite to bring alive the vital concept of the head of the *coenobium* familiar to the RB redactor and his readers. These fields of inquiry open up on a larger problem, however, that of cenobitism itself. When the place of the abbot in the monastery is subjected to examination, the following query cannot be eluded: what is the meaning of this society? The response will evidently be bound up with what is said about the abbot. If the abbot has been defined as a kind of pastor and the *coenobium* as a kind of church, it will still be necessary to inquire into the nature of the bond uniting members of the community to their head. Is the cenobitic monk principally a disciple of the abbot or a member of a social body? Is the master-disciple relation-

ship the source of the *coenobium* or does the *coenobium* owe its
existence primarily to a desire for life in common with many
brethren? Does the abbot precede and engender the community,
attracting around himself the spiritual sons who, one by one, are
drawn by his reputation as a director or does the community have
a consistency and a value of itself such that its superior seems to be
simply a part of the machinery, a necessity of social life?

Closely connected to this is the relationhip between cenobitism
and eremitism. If the *coenobium* is fundamentally a school, that
is to say, an assembly of disciples gathered round a master of the
perfect life, the passage to a higher and more solitary form of life
for the fully formed disciple is conceivable. But if the common life
is regarded as a fundamental value because of the exchanges of
charity it provides, the *coenobium* will tend to appear as an end in
itself beyond which one cannot go.

The meaning of obedience is equally involved by the standpoint
adopted regarding the *coenobium* and the abbot. According as
the accent is placed on the personal relationship of the master to
the disciple or, on the contrary, on membership in the community, motives for obedience are to be sought either from the point of
view of the subject's benefit or that of the common good. The role
of the man who commands, and consequently the act of obedience, can also be envisaged in several ways: some of the viewpoints favor mutual obedience more than others, an obedience
rendered not only to the abbot and his delegates, but to all the
brethren as well.

The abbatial office, cenobitism, and obedience are the inseparable issues whose meaning will be considered before all else
in the RB texts upon which we shall comment. But RB, as we said
before, does not lend itself to full understanding unless it is compared with its privileged source, RM. Consequently, no effort
should be spared to gain a complete understanding and an exact
appreciation of the work of the Master. For this reason our commentary will necessarily give as much attention to RM as to RB.
This simultaneous reading of the two rules results in incessant
comparison, a reverting back and forth which may sometimes tire
the reader, but which, we hope, will help us to see precisely St
Benedict's originality where it exists. There is then a final question
which will continually occupy us. In what direction is the theory of
the abbacy, or at least the situation of the abbot, modified from
one rule to the other?

Having outlined the issues with which this commentary will deal, we should say something about presuppositions and method. The spirit in which we approach RB is not wholly like that of our predecessors. St Benedict has had numerous commentators, from Paul the Deacon to Basil Steidle. Our own century is not the least fruitful in exegetes of his work. It is especially important to determine our standpoint in relationship to these recent commentators.

An intense filial piety is the common mark of all modern labors. They are for the most part works by Benedictine monks. But such reverence paid to St Benedict sometimes hinders an exact understanding of his ideas. Often, in fact, veneration leads to an exaggeration of his historical role and the importance of his rule. As a result, real overstatement which, in systematically exalting RB at the price of everything that preceded it, has proved very injurious to its interpretation. Its author is credited with a novel intention and is placed in opposition to all anterior legislators or theorists.[2]

The wide diversity of explications proffered concerning St Benedict's originality suggests that they are based on an *a priori* judgment. Some make the originality consist in the introduction of the promise of stability, others in discretion and the mitigation of austerities. Certain commentators talk about the pre-eminence given to the divine office, others insist on the wholly communal life, still others stress the importance of work or, finally, the juridical precision and practical nature of the regulations. It seems as if each author had from the beginning unconsciously taken benedictine genius for granted and gone on from there to uncover the specific element in which he could make this originality consist.

Now why do they all hold from the outset that St Benedict intended an original work or, at least, that he made profound changes? Is it not because each allowed himself to be swayed by the spread of RB and its final triumph over all the other rules, a fact which made St Benedict the 'patriarch of Western monks'? Here, certainly, we have an historical fact that calls for explanation, and we shall attempt to identify the factors that led to its success. But it should not be forgotten that St Benedict finds himself in a position very different from that which St Francis, St Dominic, or St Ignatius hold in relation to their respective spiritual families. Notwithstanding the diversity of their genius and modes of influence, these three saints may be considered founders of orders. During their lifetime a religious family characterized by their personality and the impetus of their ideals crystallized around them. This initial motion, due to their personal charism, defines and orients from generation to generation the society which bears their name. The case of St Benedict, however, is altogether different. The history of his influence is not that of a religious family gathered around his person and propagating itself from his time on, but the history of the diffusion of a document written by him, which little by little recommended itself to all Western monasteries as the most felicitous and most practical expression of the traditional wisdom of cenobitism.

To read the preface which St Benedict of Aniane prefixed to his *Concordia Regularum*[3] is enough to understand how the very person responsible for imposing unity of observance under RB on occidental monasticism conceived the relationship of RB to other cenobitic rules. We would substitute this image of St Benedict 'culling his own rule from others, and contracting into a single sheaf the sheaves of his predecessors' for the image of a genial originator drawn by modern commentators. It is only too clear that this recent representation projects on to benedictine origins something which actually came to pass at the birth of the great orders of later times. In reality, in contrast with such orders, benedictine monasticism did not emanate from the personality of a creator and it did not arise as the ingenious response to new needs of the Church and society. St Benedict came in the wake of two centuries of cenobitic experience and harvested the fruits. He legislated modestly, without pretentions of originality, making traditional themes and institutions his own.[4]

His Rule, which experienced a lengthy peregrination alongside others like it in the apparently eclectic and basically traditional perspective of the monasticism of those times,[5] came to be imposed as the sole rule to the exclusion of others only at the critical juncture of the Carolingian period, when the adoption of uniform legislation proved to be the only means of re-establishing observance among monks. It was at that time, and not at the time of St Benedict, that RB figured as the instrument of reform.[6] And the grounds on which it fulfilled this role were not its inventive character, but just the opposite, its value as a representative of the whole tradition and the relatively extensive and organized exposition of common doctrine and institutions it furnished.

If this is the real situation of St Benedict with regard to monastic tradition, we see what should be thought of attempts at a psychological portrayal which have taken RB as their starting point.[7] It is risky business to uncover in a body of legislation of this sort the characteristics of a spiritual physiognomy, and to explain the prescripts of the Rule by the personal experience or supposed psychology of the author is no less hazardous in the majority of cases. The paragraph on hermits in RB One, for example, has been interpreted as the result of personal verification by St Benedict: after having lived an eremitical life for three years at the beginning of his conversion, he came to point out in his Rule the dangers of this manner of life because he had experienced them. Actually, this passage on hermits is a simple résumé of Cassian. A more attentive consideration of sources and literary parallels should make authors of similar psychological hypotheses more circumspect. The epithet 'roman' which has been employed excessively in characterizing RB is equally susceptible to distrust. One cannot appeal to the national temperament of an author to explain his work unless one is certain that the literary genres, sources, and spiritual tradition do not furnish the explanation sought. Consideration of the literary and spiritual background out of which RB arose, which is before all else the monastic tradition, has been woefully lacking.[8]

For the same reason it seems imprudent to have recourse ceaselessly to secular analogies in order to account for some of the institutions of RB. The ancient *familia* or the decury of the roman army are not valid parallels unless the texts make explicit reference to them, or at least do not refer to scriptural or ecclesial prototypes. An explanation drawn from the Sacred Books or from the life of the Church is *a priori* more likely than one drawn from secular institutions in an environment as impregnated with Scripture and as little open to secular influence as was ancient monasticism.

But let us revert to the image of St Benedict the reformer, the innovator even, which has prevailed since the time of Cuthbert Butler. The chasm introduced between RB and its sources by a depiction of this sort seems to bring the holy patriarch closer to us. In this way present day benedictine monasticism tries to justify itself. Tendencies which in fact came to prevail among his posterity are attributed to St Benedict himself. The concern to edify (in the noblest sense of the word) which may have moved Delatte, Butler, Herwegen, must remain foreign to the commentary we are undertaking. We are not obliged, as those great abbots were, to extract from the Rule what seems most suitable to the possibilities and needs of a contemporary monastery. Even less are we writing a 'mirror for abbots'! Contemporary realities are not of immediate interest to us. RB in its own right is our concern. We shall try to reach a detached understanding of its text without a preoccupation with resolving modern monastic problems, and only in the light of the most ancient monastic documents.[9] Opinions of contemporary authors will not be discussed save in the measure in which they are presented as interpretations of the text on which we are commenting.

The break with the past effected by St Benedict consists principally, according to Butler, in two novelties: 'the elimination of austerity and the sinking of the individual into the community.'[10] The second point is of special relevance to our field of inquiry. The abbot of Downside thought the first chapter of RB was tantamount to a repudiation of eremitism. Even more, he believed St Benedict impressed a communitarian and objective character on prayer and asceticism. 'It was to the discipline of family life and the performance of a round of community exercises, rather than to personal strivings of an individual piety, that he looked for the religious formation of his monks…. The uppermost idea in his mind was God's service, rather than the self-betterment of the monks or their progress in virtue.'[11] 'St Benedict was a collectivist in the spiritual order.'[12]

This theory has found echo in other commentators. In particular, it fills the great work of Abbot Herwegen, *Sinn und Geist der Benediktinerregel.*[13] It retains a place of honor in the work of Basil Steidle,[14] in which the accent nevertheless falls forcefully on the personal effort for sanctity. I have already had occasion to assess this highly remarkable work, voicing the reservation which certain of its formulas seem to require.[15] A dozen years earlier, the 'collectivist' theory of Butler and Herwegen elicited the pertinent criticism of Léon Thiry.[16]

It would be unjust not to pay homage to the fine work expended during the last twenty years to rediscover a more authentic vision of RB. Although the theses of Butler, Herwegen and Hilpish continue to feed the ideas of popular writers,[17] and although the exaggerated idealization decried above attained a zenith in the historical novels of Cardinal Schuster,[18] the studies of Stoltz, Hausherr and Bouyer have taught us to esteem the ancient ascetical literature of monasticism and to understand St Benedict in continuity with his predecessors.[19]

At the time we were being thus re-connected to the Fathers of the desert, works dealing with the great legislators of cenobitism increased until cenobitism can no longer be conceived according to the pattern of thought so glibly proposed during the first decades of this century. Cenobitic history has customarily been represented as a progression marked out by three great names: Pachomius, Basil, Benedict. Pachomius was understood to have broken with eremitism, but in his writings there remained serious hiatuses which, it was thought, Basil undertook to amend. It was from Basil that Benedict derived his basic ideas, making them more precise in a 'roman' legislation adapted to the Italian peasants of a semi-barbaric age.[20]

The Pachomian Congregation was criticized for two defects which at first sight seem almost contradictory: the highly enforced organization in which a quasi-military sense of order and discipline prevailed and, on the other hand, the solitude and spiritual independence in which the monks lived. These two traits led commentators to conclude the absence of 'true fraternity' in those gigantic communities, a 'merely material cenobitism' in which the work schedule was given too much importance. Its dissolution for economic reasons has been seen as a verdict of history, the revelation of an intrinsic flaw which later legislators -Basil and Benedict - would fortunately remedy.

This picture does not do justice to the true physiognomy of pachomian cenobitism as it could be understood after the publication of the *Vies Coptes* and the *Catéchèses* of Pachomius.[21] The pachomian 'rule' is surely a simple body of regulations consisting of successive additions and almost devoid of spiritual annotations. But one would wholly deceive oneself if one stopped at appearances and misconstrued the admirable spiritual commentary provided by the *Liber Orsiesi*, the *Catechesis* and the *Lives*. If pachomian cenobitism retained many eremitical observances, in particular the individual cell in which the monk remained alone most of the time, the infrequency of offices celebrated in common, a certain latitude in alimentary regimen, we have no reason to conclude that pachomian monks were juxtaposed individuals lacking genuine fraternity. The texts give the opposite impression, that of a community closely united around the 'Father' and his successors, in the awareness that everything was due to the singular grace of the Founder and to the sharing of his spirit. An essential observance in pachomian monasteries was the superior's conference. This occurred several times a week, and the examples which have come down to us, as well as the testimony of the hearers recorded in the *Lives,* show to what extent the entire community lived on this almost daily catechesis. It is therefore not right to attribute to Basil the creation of the 'spiritual fraternity', and to Benedict the 'community spirit', as if these values had been missing in the *coenobia* of Egypt![22] Besides, are the elements of solitude and even of liberty which the pachomian system involves not also a part of the program of common spirituality?

It is no less unjust to see in pachomian discipline nothing more than preoccupation with organization and practical order, explicable by Pachomius' Egyptian temperament or by his previous military experience. Heinrich Bacht has clearly demonstrated -and this becomes apparent even at a first reading of the texts -the extent to which the social concept of Pachomius was ordered purely to the formation of souls.[23] Is it right to read in the decline of the Congregation a condemnation of the system, when so many centuries of monastic history have made us witnesses to repeated degeneration in even the best-ruled monasteries? No form of cenobitism is immune from this law.

Basil is thought to have reacted against such defects in pachomian cenobitism. But the important studies of Jean Gribomont no longer permit basilian work to be viewed as the follow-up and rectification of Pachomius'.[24] Basil seems to have had no direct knowledge of Egyptian cenobitism. His point of departure was the monastic movement that sprang up around Eustathius, and this placed him in a situation, and confronted him with problems, quite different from the conditions under which Pachomius' work was realized.

Other results obtained by Gribomont profoundly alter the classic image of basilian monasticism. The *Regula Basilii* translated by Rufinus and cited by St Benedict ought no longer to be reckoned a recasting of the Greek *Rules,* but rather an initial state of the *Asceticon* which later underwent further development and divided into the 'Long' and 'Short' Rules, as F. Laun had previously suggested. By comparing these various redactions, Gribomont has been able to demonstrate the singularly tentative character of the institutions which there take shape. Whereas we know the pachomian Congregation in its final state,[25] the Rules of St Basil display the settling into place of a cenobitic discipline which progressed in rhythm with experience. Another difference between the two legislators is their respective position among the monks whom they address. Pachomius is, in the full sense of the term, an Egyptian 'Father' who attracts disciples and upon whom everything depends during his life and after his death, while Basil is only the spiritual counselor of fraternities of which he is not the founder and which begin to discover little by little the laws of a common *ascesis* founded on the Gospel. In the first case, the superior is endowed from the outset with the prestige and ultimate authority of a man of God. In the second, he tends to acquire the same prerogatives, but according to a process in which he emerges gradually from the fraternity, appearing as an increasingly indispensable organ as difficulties of common life make themselves felt.

These rapid remarks on the genesis of the authority of Pachomius and Basil already augur disagreement with the opinion of Butler, according to whom 'St Benedict owed more of the ground-ideas of his rule to Basil than to any other monastic legislator'.[26] On the contrary, we believe that the Egyptian influence, communicated in its essentials through Cassian, is much more in evidence in St Benedict than that of Basil. Pachomius really seems to stand at the origin of a strong and steady Egyptian 'tradition' which is easily recognizable in the cenobites depicted by Jerome (Letter 22:35), in the *Institutes* of Cassian, and then in the Master and St Benedict. This tradition is composed of a body of characteristic institutions such as the gradated hierarchy (abbot and deans), the division of the community into 'houses' or 'decuries', and the weekly rotation of ministries. It falls within the prolongation of eremitism and remains open to it, notwithstanding certain hesitations in pachomian circles.[27] It extends to the furthest limits the pedagogical spirit which provides the fundamental theme for all ancient cenobitism, by instituting a minute discipline which is none-the-less deeply spiritual (not at all 'military', as has too often been alleged). It lays express claim to the title of 'tradition' in the highest sense of the word, both when associated with 'our Father' Pachomius, as was the case within the Congregation, and when, beginning with Cassian, efforts were made to trace its origins to the apostles.[28] It distinguishes itself from other branches of cenobitism not so much by a different orientation as by the extra strength and precision it apparently possessed from the outset and which was derived from the extraordinary figure who founded it.

In line with this tradition, transmitted through the *Institutes* of Cassian, the anonymous 'Master' composed his rule, a work remarkable for the logical vigor with which it systematized traditional doctrine and observances, for the precision with which it

treated even the least details, and also, it must be admitted, for
the exaggeration of certain themes, such as emulation, which it
went so far as to employ in questionable educational methods.
The essentials of this work are found again in the rule of St
Benedict, where the Master's superb construction lost much of its
clarity and was tempered by new values which seem to reflect the
influence of Basil and Augustine. Whatever the alterations of RM
introduced by St Benedict, which we shall try to define in this
study, the fundamental structure of the monastery regulated by
RB remains that of the Master, of Cassian, and of the great Egyptian tradition.

Did St Benedict give his monastery a 'family-like physiognomy'
which the Egyptian *coenobium* lacked? Was he, in this matter,
'the faithful heir of St Basil'?[29] This trait, in our view, does not
characterize the benedictine community any more than the
pachomian. We have here a theme common to all forms of
cenobitism. As regards institutions, it is true that the community
life of the sixth century was more intense than it had been among
Pachomians, more intense even than in Cassian's time, just a century earlier. Suppression of individual cells and the institution of
the common dormitory are typical in this respect. But this was a
general trend at that time. It is also found in Caesarius of Arles, in
the *Life* of St Eugendus, and in the legislation of Justinian, as well
as in RM and RB. The purpose of this innovation was to remedy
moral slackness and the vice of private ownership. It was not felt
to be progress towards a more communitarian kind of life, but a
palliative for laxity. The ideal of cenobitism had not turned
toward a more complete cenobitism. It remained, as in the past,
dominated by eremitical aspiration, but human weakness and a
concern for insuring at least minimal integrity led to a development of the common life. The evolution of prayer in common
from the embryonic form it had with St Pachomius is to be interpreted in the same sense, if we may believe Cassian.[30]

These indications will serve to give some idea of the spirit in
which we are undertaking this study. The ever-present
background for the text we are studying is provided by RM and
the whole body of ancient cenobitic literature. We set aside the *a
priori* judgment which holds in principle that St Benedict wanted
to create an original work. Taking account of his evident
dependence on his predecessors, we will read his rule in the
perspective of the unity of ancient monasticism, elucidating it as
much as possible by the documents issuing from the same milieu.

Only when RM and the monastic tradition provide neither source nor valid parallel do we advance the hypothesis of progress, or at least of a new element introduced by the author. To designate that author we shall usually avoid speaking of 'St Benedict', not so much to allow for doubts which have arisen in recent years about the attribution of RB to the holy Patriarch as to assist in an objective appreciation of his work. St Benedict, then, will ordinarily be for us 'the redactor of RB'. We shall, moreover, make little use of Book Two of the *Dialogues* of St Gregory to explicate the rule. The nature of that biography demands the exercise of even more prudence than does RB itself in establishing a portrait of St Benedict. Its historical data are of little help for interpreting RB, which receives much greater elucidation from the ascetical and legislative texts which relate directly to the particular genre of its various chapters.

Before concluding this Introduction, we must present the ancient texts to which this commentary will refer.

The *Regula Magistri* holds first place. The position assigned this document in relation to RB determines the idea we shall make of RB. It is therefore vital that we weigh with the greatest care the arguments that have been brought forth for and against the anteriority of RM, and even arguments favoring a joint dependence of both RM and RB on some earlier text. A consideration of this sort is now rendered very much easier because, thanks to Gregory Penco, we possess a veritable manual on this controversy.[31] Yet it is not in the enormous mass of articles summarized in his little book that we hit upon the reasons which have made us adopt the hypothesis of RM's anteriority. From the beginning of our research, we have had access to the most complete and methodical work done to date for resolving the RM-RB problem. This remarkable study, which unfortunately remains unpublished, has been forwarded to us by its author, Jacques Froger, to whom we are indebted for enabling us to make a sure and decided stand in this highly complex issue.

The public is unacquainted with Froger's labors save for a very brief note in which, at the end of a review of the diplomatic edition of RM,[32] he outlined his own thesis on the relationship between St Benedict and the Master.[33] The attention of critics was captured above all by the bold theory attributing RM to St Benedict and postponing the composition of RB until the next century. This suggestion, only the general lines of which are known even now, has not been generally well received and has been refuted several times.[34] It is not this theory which has formed our conviction and grounded our work, but rather a previous study in which Froger established only RM's anteriority to RB. We shall summarily present the chief arguments we have retained after personal critical evaluation. We add remarks of our own when the case requires it.

1. The most impressive facts, because they can be tabulated, are certainly those which result from a vocabulary study. In a series of words, the part common to the two rules (MB) turns out to be homogeneous to RM and heterogeneous to RB. The most arresting example (which Masai and Penco, following Froger, have stated) is *autem*; this conjunction figures eighty-one times in texts peculiar to RB (Bp), whereas it appears only eight times in texts peculiar to RM (Mp). MB never employs it, a fact which places the common part in obvious continuity with the Master.

Similarly, *omnino* and *aliter* are employed by Bp eighteen and six times respectively. But these two words are wholly absent from both MB and Mp.

An examination of the names given the abbot by each rule is of particular interest for our purpose. Here again the common part manifests harmony with the Master. *Doctor*, never used by Bp, figures once in MB (RM 7:6 = RB 5:6) and fourteen times in Mp.[35] This proportion is hardly unusual when the respective lengths of MB and Mp are taken into consideration. This proof assumes its full value when we observe that the single instances in which MB utilizes this expression occurs in the introduction of a citation of Lk 10:16, which is likewise the case in several instances where Mp employs the word.

In the same way, *maior*, not found in Bp, recurs four times in MB, in the sense of 'superior' and twenty-eight times in Mp; *magister*, occurring twice in Bp, figures three times in MB and twenty-three times in Mp. For anyone attentive to the relationship between the length of the common part and of the two rules (MB amounting to about one quarter of RB and one twelfth of RM), these figures indicate that *magister*, very rare in Bp, is much more frequent in both MB and Mp.[36]

Discipulus, correlative with *magister*, witnesses still more clearly to the homogeneity of the common part with the Master. It is found eleven times in MB and sixty-two times in Mp, whereas Bp uses it just twice.[37].

The counterproof is furnished by *prior,* which Bp utilizes eleven times in the sense of 'superior', whereas MB and Mp never use it in this sense.[38] Likewise, *senior,* which appears thirteen times in Bp to denote the dean or the elder, never figures in MB or Mp. Its correlative *iunior* is used eleven times by Bp, never by MB or Mp.

Besides these words designating superiors and inferiors, Froger has uncovered several terms which often figure in Mp and MB, while they are entirely missing in Bp: *actus* (eight times in MB, more than thirty in Mp), , *facta* (eleven times in MB), *adinplere* (three times), *omni hora.*[39]

For our part, we would add to this list the term *scola,* absent from Bp but found once in MB (RM Thema 45 = RB Prol 45) and at least nine times in Mp.[40]

From the standpoint of vocabulary, therefore, the common part stands in continuity with Mp and in discontinuity with Bp. Here we have proof that RM and the common part are indeed by the same author, whereas RB derives from another writer who had made this common part his own.

2. After linguistic analysis, utilization of sources also offers material for verifications which are precise and difficult to refute. The argument is this: in the common part there are a number of quotations, and these citations are generally more faithfully rendered by RM than RB. Then, too, the works quoted are sometimes utilized again by Mp, while Bp makes no further reference to them. It appears then that it was the Master who had read the sources common to the two rules and that the RB redactor was content to copy the quotations from him.

First there is the case of RM 2:32 = RB 2:30. The reading as found in RM (*creditur*) exactly reproduces Jerome's letter 14:9.[41] The RB reading (*conmittitur*) deviates from the quoted text. But the clinching force of the argument is diminished because we are unable to establish with absolute certainty that Jerome is the author cited here.

Yet it is hardly possible to avoid the conclusion which results from a comparison of RB 7 and RM 10 with Cassian, *Inst* 4:39. Jacques Froger notes six cases where Cassian and RM are in mutual accord while RB deviates. Only once does RB square with Cassian while RM does not, but in this instance it is a question of a correction *ad sensum* (RB 7:51: *affectu*). Since these are well known facts, we need not insist any further on them.[42]

The *Acta SS Agapes, Chioniae et Irenes* are cited jointly by the two rules (RM 10:44 = RB 7:33). These same Acts provide the Master with a quotation peculiar to him alone.[43]

The *Acta S. Sebastiani* are cited by RM 10:35 = RB 7:24: *mors secus introitum delectationis posita est.* This same quotation reappears in RM 7:45, and this time in a form more faithful (*iuxta* instead of *secus*) and more complete (*homini creato*). Moreover, the *Acta S. Sebastiani* include a description of paradise which is reproduced literally by RM 10:94-115, and traces of which are found in RM 3:89-90; 7:42; 90:24-25. Nothing could demonstrate better that the Master drew directly on a source, access to which the redactor of RB did not have except through RM.

Lastly, there is a source for the common part which does not figure in the *Fontes* of Butler:[44] the *Passio SS Juliani et Basilissae (Acta SS Jan.I:576).* Chapter Forty-six is cited by RM 3:68 = RB 4:62, as well as by RM 3:15-34 = RB 4:15-29. This same *Passio,* from which RB draws nothing else, is again cited by RM 90:47.

3. The argument which Froger grounds on the state of the institutions in the two rules has strong probative value also. From the viewpoint of description, RM is much more precise and detailed. Nevertheless, when the actual state of the institutions is examined, they appear simpler and less developed than in RB. In the Master we find no 'provost' or prior, no master of novices, infirmarian, permanent guestmaster, guests' cooks, roundsmen, bellringer, or elders to form the counsel of the abbot. All these officers figure in RB, notwithstanding its sobriety of detail by comparison with RM. The same contrast occurs with regard to the buildings. RB speaks of a *cella nouitiorum,* an infirmary, and a guests' kitchen, whereas RM has as yet no special places for these purposes. In RB a more complex form is given to the community by regulating the order of the brethren according to seniority, with different titles of address for seniors and juniors.

Considering the Master's tendency to spell out everything in precise detail, it would be hard to explain his restoration of institutions implemented by RB in a basically less precise and less differentiated state. It is rather the RB redactor who, taking up the Master's descriptions, was obliged to complete what he found in his source in accordance with the exigencies of a more evolved situation or of a more numerous community.

4. The plan of RM is much clearer than that of RB. Whole series

of chapters, the reason for which is not obvious from a reading of RB, become perfectly explicable in the work of the Master. Elements which are not in the same place in the two rules - the liturgical section in particular[45] - are linked to one another in RM by explicit liaisons, whereas in RB they are found in erratic blocks with no relation to what precedes or follows. It is difficult to imagine that the Master succeeded in transforming a compilation as unmethodical as RB into a coherent whole. On the contrary, the sequence of unorganized RB material is handily explained by admitting that the order established by the Master has been either broken up by the interchange of certain passages or, above all, effaced by the suppression of the greater number of logical conjunctures, the inevitable consequence of abridgement.

After these observations, we must follow out the thesis of Jacques Froger, and along with him examine the manner by which RB came to be composed from RM. Having established the anteriority of the Master, Froger asks how RB was drafted. He observes first that RB offers two strata of texts: one deriving from RM by simple transcription, abridgment, or résumé, and the other comprising 'additions' without corresponding passages in RM. He then uncovers in the RB text a large number of hiatuses and, from the standpoint of the logical sequence of grammar and style, abrupt junctions. These irregularities occur precisely where the texts which derive from RM and the 'additions' are joined. The convergence of these two series of observations gives rise to his hypothesis of a redaction in several stages. A résmé of RM was the first to be composed, and then this 'résumé' received annotations in successive layers. Froger thinks it possible to establish that the 'résumé' constituted a primitive independent writing, that the annotator responsible for the 'additions' was a person distinct from the abridger who composed the 'résumé', and that both, moreover, were distinct from the Master. The whole thesis tends to manifest this duality of authors for RB, a work which was not the result of a single stroke, but of successive reshapings. The annotator, he thinks, gives proof in many instances of having no knowledge of RM, and of working only from the 'résumé'. Not able to consult the source of the 'résumé', the annotator came to the point of not understanding it and made some blunders. This critique leaves us with a very mangled RB: 'résumé', 'notes' and 'notes on the notes' chop the text into innumerable and often minute segments.

This part of the work of Jacques Froger has not convinced me.

The facts, it is true, are ingeniously analyzed. But the thesis supposes that the 'résumé' followed RM faithfully. This postulate is indemonstrable and nothing proves that the abridger did not himself modify what he drew from the Master. Plurality of redactors cannot rightfully be alleged except when the text offers *positive* indications of later insertions, that is, abrupt junctions which allow one to suspect that violence has been done to the text. In such cases, which are numerous enough, we readily admit that the 'additional' passages are in fact notes introduced forcibly into RB by a foreign hand. But Froger also appeals to a negative indication: the continuity which the 'résumé' presents when the 'additions' are excised. The argument is then rather weak, especially in the case of detailed prescriptions which by their nature are easily detachable. Furthermore, the texts which Froger ascribes to the 'résumé' sometimes drift rather far from the RM text which they are said to represent. Has this relative liberty taken by the abridger not sometimes extended to modifications touching the very substance?

I am not persuaded, therefore, that the 'additions' are not the work of the abridger himself in the majority of cases. It ought not to be forgotten that no one has ever seen the 'résumé' in the primitive and independent form which Froger postulates. We possess only the RM and the RB texts, and it is a good policy to restrict oneself as long as possible to the writings at hand without having recourse to hypothetical intermediaries. Also, while acknowledging the interest of Froger's work, I prefer not to adopt here his reconstruction of the process by which RB was composed. Even less do I want to take up his hypotheses about the time and place of the composition of the two rules, all the more as I have not seen a detailed account of his line of reasoning in these matters. I shall be content with the minimum needed to make use of RM in this commentary on RB, that is, a working hypothesis on the chronological relationship of the two rules. The arguments presented above appear to allow the prudent acceptance of the anteriority of the Master. That will suffice for a commentary on RB.

In regard to RM, the critique has as yet made little progress. The problem of the RM-RB relationship has until now monopolized scholars' attention, not leaving much room for interest in the work of the Master itself. The most stimulating studies are those by the three editors of the diplomatic edition, Vanderhoven, Masai and Corbett. They are cited, with all the other articles published on this issue, in the Bibliography compiled by Penco at the beginning of his *Regula Sancti Benedicti.* This list needs just three further citations to bring it up to date. At the moment it appeared, Philip Corbett published at Louvain a volume entitled *The Latin of the Regula Magistri, with particular reference to its colloquial aspects.* It is in fact a philological commentary destined especially for those who attempt to establish the text. A little later, *Regula Magistri, Regula S. Benedicti, Studia Monastica cura B. Steidle* appeared in *Studia Anselmiana* 44 (Rome, 1959). In it Theresia Payr proposed, in more than eighty pages, a new theory on the relationship between the two rules. It is this important work which serves as the basis for the recent edition by Rudolf Hanslik, *Benedicti Regula* in CSEL 75 (Vienna, 1960). It has not been possible to utilize here the last two mentioned works; we propose to discuss them at a later time.[46]

The three authors of the *diplomatic edition* are busily engaged in investigating the successive stages by which the highly composite text of RM came to be constituted. We shall deal with this critique of 'interpolations' in the Master when we comment on *De generibus monachorum* and the treatise on obedience (RB One and Five). For the present, however, I would voice in this matter certain reservations similar to those formulated above about Froger's work on RB. Anomalies and incongruities can surely be detected in RM. Nevertheless, this work as a whole is striking above all for its indisputable unity. Philip Corbett himself has acknowledged that the discernment of different textual strata on the basis of linguistic study is rendered difficult 'by what I am convinced is the unifying work of the legislator-editor whose style pervades the whole rule'.[47] We retain this avowal. It fully authorizes us to consider RM in principle as a coherent whole, the work of a single redactor. Lacunae in *Paris lat. 12634,* from which it has been argued that 'interpolations' exist in the complete text, are in fact not very convincing for anyone familiar with the liberties the compiler of this anthology allowed himself. And when other indications suggest an 'interpolation', it may often be a simple revision by the author.

Until the contrary is proven, therefore, we shall speak without hesitation of the 'Master' and of the 'RB redactor' as the two authors responsible for the whole of each of the rules. As for the time and place of composition of the two works, and the identification of the two authors, one must not be too exigent. Of the numerous hypotheses turning round the person of the Master, none deserves to be kept at the present time. It is better to confess our complete ignorance and leave François Masai and Philip Corbett looking in South Gaul or Northern Spain, where they hope to be able to situate RM. The question is moreover less important than it may seem: RM is a document of such richness that precision about its author and place of origin can contribute very little additional light to its interpretation. What are the meagre facts of monastic history in comparison with the enormous mine of information contained in such a text? To identify the Master with this or that known person or to localize RM in this or that region would tell us much more about the person or the region than about the meaning of the work itself. The principal beneficiary of such an identification would not be RM. It is above all by studying the text itself and its sources that we must look for an elucidation of RM, remaining content meanwhile with the delineating dates furnished both by the texts it cites and by the age of the most ancient manuscripts. Certainly posterior to Cassian, RM must be anterior to the close of the sixth century according to the testimony of the Paris manuscripts. Between these two definite *termini* stretches a period of a century and a half. If it be admitted that the *Passio Sebastiani,* which the Master cites, was composed towards the close of the fifth century,[48] this would perhaps be the most precise tenable indication to be had at the moment. As for RB, we acknowledge it to be the work of St Benedict of Cassino whose life is narrated by Gregory the Great in Book Two of the *Dialogues.*[49] Thus RB saw the light of day not long after RM. The reasons invoked by Froger in support of an interval of several generations between the two rules do not, to me seem cogent.

We have provided a table of abbreviations designating the ancient documents to which the commentary makes continual reference. Their division into three categories (Rules, Lives, and Ascetical Treatises) has manifestly only a wholly relative value. The group of Lives contains writings as dissimilar as biographies of holy monks and the *Vitae Patrum* or *apophthegmata.* More homogeneous in appearance, the group of rules is in fact no less diverse. We stress this point, for more than one error has been committed regarding the meaning of these documents as a result of incorrectly evaluating their literary character. These ancient 'rules' assembled into a collection by Benedict of Aniane are writings of very diverse importance, with altogether different ends in view. It is difficult to institute a comparison between them because they belong to totally different literary genres. The Rule of Pachomius, as we have said, is a simple body of regulations built up through successive additions and almost devoid of spiritual annotations. The Basilian Rule takes the form of *Questions* and *Answers,* which sometimes hide thoroughgoing methodical treatises. The Rule of St Augustine is a rapid examination of conscience on some points of the common life, in which well-developed passages of an admirable finesse, envisaging all the aspects of a single spiritual problem, alternate with series of simple prescriptions on matters of detail which arise out of vague associations of ideas. The Rule of the Four Fathers is presented in the form of minutes of an abbot's synod. Thus one needs to be above all aware of the fundamental ambiguity of the term 'rule', and to seek from each only what it precisely intends to present. Much of the opposition which over-hasty historians seem to see among the legislators of cenobitism will thereby vanish.

NOTES TO THE INTRODUCTION

1. *Vita Honorati* 19 (PL 50:1260ab).

2. Cuthbert Butler had already proposed this theory in *The Lausiac History of Palladius.* Texts and Studies 6 (Cambridge University Press, 1898) 251-256; he developed it in *Benedictine Monachism* (London: Longmans, 1919 [rpt. Cambridge-New York: Barnes and Noble, 1961]) pp12-23, 45, 291-303, *et passim.* His essential ideas are to be found again in Henri Leclercq, 'Cénobitisme' in DACL,vol. 2/2, cols. 3232-3240, and in Stephanus Hilpisch, *Geschichte des benediktinischen Mönchtums* (Freiburg im Breisgau: Herder, 1929), to mention just two figures at the top of a long list.

3. PL 103:715a: *Beatum Benedictum suam a caeteris assumpsisse regulam, et ueluti ex manipulis unum strenue contraxisse manipulum.*

4. The best exposition on St Benedict's relationship to Oriental monasticism is that by Jacques Winandy, 'La Spiritualité bénédictine', *La Spiritualité catholique,* edited Jean Gautier (Paris: Rameau, 1953) 13-16.

5. From the fifth to the eighth centuries, a common conception of the monastic life prevailed which made possible a certain number of facts which may surprise us: authors of rules or treatises copied or largely utilized anterior writings, sometimes going so far as to compose anthologies like the rule of St Donatus or the cento-rules such as *Paris lat 12634.* Monasteries changed rules or even observed two rules simultaneously. Adoption of a new rule did not necessarily signify a reform, and the plurality of rules was not a syncretism, a compromise between several concepts of monasticism. These facts simply mean the monks of those days considered all the rules as expressions of the same spirit and the same doctrine. One could pass from one rule to another or have several at a time without this being of great importance. I thank Jacques Froger for having drawn my attention to these facts and their meaning. Kassius Hallinger has some useful developments on this issue of the *regula mixta.* See 'Papst Gregor der Grosse und der hl. Benedikt' in *Studia Anselmiana* 42 (1957) 259-266.

6. Cf. Jacques Winandy, 'L'oeuvre monastique de saint Benoît d'Aniane', *Mélanges Bénédictins* (Saint-Wandrille, 1947) 235-258.

7. This is the avowed intention of Ildefons Herwegen in his *Saint Benedict, A Character Study* (St Louis: Herder, 1924), but the tendency is general.

8. We owe our thanks to a layman, Denys Gorce, for one of the first studies in which the traditional character of RB was set out in full light: 'La part des *Vitae Patrum* dans l'élaboration de la Règle Bénédictine', *Revue Liturgique et monastique* (Maredsous, 1929) 338-339. Basil Steidle has developed rapprochements of this sort in his articles in *Benediktinische Monatschrift* from 1932 to 1953, and in his work *Die Regel St Benedikts* (Beuron/Hohenzollern: Beuroner Verlag, 1952), ET *The Rule of St Benedict: a Commentary*, tr. Urban Schnitzhofer (Canon City, Colorado: Holy Cross Abbey, 1967) which remains the best commentary we have on RB up to the present time.

9. This documentation extends from the Pachomian Rule to that of Fructuosus, that is, from the middle of the fourth century to about the middle of the seventh century.

10. *Benedictine Monachism*, p 45.

11. Ibid., pp 300-301. 'School of the service of God' would have an 'objective' sense (accomplishment of determined duties within a communitarian framework) in distinction to 'school of perfection', a modern formula stamped by 'subjectivism'.

12. Ibid., p 45.

13. Einsiedeln/Cologne: Benziger, 1944. Introd., p 12: 'The rule is not a manual destined for the monk, but in its entirety as in details it regards rather the community of monks.' Cf. pp 76, 189, 201-204, 220, 243 ('today the monasteries of St Benedict are still schools and ramparts of the communitarian spirit'), 268, 271 ('this precise regulation comes in reaction to the individualistic ascesis expressed, for example, in the Rule of Pachomius'), 272, 273, 296-297, 302-303, 364, 369-370, 373 ('the vocation of monasticism: to constitute a community in the service of the sovereign Lord and King'), 396, 398.

14. See above, n. 8.

15. 'Le monastère, Église du Christ', *Studia Anselmiana 43 (1957) 25-46.*

16. *'Individu et société dans la Règle de saint Benoît'*, *Mélanges Bénédictins* (Saint-Wandrille, 1947) 115-142, especially 124-126 and 138.

17. Even the excellent essay by Olivier Rousseau, *Monachisme et vie religieuse d'après l'ancienne tradition de l'Église* in the *Collection Irénikon* (Chevetogne, 1957) subscribes to these theses in Chapter three: 'La vie commune des origines au XIIe siècle'). But we would not rank among the 'popular writers' the author of this little book filled with original views and penetrating insights!

18. *St Benedict and his Times*, tr. Gregory Roettger, 2nd ed. (St. Louis: Herder, 1953). With greater charm and poetry, Cardinal Schuster follows the line of John Chapman, *Saint Benedict and the Sixth Century* (London: Sheed and Ward, 1929). These two investigators have lavished a wealth of erudition into making St Benedict the agent of the Roman Pontiff in the work of reforming the monasteries of the West.

19. Anselm Stolz, *Théologie de la mystique* (Chevetogne: Éditions des Bénédictins d'Amay, 1939), and above all *L'Ascèse Chrétienne* (idem, 1948). Of the works of Irénée Hausherr we cite only *Penthos* (Rome: Pontifical Institute of Oriental Studies, 1944) and *La direction spirituelle en Orient autrefois* (1955); this last work is of the greatest interest for a study of the abbacy. [English translations projected by Cistercian Publications.] See also Louis Bouyer, *Le sens de la vie monastique* (Turnhout: Brepols, 1950) [*The Meaning of the Monastic Life (New York: Kenedy, 1955)*] and *La vie de saint Antoine* (Saint-Wandrille: Éditions Fontenell, 1950).

20. The subsequent sentences discuss the affirmations of Rousseau in his third chapter: 'La vie commune'.

21. *Les Vies Coptes de saint Pachôme*, tr into French by L. Th. Lefort in *Bibliothèque du Muséon* (Louvain, Bureaux de Muséon, 1943). Also translated by Lefort, *Oeuvres de S. Pachôme et de ses disciples* in CSCO 164 (Louvain, 1956). [English translations forthcoming from Cistercian Publications - ed.]

22. Rousseau, pp 82 and 86.

23. Heinrich Bacht, 'Antonius und Pachomius. Von der Anachorese zum Cönobitentum' in *Antonius Magnus Eremita*, Studia Anselmiana 38 (1956) 66-107, especially 101-103. Earlier, Karl Heussi had already done full justice to the spiritual motives of Pachomius. Cf. *Der Ursprung des Mönchtums* (Tübingen: Mohr, 1936) 112-129 and 131.

24. Jean Gribomont, 'Obéissance et Évangile selon saint Basile' in *Supplément de la Vie Spirituelle* 21 (1952) 192-215; *Histoire du Texte des Ascétiques de saint Basile* (Louvain, 1953); 'Le monachisme au IVe siècle en Asie Mineure' in *Studia Patristica* 2 (Berlin: Akademie Verlag, 1957) 400-415; 'Les Règles Morales de S. Basile et le NT', *Studia Patristica* 416-426; 'Eustathe le Philosophe et les voyages du jeune Basile', RHE (1959) 115-125.

25. This may seem less true since M. M. Van Molle has striven to decipher various strata in the Pachomian Rules. See 'Essai de classement chronologique des premières règles de vie commune en chrétienté' in *Supplément de la Vie Spirituelle* 21 (1968) 108-127, along with our criticism in the papers mentioned in the Preface, notes 8 and 9.

26. Butler, *Benedictine Monachism*, p 16. Cf. Rousseau, 'Monachisme et vie religieuse,' p 83.

27. *Vies Coptes*, pp 267ff, pp 176-178. Cf. the study by Heinrich Bacht cited above (n. 23), especially p 103ff.

28. See the references in ch. 4 below n. 122. In order to impart a certain historical basis to the thesis of the apostolicity of the *coenobia*, Cassian had only to interpret Philo (the *Therapeutai* of the *De uita contemplatiua*) in accordance with an exegesis already common to Eusebius, St Epiphanius, and St Jerome. Thanks to this myth, the tradition of the *coenobia* of Egypt can present itself in Cassian with all the characteristics of the ecclesiastical tradition found in the famous *Commonitorium* of his compatriot, contemporary and ally, Vincent of Lérins. Is it in order to safeguard better the legend of the apostolic origin of cenobitism that Cassian seems to ignore the existence of Pachomius? The true founder of the *coenobia* is not even once mentioned in the *Institutes* or *Conferences*.

29. Rousseau, 'Monachisme et vie religieuse,' p 84.

30. Cassian, *Inst* 3:2

31. *Sancti Benedicti Regula: Introduzione, testo, apparati, traduzione e commento, a cura di Gregorio Penco OSB* (Florence: Nuova Italia, 1958).

32. Hubert Vanderhoven and François Masai, *La Règle du Maître: éditon diplomatique des manuscrits latins 12205 et 12634 de Paris, avec la collaboration de Philip B. Corbett* in *Les Publications de Scriptorium* (Brussels-Paris: Éditons 'Erasme', 1953).

33. 'La Règle du Maître et les sources du monachisme bénédictin', RAM 30 (1954) 275-286.

34. Christine Mohrmann, 'Regula Magistri. A propos de l'édition diplomatique des mss. lat. 12205 et 12634 de Paris', *Vigiliae Christianae* 8 (1954) 239-251. Anscari Mundó, 'L'authenticité de la Regula Sancti Benedicti', *Studia Anselmiana* 42 (1957) 105-158.

35. See the survey of these texts in ch. 2 below, *Appendix*. We do not count here RM 11:12, a quotation (though not correctly cited) of Jer 3:15.

36. If the anteriority of the Master is admitted, it will be noted that one of the two occasions when Bp employs *magister* (RB 3:6) is found in a phrase copied from a passage in MB (RM 8:37 = RB 6:6; cf. our commentary on RB 3, in ch. 3, n. 26), and the second occasion (RB Prol 1) might well be a subtle allusion to the author of RM. These two instances when Bp employs *magister* may therefore be considered indirect traces of RM vocabulary, and the statistic of this word is no less striking than that of *major*.

37. RB 3:6(see preceding note) and 36:10. Penco remarks (*Regula*, p xxxvii) that RB 7:13 substitutes *homo* for *discipulus*, which is read in RM 10:13. By making such an alteration the RB redactor has let his disfavor for this term appear.

38. RM 93-94 uses *prior* seven times, but in the sense of the 'former' abbot. Note that RB 7:41 substitutes *prior* for *major*, which is read in RM 10:58.

39. For Mp, Froger indicates here seventeen cases, Penco only fifteen. The latter sum (*Regula*, pp xxxviii-xxxix) is due to the fact that RB 7:10 substitutes *omnino* for *omni hora*, which is read in RM 10:10. A similar correction in RB Prol 6 (cf. RM Ths 3). Evidently the redactor of RB only uses *omni hora* reluctantly.

40. Thus Penco (*Regula*,, p xxxvii), but the references he gives are incorrect in four out of eight cases. The exact accounting is as follows: RM 1:83; 87:9; 90:12, 29, 46, 55; 92:26, 29, 62.

41. See Cuthbert Butler, *Sancti Benedicti Regula Monasteriorum*, third edition (Freiburg-im-Breisgau: Herder, 1935). I have noted the same quotation in RM 93:20, where the inversion of *plus* and *cui* seems due to a simple error of transcription.

42. Cf. Penco, *Regula*, pp lxxvii-lxxix and 249-253.

43. RM 90:76. It may be objected that the quotation is doubtful, for the Master speaks of 'being possessed by God', whereas the *Passio* means possession by the devil. But there are other instances of RM transforming quoted texts in this way. See for example RM 10:35, which will be studied in the next paragraph.

44. Butler, *Regula*. See above, n. 41.

45. See Corbinian Gindele, 'Die römische und monastische Ueberlieferung im *Ordo Officii* der Regel St Benedikts', *Studia Anselmiana* 42 (1957) 171-222, especially p 208. This author rightly assesses the posteriority of the *Ordo* of St Benedict in relation to that of the Master, but we cannot assent unreservedly to the demonstration he offers for this thesis.

46. [Three years after *The Community and the Abbot* was published in French, Adalbert de Vogüé, in collaboration with Jean-Marie Clément, Jean Neufville, and Daniel Demeslay, published *La Règle du Maître: Introduction, Texte, Traduction, Notes, et Concordance Verbale du Texte Critique*. Sources Chrétiennes, nos. 105-107 (Paris: Les Éditions du Cerf, 1964-1965). This three volume edition of the Rule of the Master has as its main purpose a study of RM itself, prescinding from its relations with RB. The English translation, *The Rule of the Master*, Cistercian Studies Nbr. 6, appeared in 1977-tr.].

47. 'The *Regula Magistri* and Some of Its Problems', *Studia Patristica*, 1 (Berlin: Akademie Verlag, 1957) p 91.

48. Cf. François Vandenbroucke, 'Sur les sources de la Règle Bénédictine et de la Regula Magistri', *Rev Ben* 62 (1952) p 251, n. 9.

49. See the arguments tendered by Anscari Mundó against the hypothesis of Froger: 'L'authenticité de la Regula Sancti Benedicti', *Studia Anselmiana* 42 (1957) 105-158.

Chapter 1

CENOBITISM AND SOLITUDE (RB 1)

A CRITICAL NOTE

T HE TEXT OF RM has been studied in detail by Hubert Vanderhoven and François Masai. The former has tried to show that *De generibus monachorum* in its entirety was an interpolation. The latter has sought to prove that the famous digression on gyrovagues was itself an interpolation within *De generibus*.[1] At the conclusion of these critical labors, RM One assumes the appearance of an excavation site in which the following strata are allegedly identified:

1. A Primitive stratum constituted by verses 76-92. This exhortation would be a continuation of the *Thema*. More precisely, if the data of manuscript E may be trusted, it is necessary to restore it after Ths 39 and follow it up with 40-46. It would be, therefore, a page of the *Thema* forced out of its original context as a result of the insertion of *De generibus*. Its present position, however, just before the treatise on the abbot, corresponds well with its primitive purpose of introducing this treatise.[2]

2. *De generibus* (vss 1-15, 72-74), a description of the four kinds of monks. The fourth kind, gyrovagues, is characterized in the most sober terms. This pericope once constituted a separate little work, then came to be inserted within the rule as a third introduction (after the Prologue and the *Thema*), and finally took its place among the chapters of the rule, thereby displacing the abbatial treatise, which had originally headed the text, to its present position as Chapter Two. A connecting sentence (vs 75) fused it to the interrupted rule.

3. The digression on gyrovagues (vss 16-71). This highly colorful text is missing in E. It is what gives the fourth kind of monks the boundless importance they have in P.

This analysis of RM One rests on a certain number of solid facts. But for all that, one cannot close one's eyes to the fact that the testimony of E, invoked time and again by the critics, always remains rather suspect because of the liberties this manuscript takes with the texts it copies. The argument based on vocabulary is not as decisive as one might wish. No doubt *De generibus* employs words which are seldom found again in the rule: *monachus, coenobium, anachorita, eremita, sarabaita, gyrouagus*; but all these terms, the last excepted, are derived from the sources of this description, Jerome and Cassian. A satisfactory explanation is that the redactor was here using the special terminology of his sources without however making it his own to the extent that he used it elsewhere when he was no longer following them.[3] The fact that *De generibus* concludes with a connecting phrase announcing a return to the *Regula* cannot be proffered as proof of an interpolation as long as analogous junctures found here and there throughout the rule are not also explained.[4] Examination of the rule as a whole would be necessary before a pronouncement on the sentence here in question could be made with security.

In any case, the incontestable merit of these analyses is that they reveal the composite character of this chapter. The three 'strata' indicated above are surely, at the very least, distinct pericopes arising from different genres.

Once this evidence is noted, the attribution of the three pericopes to distinct authors is nothing but a more or less probable hypothesis. According to Vanderhoven, *De generibus* had been inserted by an interpolator preoccupied with disposing his listeners favorably to the call to cenobitism which resounds at the end of the *Thema*. Due respect was rendered to anchorites while cenobites were so highly exalted. Masai saw the digression on gyrovagues as the work of the redactor of the rule and Corbett saw it as the work of the 'legislator-editor', which amounts to the same thing.[5] Prudence prompts us not to multiply authors, all the more as this digression presents many a resemblance with other pericopes of the rule.[6]

With a commentary on RB in mind, we should determine first of all which are the pericopes the redactor of the rule had before him, and in which order he saw them. It is certain the redactor read the texts successively arranged as we read them in P, not as in E. The conclusion of the RB Prologue corresponds to that of the *Thema* in P.[7] *De generibus* then follows, with its four kinds of monks. The third kind, as we shall see, is described more briefly than in RM and the fourth receives an even more summary treatment. Yet if one considers this last paragraph attentively, one cannot escape the conclusion that it summarizes not only the passage devoted to gyrovagues in the 'primitive' redaction of the Master's *De generibus* (RM 1:13-15, 72-74), but also the 'digression' on gyrovagues (RM 1:16-71). In effect, when RB says of wandering monks that they are *propriis uoluntatibus et gulae inlecebris seruientes*, it is alluding to two faults mentioned not in the 'primitive' RM text of *De generibus* but rather in the 'digression'.[8]

Once it is established that the RB redactor read this digression in RM, a remarkable peculiarity of RB One can be readily explained: the first two kinds of monks are described in terms identical with RM's, the third is also, but with the last verses of the text amputated (RM 1:10-12). As for the passage on gyrovagues, it was drafted first in the terms of the Master (RB 1:10 = RM 1:13-14), then in terms which are not found in RM but which summarize it. Why did the redactor have recourse to such a procedure, when he had previously been satisfied to recopy or abridge? To all appearances, because he found himself before a pericope of unusual proportions. Had he been faced with only the brief passage of the 'primitive' *De generibus*, he would have been content to recopy it while pruning this stock of some verses as he did the passage on sarabaites. But the immense size of the description of gyrovagues did not lend itself to this method of transcription and abridgment. Thus we have the résumé we read in RB 1:11-12.

Certainly, therefore, the RB redactor found himself in the presence of *De generibus* as we read it in P, that is, in its 'interpolated' form which includes the digression on gyrovagues. The connecting phrase (RM 1:75), attested by all the RM manuscripts, is likewise repeated in RB (vs 13), but its redaction is modified, as was previously true at the end of the passage on gyrovagues. As for the Master's final exhortation (RM 1:76-92), even though no trace of it remains in RB, nothing prevents our supposing that the redactor knew it, since both E and P include it. It must have concluded as in P, however, and not have been followed by the end of the *Thema* as in E, since this conclusion is already to be read at the end of the RB Prologue.

If it is admitted that the Master served as the source for RB, it was without doubt in the form attested by P, including all the texts furnished by this manuscript and in the order in which it arranges them. As a consequence, it is of relatively little importance for us to criticize this version of RM One according to P. We ought to consider the various pericopes contained in this chapter, whatever their origin, with the same eyes as did the RB redactor. He probably looked on them all as the work of the same author. If he abridged, summarized and omitted in spontaneously reckoning the natural divisions in the text and the difference of outlook which these manifestly disparate pericopes presented, his particular instinct as author guided him in this work of restatement. The selection he made resulted from his intention to abridge and from his personal preoccupations, but the text of the Master must have appeared to him a unified whole. We ourselves ought to regard RM in the same way. Together with the redactor, we read the P text as if it flowed from the pen of a single author, though not without taking account of the discrepancies and collisions. We attribute everything to this conventional author, whom for lack of anything better we must call the Master.

A last remark about method. Since the RB redactor appropriated the text of his source, being content to abridge or summarize it in the measure that served his purpose, but without introducing substantial additions or modifications, we are justified in thinking that he made the Master's doctrine his own. When commenting on passages common to both, we shall therefore speak indiscriminately of 'St Benedict' and of 'the Master', attributing to one or the other, even to both together as the necessities of the commentary may require, what is in fact their indivisible property. It sould come as no surprise, then, that we use these two names as interchangeable synonyms.

COMMENTARY

This chapter develops a theme which already had a long history: the 'various kinds of monks'. The origin of the genre, and its most brilliant exemplar, is the famous text of St Jerome on Egyptian monks.[9] Shortly after its appearance, St Augustine used it, with some retouches, in his polemic against the Manichaeans.[10] Cassian in turn came to treat the subject, but much more independently, and here the immediate source for the present chapter is to be sought.[11]

The texts of these three authors concern monks *in Egypt*. A more general description, without particular localization, is given by the *Consultationes Zacchaei*.[12] We simply mention it in passing, for it seems to owe nothing to what St Jerome wrote, and to furnish nothing to what we are commenting upon here. The only trait it shares with our text is that it describes not Egyptian monks but monks in general, or more exactly, since this is a Latin writing, Western monks, in principle at least.

Each of these descriptions is executed somewhat differently, according to the context in which it is inserted. With Jerome it is really a digression, one of those brilliant asides which no writer misses when he is put at his ease by the highly supple laws of the epistolary genre. An affair of 'avarice' at Nitria provided the occasion. Jerome went on to depict the bad monks or *remnuoth*, then the cenobites, and finally, quite briefly, the hermits. The description of cenobites thus comes in the center of the pericope, and on it Jerome willingly lingered and devoted much thought, even though anchorites held a higher place in his estimation. The portrayal of the *remnuoth* at the outset serves only for contrast.

What impression was Jerome trying to create when he described cenobites? A community in which reign order, peace, virtue, in which fervor is expressed through austere renunciations and ardent aspirations for the things above. Moreover, Jerome heavily stressed the role played by the hierarchy of the *coenobium*. Not only is obedience mentioned from the beginning as the fundamental pact of this society, but the depiction first of the day and then of the week and the year is centered on the educational role of the 'Father', of the deans or provosts, of the bursar and the infirmarians. It is a strongly structured community in which the monk, even during the long hours he spends alone in his cell, is under the incessant supervision of educators who are both competent and full of solicitude. They take him completely into their charge, body and soul, to teach him to live well. This deserves notice, for we shall find no other image of cenobitism in the two rules on which we are commenting. This image will only be magnified by the suppression of the individual cell and by an all-pervading community life.

It is understandable that Augustine appropriated this enticing passage. It offered him a good apologetical argument in favor of the Catholic Church, a useful picture to oppose to the vauntings of Manichaeans only too proud of the ascetical feats of their 'elect'. In such an apologetic context there is no longer any question, to be sure, of the bad monks, the *remnuoth*. Anchorites and cenobites undergo an inversion. For the former, Augustine declared his refusal to produce an argument because of their sublimity, which to some seemed inhuman.[13] Anchorites apart then, the description of cenobites comes even more to the forefront than it does in Jerome. Augustine took over the essentials of his source but modified details. The plan he followed lifts the economic aspect into sharper relief. There is community of goods, manual work and distribution of alms to the indigent. His concern was to emphasize the charity practiced by these Catholic communities, a trait which for the rest of the book he never ceased to underscore with regard to the ascetics of Rome and Milan.[14]

Taking up this theme in *Conference Eighteen,* Cassian did not try to create a lifelike depiction either from motives of edification, as did Jerome, or for controversy, as did Augustine. His purpose was more didactic and his style more abstract. With him the issue was to establish an historical thesis that based the authority of cenobitic tradition on the primitive Church itself: the *coenobia* of Egypt originate through uninterrupted succession with the apostles. Anchoritism is a branch which has sprouted from this stock and which brings its virtues to their highest perfection. Sarabaites, on the contrary, constitute its degeneracy. There is even a fourth kind, as Cassian added in Chapter Eight. (He counted only three in the first enumeration in Chapter Four, no doubt out of regard for the number become traditional since Jerome. We shall encounter a similar scruple in the Master, who enumerated four kinds while describing five.) This fourth kind bears no special name; it counterfeits anchoritism just as sarabaites counterfeit cenobites.

More abstract than the preceding descriptions, this one stresses the characteristic virtues of the cenobite: *aktèmosunè*, obedience, patience, without painting a detailed portrait of cenobitic life.[15] As for the historical thesis it develops, one can easily see that Cassian is only projecting a bundle of theories on to the course of history. If he has cenobitism originate with the apostles, it is because he believed–and in this he was not mistaken–that the apostolic teaching was heeded and practised there in full. If he places the debut of anchorites long after that of the *coenobia,* it is because the monk, in the individual course of his own life, ought to follow such a progression and pass through the *coenobium* before encountering the desert. If the sarabaites do not enter the

scene until a still later period, this is because such a corruption of
the cenobitic ideal, far removed from the first fervor, could not
have set in until afterwards. And since anchoritism is
chronologically posterior to cenobitism, its degeneration (the
fourth kind) would duly have set in after the decline of cenobitic
life.

Three valid ideas, therefore, form the substance of this myth:
first, the authority of cenobitic tradition founded on the teaching
of the apostles and the example of the primitive Church; second,
the necessity of an apprenticeship in the *coenobium* before any
eremitical experience; and finally, that sarabaites are nothing but
false monks, a caricature of the authentic ideal. The historical
thesis which serves as the expression of these ideas contradicts the
most certain data of history. We know that cenobitism did not appear until Pachomius as the extension of anchoritic experience
which he endeavored to place within reach of a greater number by
developing some of its elements. If it can be traced back to the
apostles, it is not by virtue of historical continuity, but in the
sense, quite true in itself, that its founders had no other model
than the primitive Church and no other law than Scripture. The
myth Cassian constructed was all the easier to fabricate as the accounts narrated in the Acts lent their full support. Cassian did not
even take the trouble here, as he did in Book Two of the *Institutes,* to have recourse to the *Church History* by Eusebius and to
the *Therapeutai* of Philo to back up his thesis.[16]

This rapid survey allows us to determine the relationship between Chapter One of RM-RB and its predecessors. It obviously
owes nothing to Augustine's presentation. As for Jerome and Cassian, both of whom are cited by Butler in his notes, only the latter
served as the immediate source. The way in which the various
kinds of monks are characterized bears closer resemblance to Cassian's abstract presentation than to the picturesque description by
Jerome. Like Cassian, these rules list four kinds and not three as
did Jerome. Like the author of the *Conferences,* they entitle the
third kind 'sarabaites' (not *remnuoth*). Like him, lastly, they successively enumerate cenobites, anchorites and sarabaites, whereas
Jerome, after having arranged the three categories in this same
order in an initial enumeration, later switched sarabaites to the
head of the list in the description itself.

This last trait permits us to interpret the *primum coenobitarum*
of RB, which has already occasioned two tendentious explana-

tions. The 'priority' of cenobites is not, as Herwegen would have it, a primacy of values, as if anchorites constitute an inferior kind of monk because they lack an abbot. The enumeration does not follow an order of descending value. It is true that RB (not RM) inserts between the sarabaites and gyrovagues a *decrescendo* of this sort (*in omnibus deteriores sarabaitis*).[17] But nothing indicates that an analogous gradation prevails between the first two kinds. The paragraph on anchorites was manifestly written in an enthusiastic style which reveals no disesteem. It even affirms with great clarity that anchorites wage a harder and more admirable warfare than their brothers in the *coenobia,* where they themselves had fought their first campaign. The thought here is identical with that of Jerome, Cassian, and the quasi-unanimity of tradition.

If we are not dealing with an order of *values,* then what does this order signify? Quite simply that which Jerome followed in his first enumeration and which Cassian took up in Chapter Four of his *Conference.* The four following chapters (*Conf* 18:5-8) expound at length the genesis of the four kinds of monks, which Cassian reckoned made their appearance successively from the time of the apostles down to his own epoch. But in the introduction, which Chapter Four in fact is, the 'historical' significance of this order is not yet disclosed. Nor does our text make any allusion to the period in which each kind emerged. So RM and RB seemingly attach no determinable sense to *primum...secundum...tertium ...quartum....* They are following Cassian (and through him Jerome's initial exposition) without regard for the historical myth. But they expressly propose two of the ideas which formed the substance of that myth: the hermit ought to undergo cenobitic probation; sarabaites are nothing else than frauds, utterly deficient cenobites.

Each paragraph demands closer attention. The famous definition of cenobites was understood by Herwegen in a sense we cannot accept. The three terms *monasteriale-regula-abbas* allegedly square with the three types of monks: hermits lack obedience to an abbot, sarabaites lack in addition the 'regulated' life, and gyrovagues have not even the *monasteriale,* which Herwegen understood as stability.

Furthermore, according to Herwegen, St Benedict was thinking of these three characteristics of cenobitism and of the three kinds of monks they excluded, when he prescribed in Chapter Fifty-eight the three vows of obedience, *conversio morum,* and stability. This last comparison cannot in any event be of use to us in commenting on the text, since the 'three vows' of RB Fifty-eight, no matter what their meaning, are not found in RM. They have perhaps been conceived in terms of what we read in Chapter One, but the Master was surely not thinking of them when he drafted the pertinent chapter.[18]

As for the relationship between the characteristics of cenobites and of the other kinds of monks, this construction also seems not to have existed in the mind of the Master. To be convinced of this one need only examine the meaning of *monasteriale.* This term, we hasten to remark, is only an attempt, an awkward attempt in fact,[19] to translate the *coenobitarum.* The copulative *hoc est* proves it.[20] The Master expressed himself in similar fashion when he tried to render 'anchorites' by a more familiar term in Latin, *anachoritarum, id est heremitarum.*[21] Now, if *monasteriale* was intended to translate *coenobitarum,*[22] we are already oriented more towards common life than towards stability. There is no question of *a* determined characteristic of cenobites reckoned on the same plane as the rule and the abbot, but of a simple translation of their name, expressing globally what is their way of life.[23] Rule and abbot then serve to clarify this appellation by specifying two essential elements which the etymology did not reveal.

This is confirmed by recourse to the corresponding declaration in Cassian (*Conf* 18:4): *coenobitarum qui scilicet in congregatione pariter consistentes unius senioris iudicio gubernantur.* The first part of this sentence endeavors to give the etymology of the word which the Master replaces with *monasteriale.* Next comes mention of government by a single elder, which our *sub...abbate* echoes, the *sub regula* being an addition by the Master. *Monasteriale* therefore does not indicate stability in some special way. It defines cenobites not by opposition to gyrovagues (of whom Cassian never speaks) but in distinction to solitary-living anchorites. This becomes evident a few lines later when we are told about the *monasterii probatione diuturna* undergone by authentic hermits (RM 1:3). This term then refers primarily to a certain number (*multorum solacio,* vs 4) opposed to isolation. More precisely, the sarabaites are reproached immediately afterwards for living 'in twos and threes' (vs 8). The cenobitic 'monastery' is normally then a rather numerous community.[24]

We would be mistaken however to continue our investigation in this direction. The essential point here is not numbers but internal structure and a certain quality of life - a fully 'common' life with the absence of all personal ownership and in obedience rendered to a single master who teaches the authentic doctrine of Christ. Already the expression *monasterii probatio diuturna* cited above had made us aware of this. The paragraph on sarabaites makes still more obvious what the Master intended by 'monasteries'; they are 'the sheepfolds of the Lord' guarded by a 'pastor' worthy of the name, distinct from those habitations of self-will, those 'private folds' within which the sarabaites shut themselves (vs 8).

In a passage proper to it at the end of the chapter, RM again speaks of the 'holy sheepfold' which is the monastery. That passage (vss 82-84) is particularly instructive. There the Master drew a parallel between 'churches and schools of Christ', secular communities and monastic communities, both defined by the authority exercised in them by a teacher instituted by Christ and speaking in his name. The 'monastery', previously defined at the end of the *Thema* as a 'school of the Lord's service', appears in the last analysis, therefore, as the church of the perfect faithful, the community assembled to hear and practise in all fullness the directives of someone representing Christ.

Monasteriale, then, harbors two elements. It cannot be analyzed unless one confronts the rule and the abbot. Cassian had already mentioned government by a single 'elder' in the same sentence in which he tried to translate the name cenobite. In addition, RM mentions the *regula.* Although this term is lacking in the corresponding phrase of Cassian, RM is far from constituting an innovation. The idea of a *disciplina coenobitarum,* of a traditional rule for cenobites, is familiar to the author of the *Institutes* and *Conferences. Conference Eighteen,* the immediate source of our text, speaks of it at the beginning of chapter Five ('The *disciplina coenobitarum* began at the time of the apostles...') and still more clearly in chapter Seven, where the sarabaites are accused of not seeking the *disciplina coenobitarum,* of not submitting to the judgement of the elders, 'of not conquering their own will and allowing themselves to be formed by the tradition of the elders, of receiving no rule of sound discernment through the normal way of instruction'.

What we have said up to now discloses the network of complex bonds which unite the abbot inseparably to a certain ascetical and communitarian tradition - bonds which are more explicitly indicated in the first Books of the *Institutes*. The abbot is the enunciator of a tradition, the possessor of the wisdom and experience accumulated by the elders, or better, the heir of the doctrine of Christ transmitted from the time of the apostles by uninterrupted succession. The tradition in its turn has as a fundamental precept the disciple's absolute obedience to a single master.

Mention of *regula*, inserted here by RM, does not therefore lack solid ties with Cassian's thought. However, the word may have a more precise meaning than the analogous terms in *Conference Eighteen*. There is here the question not only of the ascetical and communitarian tradition of the *coenobia*, but also of a *written* document to stabilize it. RM is intended to be just such a document. Previously, the Rule of St Augustine had presented itself as an authoritative text to be read weekly to the community.[25] In the same period as St Benedict, Caesarius of Arles inculcated in his nuns a genuine religious veneration for the 'holy rule' he wrote for them.[26] Even if the Master went beyond Cassian by speaking of a written text, he was not introducing an original element into the definition of cenobitism.

The paragraph on anchorites demands careful examination. The recent opinions we cited on the meaning of *primum...secundum* and on the relationship among the elements which distinguish cenobites from the other three kinds of monks have prepared us for it. With Herwegen, ought we to see in hermits a category inferior to cenobites because lacking obedience? Should we at least think, along with the majority of modern commentators, that St Benedict accords the cenobites a 'practical preference' out of regard for the weaknesses of most men or should we on the contrary underscore with Anselm Stolz the significance of the panegyric of hermits which we read here?[27]

In order to appreciate this pericope thoroughly, we should first note its very modest proportions. Anchorites are characterized by the Master as summarily as possible. Of Cassian's numerous annotations in *Conference* 18:4 and 6 (Cassian in particular has frequent recourse to the action-contemplation theme) the Master has retained only the theme of combat, seen solely as a *singular* combat in distinction to the *collective* combat of the *coenobium*. RM is not concerned with anchorites except to underscore, like Cassian, the need of passing through a long cenobitic probation before facing the perils of the desert. So it is not a matter of recommending anchoritism as the end of cenobitic ascesis. The idea is certainly present but the point of the text is rather the indispensable cenobitic formation which alone renders such prowess possible. The panegyric is therefore intended for anchoritism certainly, but still more, in using anchoritism as a starting point, for cenobitism.

The paragraph's significance seems even further restricted when it is re-inserted into the total context of RM One. By abridging what is said about sarabaites and summarizing the part on gyrovagues, RB has produced three paragraphs of almost equal length. This is not the case in RM, where there are three verses for anchorites, seven for sarabaites and false hermits, and sixty-two for gyrovagues. A long doctrinal conclusion of eighteen verses then recalls attention to the cenobites and proposes the fundamental principle of their life - obedience to a teacher. Transition to the chapter on the abbot thus comes very naturally. In all this, the brief word on anchorites occupies only a minimal place.[28] RM introduces this subject for the first time here, barely touching it, and does not revert to it again. Nowhere, either in RM or RB, is the concrete case of a cenobite who would like to become a hermit encountered.

We note lastly, in line with these restrictive considerations, that this stray mention of anchorites was required by the theme of 'various kinds of monks'. It was not deliberately chosen for its own sake but made up part of a theme which necessarily included it and which was in fact centered upon a panegyric of cenobites.

Having avoided exaggerating the importance of the pericope, we must now recognize its full doctrinal significance. One cannot but agree with Anselm Stolz in his insistence on this point in opposition to the tendentious exegeses of so many modern commentators. That RM and RB in no wise intended to rank hermits beneath cenobites has already been demonstrated. Do they at least accord cenobites a practical preference? Certainly the idea that cenobitism is a safer way, and normal for the majority, is frequently met in tradition even among authors who consider eremitism superior in absolute value.[29] But that idea does not seem to be present here. We do not find St Benedict in the position of having to make a decision, as commentators ordinarily represent him. He was not in fact in the position of choosing. He was simply writing a rule for a monastery of cenobites, at the beginning of which he sought to define that type of life in contrast to that of other kinds of monks. He intended no reflections on the comparative advantages of cenobitism and anchoritism as Cassian, for example, had offered in his *Conference Nineteen,* when he put in the mouth of Abbot John a highly subtle discourse on the respective values of the two states of life. Our author, like Cassian in *Conference Eighteen,* was satisfied with characterizing them summarily, indicating by a simple stroke the relationship of the one to the other and emphasizing that, if anchoritism is a higher degree, it demands by that very fact a passage through the preliminary initiation of the *coenobium.* And, if that is the way things are, legislating for cenobites means at the same time giving eremitism its real chance.

Writing for cenobites and seeking to give them an understanding and esteem for their kind of life, our author could have been inspired here by considerations developed by St Basil in Question Three of his *Regula,* if he knew of them.[30] Basil, we know, peremptorily established cenobitic life as the indispensable framework of *every* search for perfection. Man is a social being. This natural law alone is enough to recommend life in a community. But there is much more. This fact of nature corresponds to divine law. Christ made fraternal charity the second commandment. Only in community life can the Christian love his brother with an effective love, forgetting himself entirely and fulfilling the many injunctions which concern relations with one's neighbor. A member of human society by virtue of his nature, the Christian is a member of a body from which, by virtue of belonging to Christ, he has no right to dissociate himself. He cannot mature except within this body, by means of the life-giving exchanges among its members. His personal charisms cannot unfold except through their exercise for the benefit of his neighbor, but on the other hand these charisms are limited. Each individual needs others to make up for what he lacks. In this respect Basil is particularly keen to secure for the ascetic the benefit of fraternal correction.

For Basil then there exists nothing beyond community life.[31] RM, on the other hand, expressly envisages just such a 'beyond', following Cassian and the whole of tradition. Community life is a school for learning to serve God. It enables the beginner to enter the battle against the devil without being exposed to sure defeat. But the mature monk is capable of a harder and more dangerous fight–single combat. Only there do human virtue and the strength of grace give full measure to the glory of God (*Deo auxiliante pugnare sufficiunt*).[32]

Throughout RM we re-encounter this concept of community
life as an educational environment in which every resource is
brought into play to stimulate the unsteady will of the individual
monk. Nowhere is it presented to us as a terminus. Regardless of
recent opinions,[33] at the center of our two rules stands not the
realization of the monastic community, but the monk himself and
his education. To promote that, cenobitic life is a precious, even
an indispensable, means. No more than any school does the community constitute a closed and consummated society in which the
individual finds his definitive place. There is something of an
analogy here with the Church militant, whose role is to beget the
elect for heaven, not to retain them forever as captives in her terrestrial womb. In the case of the *coenobium,* only death marks the
end of membership in terrestrial society and entry into the state of
perfection. Even here below such a break is possible, even
desirable, when the monk has derived from the fostering society of
the community enough strength to confront the risks of
autonomy. Anchoritism is for cenobitic society a 'beyond' which
gives it meaning, as heaven gives the Church militant meaning.
The difference is that, by an extraordinary anticipation, the
'beyond' can be realized here below. The monk alone in the desert
is the heavenly condition prefigured and in some measure already
attained, an initial face-to-face encounter with God, contemplated undistractedly by a pure soul.

Such indeed, in the eyes of Cassian, is the most profound meaning of anchoritism: contemplation, crowning the attainment of
virtues acquired through cenobitic training. But to imagine
solitary life only as contemplative repose following the ascetical effort of the common life would be a mistake. In reality, this
celestial life is at the summit of militant life. For although the
anchorite means to anticipate heavenly beatitude, the cost of such
audacity is easy to foresee. Seeking to lay hold of beatitude during
the time of testing, he will undergo proving to its maximum inten-
sity. To withdraw from terrestrial society is not only to liberate
oneself from the association of human beings in order to converse
with the Divine Persons and with angels, it is also to enter into a
fearful *tête-à-tête* with the devil. In breaking every bond with the
world, the anchorite deprives himself to some degree of that society of grace which is the Church, of that school of perfection which
is the monastic community.[34] With the last shackle he loses the last
support.

In RM only this ascetical and warlike aspect is envisaged.

Nothing is said of contemplation and even the word is never uttered either in RM or RB. Some have wanted to see in this a sign of a lack of interest for the spiritual theories developed by Cassian. St Benedict, they say, was a practical man, a Roman realist, oriented towards social life and the virtues it demands.[35] Here again we are positing a *decision* prompted by hypothetical psychology (the Roman temperament is made to bear quite a lot!), whereas this is simply a question of situation. The silence of the rule on contemplation is to be explained very naturally by the literary nature of a writing destined for cenobites, that is to say, beginners whom pains are being taken to 'convert' and educate. A cenobitic rule is not the sum-total of monastic life any more than cenobitism is the whole of monasticism. In characterizing eremitism summarily, the author was satisfied with bringing up just one of its aspects, that which most obviously prolongs the ascetical effort demanded of the cenobite.

Some have also wanted to see a sort of contradiction between perseverance *usque ad mortem* required by the Prologue, and the possibility of passage to eremitism conceded here. The true mind of St Benedict should be sought, they say, in the express exhortation of the Prologue, not in the eventuality envisaged in this chapter, in which it is no more than common ground touched only in passing. In reality, there is no opposition between the two themes of perseverance in the *coenobium* and passage to eremitism. Cassian treated both with equal energy in various places.[36] He even came to the point of uniting them.[37] Perseverance is opposed to flight to something lower, not to an authentic rising above and beyond. Cassian offers no information, however, on the conditions under which the passage of the cenobite to eremitism legitimately transpires. According to Sulpitius Severus,[38] cenobites of the Thebaid could not change their state without the authorization of their abbot, on whom they remained dependent in their new state of life. As we said, the issue is never again raised either in RM or RB, nor is the death of a monk in the *coenobium* treated. To all appearances, these two affairs simply exceed the limits of their draft.

After all, cases of anchoritism may have been extremely rare in the communities for which these rules were written, and perhaps they were never even an issue. The important thing is not to investigate what existed in fact, but rather to keep before our eyes the *meaning* imparted by the anchoritic ideal to cenobitic life. The fact that the hermit is here considered the perfect monk in-

vites us to recognize the profound dynamism of cenobitic ascesis.
Always tending to go further, it has no other *terminus* than absolute union with God. Cenobitic life is oriented toward contemplation, toward solitude and total intimacy with the Divine
Persons. When Basil Steidle asserts that 'at the center of monastic
life is found the perfect realization of the idea of the Church', we
cannot agree unreservedly with him. The Church is surely the exemplar of cenobitic society, in which it seeks to realize itself
perfectly. But this society is not an end in itself, and the impetus
of monasticism passes through it without stopping there. Before
the end of this chapter, RM itself indicates the precise and well-
defined sense in which it likens a monastery to a church.[39]

Sarabaites are the living antithesis of cenobites. Cassian, who
introduced their name into Latin, indicated the Coptic
etymology: 'They *keep aloof* from cenobitic communities and
fend, each for himself, for their own needs'.[40] In these words the
historical theory of Cassian may be divided. In such free-lancers,
he saw fugitives from cenobitism.[41] Cut off from cenobitic communities, sarabaites suffer in consequence two fundamental evils:
they fail to benefit from the formation given by the qualified
masters of the *coenobium,* and they are not dead to earthly
anxieties, since they provide what they need themselves.

This second trait is closely connected with the first in Cassian's
mind. The first reason for stripping the monk of all property is
that he must burn bridges behind himself as a safeguard against
the temptation to turn back. Only after burning his boats will the
cenobite have a chance of persevering in his humble and painful
condition of disciple, relinquishing himself to the teaching of the
elders, surrendering his will to them in obedience and supporting
all the trials they impose on him. More profoundly, this stripping
signifies deliverance from all corporal anxiety and all egoistic
preoccupation. The cenobite is in the hands of his superior, body
and soul, for life and death. He no longer has charge of himself.
Someone is watching over him, someone who has taken complete
charge of him. Thus he accomplishes to the letter the divine precept to 'take no thought for your life'.[42] The monk is then free to
attend entirely to his conversion, to the accomplishment of the divine will as it is manifested to him through his abbot's command.

Developed at great length in Book Four of the *Institutes,* these
views reappear in the description Cassian gives of sarabaites.[43] The
'economic' aspect of their evilness (personal property, anxieties

about self) is underscored with particular force. Sarabaites are a resurgence of Ananias and Sapphira.

In its turn RM has clearly noted the two elements: first, the lack of formation under a rule and a pastor in an authentic monastery, that is, the sarabaites setting up instead their own will as law;[44] second, property (*et dum in proprio arbitrio quaerunt habere cellas, arcellas et rescellas, ignorant quia perdunt suas animellas*).[45] Abridging the text, RM left out this second element. Prohibition of property remains nonetheless implied by the very definition of cenobites.

The verses which follow in RM (11-12) have also been omitted by RB. They affiliate to the sarabaite category, those whom Cassian calls the 'fourth kind': false hermits. These are the *nuper conuersi* who embark without preparation on the solitary life and throw themselves as it were into the lion's mouth. In this regard, RM is content to repeat what it said in the paragraph on hermits. The fact that it mentions false hermits proves its intention to follow *Conference Eighteen* step by step. It was necessary to squeeze Cassian's 'fourth kind' in here! Note, however, that the Master's fidelity to his source comes off somewhat awkwardly. Our author apparently wanted to conserve two elements of Cassian's presentation, the category of false hermits and the total of four kinds, while at the same time importing a new kind unknown to Cassian, the gyrovagues.[46] So he amalgamated the third and fourth kinds, making false hermits a variety of sarabaites. For Cassian the sarabaites were essentially false cenobites, living in twos and threes at least, so there is some awkwardness in classifying them with hermits. This confusion in RM appeared earlier in the words *aut certe singuli* (vs 8).[47]

Because of this little accident, RM is able to present us with a new sort of monk, unknown to its source, without departing from the outline of the 'four kinds' taken from *Conference Eighteen*. Plainly, the description of these gyrovagues elicits from the author a literary outburst which obliterates all sense of due measure. For all of sixty-two verses he showers them with ridicule! This expressive vehemence could claim a foretype in Jerome or Sulpitius Severus, but prolixity is a typical fault of the Master's and we shall come across it time and again. Prudently, RB summarized this interminable satire into a few verses. The full content of the RM development is recovered, but literal copying ceases after *per diuersorum cellas hospitantes* (vs 10).

For its description of gyrovagues RM does not seem to have utilized any source, although St Augustine had already spoken of some wandering monks of this sort.[48] The very word 'gyrovagues' does not appear prior to these two rules. Why did RM introduce this new kind of monk, and why did it spend so much time abusing them? The question is more pressing as the first three kinds had been described very summarily in a kind of résumé, leaving out many of Cassian's developments. Such conciseness makes the prolixity we find here all the more surprising.

Our author plainly had in mind certain disorders he had witnessed and from which both he and his community had suffered. When he treats of guests and postulants, we see him encircle their reception with numerous precautions connected with what we read in this paragraph. Furthermore, as Jacques Froger has remarked, a lively pericope of this sort may have been conceived as a pleasant anecdote meant to relax the listeners. Let us not forget that the rule is read in continuous fashion in refectory. There was in this a method similar to that of every experienced speaker who knows how to bring in 'stories' at the right moment in order to relax his audience and regain attention.

'Of the lamentable ways of all those people [gyrovagues and sarabaites] it is better to say nothing than to speak' concludes RB, using a literary cliché which RM had employed at the beginning of its development on gyrovagues.[49] 'Leaving them on one side therefore, we intend to formulate a rule with the assistance of the Lord for the very strong kind of cenobites.'[50] It is difficult not to hear in this last sentence an echo of Jerome.[51] This would be the only direct trace his description had left in these rules. Curiously this trace appears in RB, but not in RM. A sentence to the same effect appears in RM (vs 75), but the reminiscence of Jerome is missing. One may allow that the RB redactor re-phrased the RM sentence, recalling that he had read something similar in Jerome.

In RB, Chapter One ends here. In RM another seventeen verses[52] form a conclusion of great doctrinal importance which clarifies the entire chapter and permits us to situate it within the whole rule. The Master here resumes the exhortatory tone he had relinquished at the end of the *Thema* in favor of a descriptive one. *Fratres, clamat nobis cottidie Dominus....* These words recall the *Thema* and also the beginning of Chapter Ten (= RB 7). In fact the call to conversion heard in the *Thema* is taken up again here: 'Never yield to evil, practice good.'[53] God lavishes his favor on those who turn to him and decide to do his will, not their own. A choice must be made. What the Lord commands in the spirit is one thing; what the flesh in the soul urges us to do is another. Servitude to the flesh or service of the Lord—the Master faces his disciples with this alternative.[54] But this time doctrine advances a step. The school of the Lord's service instituted at the end of the *Thema* is practically already defined by the first lines of Chapter One and is clarified in turn by the developments of the other kinds of monks. We are therefore not obliged to state the fundamental principle of obedience to God. The monastery, the rule, the abbot have all now been brought forward. Obedience to God concretizes itself in obedience to the abbot. Verses 82-89 are meant to bring about this transition from the will of God to that of the superior:

> Now, the Lord has given his Church, in conformity with the Trinity, three series of doctrine—first that of the prophets, secondly that of the apostles, thirdly that of the teachers —and according to their authority and teaching, the churches and schools of Christ are governed.[55]

> Like shepherds they enclose and teach the sheep of God in holy sheepfolds, as the Lord says through the prophet Isaiah: 'I will give you shepherds after my own heart, and these shall feed you with knowledge and discretion.'[56] And the Lord himself says to Peter, 'Simon, son of John, feed my sheep, teaching them to observe all the commands I gave you. And know that I am with you always; yes, to the end of time.'[57]

> Therefore all who still have folly as their mother ought to be subject to the authority of a superior so that, guided on their way by the judgment of a teacher, they may learn to avoid the way of self-will. For the Lord gives us his commands through a teacher since, as he said above, he is always with these teachers to the end of time, certainly for no other purpose than to instruct us through them, as the Lord himself says to his disciples who are our teachers: 'Anyone who listens to you listens to me; anyone who rejects you rejects me'.[58]

The conclusion ultimately brings this development to its eschatological term. If the instruction of the teacher takes the place of our self-will, the devil will have nothing to claim in us on the day of judgment and the Lord will be able to reward with glory what he himself will ceaselessly have accomplished in us.

This eschatological finale brings us back to the *Thema*.[59] But it is noteworthy that 'the school of the Lord's service', the 'monastery', is here replaced by 'the teachers'. This is precisely the new element introduced by Chapter One. It has enabled us to penetrate into the monastic school to introduce us to its chief personage, this 'teacher' instituted by Christ and speaking in his name. The next chapter (*What the abbot ought to be*) is entirely devoted to him. Chapters Three through Six merely propound what his skill as craftsman of souls should be, and Chapters Seven through Ten how such souls ought to let themselves be worked upon by him

We find ourselves in the presence of a major articulation here. The finale of Chapter One serves as introduction for the whole treatise *actus militiae cordis: pro timore Dei quomodo fugiantur peccata*,[60] a doctrinal tract totally dominated by the figure of the abbot. When the Master passes in Chapter Eleven to the *ordo monasterii*, he will repeat, as a sort of introduction to this new treatise, the considerations we have already read, while expanding them in such a way as to make place beneath the abbot for that subordinate grade of the claustral hierarchy, the provosts. From a consideration of only these facts of literary order, we are already sure of reaching here the foundation upon which the entire doctrinal edifice of these rules rests. In these lines we are furnished with a complete justification for cenobitic obedience, with a force and clarity that leave nothing to be desired. The monastery, *schola Christi*, is likened to a church of Christ, the abbot to the 'teachers' who govern it in the name of Christ, following after the prophets and apostles. Obedience is presented essentially as a necessity for the 'senseless', for the man still incapable of governing himself according to God. In order not to be the slave of his own will, that is to say, the devil, he delivers over his will entirely to a *unique*[61] master charged with guiding him in everything. Through the mediation of such a master, Christ himself acts in him,[62] and he may advance securely to glory.

What is most striking in this doctrine is the tranquil assurance with which our author inserts the monastic 'teacher' into the hierarchy of the Church and makes him the beneficiary of the promises addressed by Christ to the apostles and their successors. The very words of Christ to Peter and the twelve are utilized during the investiture of the abbot. We shall have to inquire about the legitimacy of this assimilation and its consequences,[63] but it must be immediately noted that the entire rule is based on these affirmations. Though it omitted the two passages which develop the theme *ex professo,*[64] RB has nonetheless kept clear traces of this doctrine in Chapters Five and Seven. In this we possess one of the most important keys furnished by RM for an understanding of RB.

It would be well to observe also, in vss 82-84, the aspect under which the monastery is likened to a church of Christ. The *coenobium* is set in parallel with a church in that it is a school meant for the education of feeble souls. The only thing which arrests our attention in this comparison is the master-disciple relationship. It is on the level of the parallel roles of the bishop and the abbot, both of them 'pastors', that comparison can be made of the two institutions which they bring to life. Throughout RM we shall find the accent placed almost uniquely on the role of the abbot and his officers in the education of the monk, with little attention devoted to fraternal relations among the monks themselves. The *coenobium* is built upon a vertical plan, the dependence of all upon the abbot is the only liaison which seems to count in the eyes of the Master. The monastery is a church, the Master declares to us here. Steidle had good reason for noting every trace of this theme. But the author does not seem to have conceived of the church-monastery as a society of brethren united by charity. We may regret that this aspect is not better set in relief and estimate that it does constitute the deepest reality of cenobitic life and its ultimate justification. Yet the fact is that the Master appears to have found in the 'school' the most suitable image for expressing the essence of the *coenobium*. If there be anything beyond this school, it ought not be sought in a new deepening of the community, but rather, as we have said, in the solitude of the hermit.

We must now form an over-all view of this chapter as it presents itself in each of the rules.

Between the *Thema* and the chapter on the abbot, at the outset of its great ascetical treatise Chapters One through Ten, RM sought to define the 'school of the Lord's service' through recourse to the traditional description of cenobitism as distinguished from other kinds of monasticism. Cassian's *Eighteenth Conference* served as the immediate source. Chapters One through Eight were very swiftly summarized in vss 1-12, then, yielding to an excess of satirical spirit, the Master vehemently ridiculed gyrovagues (vss 13-74). Finally, returning to the cenobites and resuming the *Thema*'s appeal to conversion, he set before their eyes the master of their school, the *raison d'être* of their kind of life, the 'teacher'. Having thus proposed the abbot to the faith of the monks, he returns to the abbot in the next chapter in order to draw up the plan of his obligations.

The treatment to which RB subjected this text is interesting. The first part, in which the Master summarized Cassian, is *copied* almost unchanged up to vs 9. When the part on the sarabaites has reached the same length as that on anchorites, the text is abridged and passes to gyrovagues. The interminable development of these is *summarized* in a paragraph even shorter than those previous. In conclusion, a return to the cenobites is announced, but after this articulation the doctrinal pericope of vss 76-92 is purely and simply *omitted*. The redactor has perhaps yielded to an ever more pressing need to abridge.

In considering the result, one is struck by the importance given by the new redaction to the initial part. On the whole, Benedict preserved it nearly intact. He then moulded the passage on gyrovagues to bring it into conformity with the passage on the other kinds of monks, while suppressing the final exhortation, disparate with the descriptive whole and apparently having no necessary connection with it. This streamlining has resulted in a correct and well-proportioned little treatise on the various kinds of monks in which each kind receives nearly equal treatment. The Master's composition, in which three very different pericopes succeed one another—a rather abstract classification of the kinds of monks taken from Cassian, an original and picturesque satire on gyrovagues, and an exhortation to cenobites in the style of the *Thema*—have been reduced to the unity of a single tableau of a demeanor as classic as it is impersonal. What RB has especially conserved of RM is the least original and most traditional element, the one which RM derived from Cassian. What had most strongly borne the impress of the Master's personality was toned down (the résumé on gyrovagues), or simply disappeared (the final doctrinal considerations).

Can we assess the losses this re-working entails? The description of sarabaites loses one of its essential components, the economic element, which indirectly impoverishes the definition of cenobitism. The dependence on Cassian becomes slightly blurred by the loss of the fourth kind of monk, the false hermit. The satire on gyrovagues which occupied more than two-thirds of the chapter disappears as such and with it the note of verbal intemperance and triviality which is repeated on many occasions in the Master. Above all, we lose a pericope of great interest, in which the Master established on a scriptural basis the necessity of subjecting oneself to a 'teacher' instituted by Christ and speaking in his name. The essentials of this doctrine, however, have been preserved for us in the celebrated opening formula of Chapter Two, *Abbas...Christi agere uices in monasterio creditur,* as well as in an allusion to the 'teacher' to whom the Lord says, 'Anyone who listens to you listens to me' (RB 5:6).

We would remark finally that RB, by omitting the Master's note on the 'economic' aspect of sarabaites (RM 1:10) as well as the paragraph on false hermits (RM 1:11-12), departs to the same degree from Cassian's *Conference Eighteen.* Thus the RM text appears to adhere more faithfully to the source of *De generibus* than does RB. Absence of these passages in RB is better explained as the result of a process of abridgment than their presence in RM is explained as an addition based on Cassian. We have here no slight argument in favor of the anteriority of the Master relative to RB — the text adhering more faithfully to the source is very likely the more ancient.

NOTES TO CHAPTER ONE

1. Hubert Vanderhoven, 'Les plus anciens manuscrits de la Règle du Maître transmettent un texte déja interpolé', *Scriptorium* 1 (Brussels: Editions 'Erasme', 1946-1947) 201-212; François Masai, 'La règle de s. Benoît et la *Regula Magistri*', *Latomus* 6 (1947) 211-214. Masai's hypothesis concerning the interpolatory character of the digression on gyrovagues is corroborated by Philip B. Corbett, *The Latin of the* Regula Magistri, *with particular reference to its colloquial aspects: A Guide to the Establishment of the Text* (Louvain, 1958) 121-122 and 131-133. Corbett discerns two different meanings of the word *monachus,* according to its use either by the author of *De generibus* and of Chapter 7, or by that of the digression. These remarks seem inconclusive to us: *monachus* in the digression surely does signify 'a monk who lives alone', but one cannot infer from such a declaration that for the author the term had solely this limited meaning to the exclusion of the broader acceptance (every kind of monk). A good résumé of these theses of Masai-Vanderhoven appears in *Sancti Benedicti Regula, Introduzione, testo, apparati, traduzione e commento, a cura di Gregorio Penco OSB* (Florence: Nuova Italia, 1958) 208-213.

2. It was separated from the abbatial treatise only by Ths 40-46, a conclusion which, according to Vanderhoven, summarizes both the whole of the *Thema* and the particular considerations of vss 76-92.

3. The case of gyrovagues, however, raises a difficulty. This term does not come from Jerome-Cassian or from any other known source. Apparently, then, it derives from the author's environment. But if it were familiar to the author of RM, one would expect to find it again in other passages, notably in Chapters 78-79, where vagrant monks reappear. Yet such is not the case. This fact lends some weight to the thesis of the interpolation of *De generibus.*

4. See for example RM 13:74-75, referring back to RM 13:65; RM 3:95, referring back to RM 3:78. Cf. RM 11:1.

5. François Masai, 'Cassiodore peut-il être l'auteur de la *Regula Magistri?*' *Scriptorium* 2 (1948) 295, N. 9. cf. Philip Corbett, 'The *Regula Magistri* and Some of its Problems', *Stud. Patr.* 1 (1957) 82-93.

6. Cf. *hospitalitatem sectantes* (Rom 12:13) in RM 1:18; 78:17; *sub imperio monasterii* (1:68) and *sub potestate monasterii* (89:20).

7. Save for the addition in RB Prol 46-49. Note also that the mss of the so-called 'interpolated' class stop after the words *si compleamus habitatoris officium* (RB Prol 39), that is to say, at the very spot where the passage begins which E transposes to the end of the exhortation *'Fratres, clamat'*. On this point see the highly provocative remarks of Vanderhoven (*Scriptorium* 1, p 212).

8. Cf. *gylae* in RM 1:21, 30, 59, 60 (63: *gylosae*); the idea of self-will, if not the word, permeates RM 1:27, 60, 68, 73. This last citation would pertain to the 'primitive' *De generibus.* The RB redactor would therefore have been able to draw the theme of self-will from this non-interpolated text, but the notion of the *gula,* in other respects much more characteristic, cannot have come to him save from the interpolation.

9. St Jerome, *Letter* 22, 34-36 (Date: 384). In the description of cenobites, we think that the words *unusquisque cum suis loquitur* apply not to all monks indiscriminately, as one would be led to believe from the translation by Jérôme Labourt (Paris: 'Belles Lettres', 1949) p 151, but only to the 'provost' or 'dean'. The dean, too, is the one who consoles, exhorts, and maks the night rounds.

10. St Augustine, *De moribus ecclesiae* 1; PL 31:66-68 (Date: 388).

11. Cassian, *Conf* 18:4-8.

12. *Consult. Zacch.,* 3:3 (PL 20:1152-1154).

13. This did not prevent him from mentioning them and from proposing, without it appearing so, the apologetical argument which he said he declined to tender. After all, he did not make his own the criticisms of which he spoke. We know the effect that the account of the life of St Anthony had on him two years earlier, and he was to make an allusion full of veneration for solitaries in *De opere monachorum* (23:29) some fifteen years later.

14. Is it necessary to conclude with A. Zumkeller (*Augustinus Magister,* vol. 1, 265) that Augustine diverges from Jerome and oriental monasticism, the latter placing the accent more on obedience, whereas Augustine proposes an original concept centered on charity? To us the apologetical standpoint of *De moribus* seems sufficient to explain the modifications Augustine made on his source. His concern is not to give a theory of monasticism, for which, moreover, he was much less qualified than Jerome himself.

15. Cassian had already done so in Book 4 of the *Institutes.*

16. *Inst* 2:5. See our study 'Monachisme et Eglise dans la pensée de Cassien', *Théologie de la vie monastique* (Paris: Aubier, 1961).

17. These words of RB have no exact correspondent in RM. The idea they express is nevertheless implied by a remark of RM in vs 69.

18. According to Ildefons Herwegen, *Sinn und Geist der Benediktinerregel* (Einsiedeln/Cologne: Benziger, 1944) p 57, *stabilitas* is envisaged by *monasteriale, conversio morum* by *militans sub regula,* and *obedientia* by *abbate.* For O. Lottin, 'Le voeu de *"conversatio morum"* dans la Règle de Saint Benoît', *RTAM* 26 (1959) 5-16: 'the third vow (*conversatio morum*) can mean only one thing: exclusion of eremitical life', whereas *stabilitas* has gyrovagues in mind and *obedientia* sarabaites. Similarly aligned with this opinion, but less categorical, is Basil Steidle, 'De conversatione morum meorum', *Studia Anselmiana* 44 (1959) 137-144: by such commitments Benedict defends his cenobitic ideal against hermits as well as gyrovagues and sarabaites.

19. The Master is evidently unaware of the etymology of *monasterium*.

20. Benno Linderbauer, *S Benedicti Regula Monachorum: herausgegeben und philologisch erklärt* (Metten: Verlag des Benediktinerstiftes, 1922) p 151, points out that *hoc est* occurs only here in RB, whereas the equivalent expression *id est* occurs very frequently in it. In RM, *hoc est* and *id est* occur alternately. Corbett has observed (*The Latin*, p 90) that the presence of this unique *hoc est* in RB alone proves that Benedict is not the author of this text.

21. Although *eremita* is just as much taken from the Greek as *anachoreta*, the latter was always harder sounding to Latin ears. Sulpitius Severus had already introduced their name by means of a paraphrase: *quos anachoretas uocant* (*Dial* 1:15), whereas *eremita*, like *eremus*, seems to require no explanation (*Dial* 1:12). It is known that hermits and anchorites form, in the thought of Sulpitius Severus, two distinct kinds. Isidore of Seville takes up this distinction (*De ecclesiasticis officiis* 2:16).

22. RM has *coenobiorum* (P, A) *coenobitarum* (E); RB, *coenobitarum*. Jerome uses this last form, whereas Cassian writes *coenobiotarum*. Would not both the P, A and E readings derive from the form used by Cassian? It is true that P, A also gives it as *coenobitarum* in vs 75 (*coenouitarum* E).

23. The ineptitude of this translation has already been pointed out. *Monasterium* is not in practice reserved to the cenobitic community in contemporary terminology (cf. Cassian, *Conf* 18:9-10: the dwelling of every kind of monk, even of a hermit or of some sarabaites), or in the Master himself (cf. RM 1:88: the house of an isolated monk?). However, *monasterium* is already made synonymous for *coenobium*, in distinction to eremitical life, by Jerome, *Letter* 125 (*ad Rusticum*) 9-17, and by VP 3:5 (PL 73:741c), to cite only two of numerous examples. In RM itself, within the strict confines of our text, we find *monasterium* taken in this sense twice (RM Ths 46; 1:3). As a result we can handily explain how *monasterium* here figures as the translation of *coenobitarum*. This 'cenobitic' meaning is nearly that which Cassian gives to *monasteriale* in *Inst* 4:7 (*habitus monasterialis*, in speaking of the Tabennesiotes). Likewise in the *Vita Caesarii* 1:8 (PL 67:1005a) *simplicitas monasterialis*, the holy ignorance Caesarius fostered at Lérins.

24. Cassian again speaks of the *coenobium* with regard to communities comprising only 8 or 10 monks. But it concerns the heroic period of beginnings, when monks were not yet numerous in the desert (*Conf* 7:23). Jerome, followed by Augustine, expressly notes the large number of brethren accommodated within a single *coenobium*. They are divided into tens and hundreds, like Israel in the desert. Sulpitius Severus (*Dial* 1:10) and Cassian (*Inst* 4:1, 7) also call attention to the fact that monasteries of the Thebaid are highly populated, as we know also from Pachomian documents. So the idea formed of a *coenobium* is normally that of a numerous community, easily surpassing the hundred mark. Masters capable of teaching perfection are rare!

25. R Aug 16: 207-213.

26. R Caes V 62-63 and *passim*.

27. Preference of esteem for cenobitic life: cf. Herwegen, *Sinn und Geist*, p 57ff, and recently René Dolle, '*Fraterna ex acie*. A propos du chapitre 1 de la Règle bénédictine', *Studia Anselmiana* 44 (1959) 126-128. Practical preference: cf. Olivier Rousseau, 'Monachisme et vie religieuse' *Collection Irénikon* (Chevetogne, 1957) p 84. On the superiority of eremitical life, see Anselm Stolz, *L'Ascèse chrétienne* (Chevetogne: Bénédictins d'Amay, 1948).

28. Even if we add what is said about false hermits (1:11-12), which takes up the same ideas again.

29. For example, St Jerome, *Letter* 130:17.

30. The *regula sancti patris nostri Basilii* is recommended by RB 73. The relations between that rule and RM require special examination. For now it suffices to say that the Master seems to have taken nothing from him directly.

62   *Community and Abbot*

31. Community life is also given as a *ne plus ultra* by certain Pachomian texts. Cf. *Vies Coptes* pp 176-178, 267-269.

32. Thus RB. In RM vs 5: *cum Deo et spiritu repugnare sufficiunt.* The anthropology of the Master is recognizable in these words, which occur again at the end of the chapter: *aliud nobis Dominus in spiritu imperat, aliud caro cogit in anima* (vs 80).

33. Basil Steidle, *The Rule of St Benedict: A Commentary,* tr. Urban Schnitzhofer (Canon City, Colorado: Holy Cross Abbey, 1967). We have cited and discussed these expressions in 'Le monastère, Eglise du Christ' in *Studia Anselmiana* 42 (1957) pp 44ff.

34. Up to a certain point, for authentic eremitism has never deprecated the sacraments of the Church and the teaching of the Elders. Some community life plays a part in the normal condition of a hermit.

35. Ciprian Vagaggini, 'S. Benedetto e la questione semipelagiana', *Studia Anselmiana* 18-19 (1947) pp 55-56, note 39.

36. *Inst* 4:1-7 and *passim*; 5:4, 36.

37. *Conf* 19:1-10. (See below, Chapter 4, p 226).

38. *Dial* 1:10-11.

39. See at greater length p 55. In this discussion with Steidle, we grant him that cenobitic life is the highest realization of the ecclesial community here below. This postulate would itself also require examination. Is there an intrinsic perfection for the Church in the visible, tangible community, in the daily give-and-take among its members? Is it not essentially his love for God which unites a Christian to his brothers? Is the hermit, according to the degree of his holiness, not at the center of the ecclesial community? See the profound remarks by Heinrich Bacht, 'Von der Anachorese zum Cönobitentum', *Studia Anselmiana* 38 (1956) 84.

40. *Conf* 18:7. This translation is ratified today by Copticists: *sar* = dispersed (qualificative); *abet* = monastery. 'Dispersed with regard to a monastery, dispersed each in his own cell.' Cf. Herwegen, *Sinn und Geist,* p 61, n. 4.

41. In fact, it would be more exact to present cenobitism as an effort to organize the liberty of the beginnings.

42. Mt 6:25.

43. *Conf* 18:7.

44. Vss 6-9.

45. Vs 10.

46. Cassian (*Conf* 18:4), like Jerome, had initially reckoned three kinds, and did not mention the fourth kind except in a sort of appendix (18:8).

47. RM reverts to this point in Chapter 7:25 in the course of another description of sarabaites-gyrovagues.

48. See the reference in Butler.

49. RM 1:13.

50. 'Very strong', not 'the strongest'. We do not have here an affirmation of the superiority of cenobitism, as Rousseau would have it (*Monachisme et vie religieuse,* pp 84, 121).

51. *Letter* 22.35, cited by Butler *in loco.*

52. Vss 76-92.

53. Ps 34 (33):14, cf. Ths 11.

54. Vss 80-81, cf. Thp 24-53.

55. Artificial as this comparison with the Trinity may seem, it is noteworthy that

something very similar is found in R Fer 3: after having recommended two fundamental virtues (obedience and respect), Feriolus adds charity *tertio loco propter ipsum etiam sacratum numerum Trinitatis.* A little before (vs 83), we read *regerentur* with E and A, as against *regenerentur* (P). See below, Chapter 2, Appendix.

56. Jer 3:15. The erroneous attribution to Isaiah should be noted; it happens habitually when the Master cites this text. Cf. RM 11:12. Before him, the *Lib Ors* (Chapter 47, p 140, 1. 25) had already applied these words to cenobitic superiors. Cf. also R Fer 37, which adds almost immediately, as here, Jn 21:17 ('Feed my sheep').

57. Jn 21:17; Mt 28:20.

58. Lk 10:16.

59. Ths 46; Thp 53.

60. RM 10:123.

61. *Unius,* vs 87. That there be but one master is characteristic of cenobitic *charisma,* according to Cassian (*Inst* 4:40). The hermit, on the contrary, ought to address himself to different masters according to the virtues he wants to acquire (*Inst* 5:4). Jerome also insists on the unicity of a master (*Letter* 125:15).

62. The Master depicts this substitution of the will of the superior for that of the disciple with a realism which disconcerts us. Cf. RM 2:32-36; 7:52-56. On this theme of transfer of responsibility, entirely surrendered by the disciples and assumed by the master, see Irénée Hausherr, *La direction spirituelle en Orient autrefois* (Rome: Pontifical Institute of Oriental Studies, 1955) pp 144-147.

63. See below, Chapters 2 and 4. The Master's theory is in any case to be compared with Cassian's on the apostolic origin of the *coenobia.*

64. Here and Chapter 2:1-14.

Chapter Two

THE ABBOT (RB 2)

STRUCTURE OF THE TEXT[1]

I F ONE EXAMINES the structure of the chapter on the abbot in the rules and compares these two presentations of the same text, it is difficult not to attribute to RM an orderly and cohesive character which is not found to the same degree in RB. The construction of the chapter in RM is so strong and simple that it would defy explanation were it not the expression of a single person's mind. In this we have an argument in favor of its anteriority to the RB text, the peculiarities of which are better explained as revisions than as primitive elements. Let us try to reconstruct the plan of the two texts, leaving to one side for the present vss 41-52 of RM, to which Chapter Three of RB corresponds.

Two paragraphs of equal length (vss 1-10 and 32-40) open and close RM. Taking their start from the name 'abbot' they develop similar reflections on the account he shall have to render at the last judgment both for his teaching and for the acts of his disciples.[2] We shall entitle these two paragraphs the Introduction and the Conclusion.

Between them (vss 11-31) are two parallel pericopes (vss 11-22 and 23-31) almost equal in length to one another and to the above paragraphs. They develop the same themes in the same order. The second pericope, however, renews and enriches the first by the introduction of new elements.[3]

The two fundamental themes which succeed each other in the same order within each pericope are:

     1. Words and acts (commands and example): vss 11-15 and 23-29.

     2. Equal love for everyone (no favorites!): vss 16-22 and 30-31.

A third theme common to both pericopes should be noted, although it does not enter into each part in exactly the same way: the diversity of methods to be employed by the abbot according to the diversity of character in his monks. We shall call this the annexed theme. In the first pericope, it is attached to what we called the first theme: words are for intelligent disciples, example for disciples who are hard of heart. In the second pericope it also adheres to the first theme, but with a difference. Oral teaching itself assumes a triple form in conformity with the reading from the Apostle: *arguere* for the undisciplined, *obsecrare* for the obedient, *increpare* for the negligent. From one pericope to the other, therefore, the annexed theme is varied. The abbot's teaching, we are told initially, is disseminated by word and example, a double form reading of the two categories of disciples. Then within the oral teaching itself three different manners are distinguished, adapted to three categories of hearers.[4]

Let us return to the two fundamental themes. They acquire further nuances in passing from one pericope to the other.

1. *Words and acts (commands and example).*

In the first pericope, this couplet appears successively under two aspects:

a) first, to ensure successful pedagogy, the master's teaching ought not to be only oral, but lived (vss 11-13). The acts of the abbot must themselves square with what he enjoins in the name of Scripture, either positively (vss 11-12) or negatively (vs 13).

b) furthermore, in his own interest the abbot must foresee that he shall be judged not only on what he says, but on his acts as well (vss 13-15): 'lest while preaching to others, he himself should be rejected'. His own salvation is at stake.

In the second pericope the 'words and acts' couplet is supported by another couplet: 'form' of the Apostle (vss 23-25) and 'form' of the Lord (vss 26-29). Oral teaching should vary according to the three types indicated by the Apostle (2 Tim 4:2). Teaching by example must consist above all in humility corresponding to the Lord's teaching to the Twelve (Mt 18:4).

2. *Equal love for everyone (no favourites!).*

The first pericope refers to the example of God himself, the second to that of human parents, father and mother. The first (vss 16-22) shows how God has no preferences save by reason of good actions, which nevertheless do not prevent his placing creation at the service of sinners as well as of the just. The abbot, in the likeness of God, should avoid all preference of persons, every sort of favoritism based on other than supernatural motives and especially on social origin. Still more, he ought to overcome even legitimate preferences based on real superiority, to love all his sons with an equal love and to show each identical treatment on every occasion.[5]

In the second pericope, the theme is dealt with much more briefly (vss 30-31) and under a new form. Like a mother, the abbot ought to love all his sons with an equal love; like a father, he ought to know how to 'mete out' his goodness.[6]

The following outline shows the structure of the chapter as we have analyzed it.

Introduction (1-10).
The name of abbot: Christ's lieutenant. He must therefore match his doctrine to divine precepts. He is responsible for this doctrine and consequently for the obedience of his disciples. He shall have to render account for the flock at the final judgment.

First Pericope (11-22).
1) *First theme* (11-15). Words and acts, commands and example.
Annexed theme: diversity of teaching forms corresponding to the variety of character (12).
2) *Second theme* (16-22). Equal love for everyone. No favorites!

Second Pericope (23-31).
1) *First theme* (23-29). Words and acts, commands and example.
23-25: *forma apostolica in doctrina.*
26-29: *forma humilitatis in se*
Annexed theme: diversity of teaching forms corresponding to the variety of character (23-25).
2) *Second theme* (30-31). Equal love for everyone. No favorites!

Conclusion (32-40).

> The abbot's name. He shall have to render account at the judgment for the souls of all his disciples and for all their actions which were performed at his order. He ought therefore to match his doctrine to the divine precepts. Besides the souls of his disciples, he shall have to render account for his own (cf. first pericope, first theme).

We apologize to the reader for having executed so scholastic an analysis, but it seems to us indispensable if we are to reveal the very solid construction of the text. The fact that so clear an outline can be made when one allows oneself to be guided by the most obvious parallels demonstrates quite well that we are dealing with a compositional work as methodical as it is supple, which in fact seems to postulate a single author. This point established, there remains the task of elucidating the cohesion of the different parts.

The connection between the introduction and the first pericope is clear: having treated *doctrina* in general, the author proceeded to distinguish a duplex doctrine: words and acts (vs 11).

How does the second theme relate to the first? Actually, it makes a rather sudden appearance (vs 17: *non unus plus ametur*). This asyndeton can no doubt be explained by the fact that it comes in the context of faults the abbot should avoid. Would the gravest of them not be preference of persons? In this way the second theme ties in with the idea of the divine commandments in the first part.[7] Possibly too, the 'equality' demanded here forms a couplet with the pedagogical 'diversity' suggested just before. In any case, this is the only plausible explanation for the affiliation of the two themes in the second pericope (vs 30: *caritatem uero...*).

The logical sequence between the first and second pericopes does not appear clear. The structural identity of the two pericopes would make one think they had been composed separately, like parallel variations on the same canvas, and later juxtaposed.[8] But a logical connection between the end of the first pericope and the beginning of the second is discernible. The first closes in recommending an equal love, an identical *discipline*. The author then immediately corrects this prescript by distinguishing for the abbot several teaching methods corresponding to the character of his disciples, thus beginning the second pericope, the 'equality -diversity' couplet which counterbalances the two themes within each pericope.[9]

Between the second pericope and the conclusion there is no explicit transposition (vs 32: *Meminere debet abbas...*). This new asyndeton does neverthelss form an evident parallel with the introduction.

vs   1: *abbas...semper meminere debet quod dicitur.*
vs 32: *meminere debet abbas semper...quod dicitur.*

At the same time there is also a brusque rupture with what immediately preceded and a reversion to the introduction - the usual technique for drawing to a conclusion. The logical sequence of this paragraph, as we have said, displays identical parallelism with the introduction. The same theme is developed in each, to wit, the final judgment. But it is not a question of mere repetition. The Master was content to suggest by the first words what he had developed at length in vss 2-6: the abbot, vicar of Christ, ought to conform his teaching with the Lord's. But here the judgment theme is enriched by an annotation which had already appeared in the course of the first pericope (vss 13-15): the abbot must prepare himself to give account not only of the sheep and of all their actions, but of his own soul as well.[10]

One peculiarity which distinguishes RM from RB merits notice. The RM chapter on the abbot extends beyond this conclusion, which becomes Chapter Three in RB. If the analysis we have proposed is accepted, vss 1-40 of RM appear as a homogeneous entity, solidly built and in some sense complete in itself. After the treatise on the abbot, the little treatise on the council of the brethren is certainly well-placed. It is nonetheless an appendix. One has no difficulty explaining why RB detached it to make it a separate chapter from the foregoing.

Verses 41-50 are clearly separate from the abbatial treatise. Not only is a new institution introduced, but the instruction is no longer addressed to the abbot exclusively, turning at times toward the brethren. Again, spiritual terrain is abandoned for temporal administration, which is the real meaning of the new terms *utilitas monasterii* (twice in vs 41) and *communis utilitas* (vs 45). The Master wanted to speak here not indiscriminately of all community interests, but precisely of temporal affairs, administration of the monastic patrimony (vs 48: *res monasterii*). That, and only that, is the abbot obliged to handle in council with all the brethren.

We put off to the next chapter a detailed analysis of this paragraph. It is enough here to have outlined its place within Chapter Two of RM.[11]

Finally in vss 51-52 the Master introduces the *ars sancta* theme, which will receive further development in Chapters Three to Six. This manner of concluding one chapter by anticipating the next reminds us of the end of Chapter One (vss 76-92). The Master was fond of transitions and he strove to give his entire work the stamp of a homogeneous and highly coherent development. Though these two verses incline toward what follows rather than to what precedes, they do nevertheless relate, prior to vss 41-50, to the *doctrina* theme of vss 1-40. This confirms that the treatise on the council of the brethren constitutes a sort of appendix or parenthesis.

Having concluded our analysis of Chapter Two of RM, let us now take up the same chapter in RB. Had it presented us with a succession of well-defined ideas, commentators would certainly not have failed to call attention to it. But, in fact, Delatte prudently abstained from proposing an outline and Herwegen seemed to attach little worth to the divisions he worked out.[12] Herwegen's schema rests on the triple reference to the name the abbot bears.[13] He thus discerned three parts which correspond to what we have called the introduction, first and second pericopes, and conclusion. Within the second part, the RB additions and suppressions did not permit him to distinguish parallel pericopes.[14]

The chapter plan, therefore, is much less prominent in RB than in RM. Then too, RB variations compared to RM consist sometimes of omissions and sometimes of additions. This is new compared with the preceding chapter in which variants were all the same type (omission or résumé). All told, RB has a text slightly longer than RM (the treatise on the council of the brethren aside) by about ten lines, or approximately ten per cent of the whole. We shall give separate consideration to the two types of variants, first omissions, then additions. Only variants of notable length (of more than one line) will occupy our attention.

On that scale, three omissions are discernible in RB. The first bears upon vs 21, the end of the first pericope. The Master's thought in this passage meanders a bit. Having established that God gives no preference to persons (A), he allows a distinction based on superiority of works (B), then shows how this distinction is itself surmounted by the universal goodness of God toward everyone, good and bad alike (C); from this he concludes that the abbot ought to have equal love and consistent conduct (D). Pas-

sing immediately from (B) to (D) RB omits (C). This omission is
not made without changing the sense of the conclusion somewhat.
Basing himself on the divine example, the Master prescribed that
the abbot have an equal love in every respect,[15] a single discipline
on every occasion.[16] By omitting the considerations of the divine
example (C), RB was led to modify the conclusion by adding
secundum merita, which is in line with (B). The abbot, like God,
takes account of works and merits. So RB stops at a point which,
in the dialectic of the Master, was surmounted and outstripped by
the unconditional affirmation of the equal goodness of Providence
for all men regardless of merit.

The second, and much more important omission bears upon vss
26-31, that is, on the greater part of the second pericope. In it
disappear: 1) the end of the first theme: the example of humility
which the abbot ought to manifest in himself, making himself little as a child, and the conclusion on the example the abbot ought
to set in all that he commands so as to draw his disciples after him,
as the head leads the members (vss 26-29);[17] 2) the second theme:
love for everyone, without preference, as equal as a mother's love,
meted out with a father's tenderness (vss 30-31).

Of the second pericope, RB retained only the beginning, the
theme of diversity of teaching methods, developed in the form of a
commentary on 2 Tim 4:2 (vss 23-25). What could be the reasons
for this important suppression? Perhaps the redactor was
disconcerted, as we are today, by the juxtaposition of images: the
abbot described successively as child, mother, father. Besides, the
omission of the passage on the child may be explained by a feeling
of embarrassment. How could anyone require such an attitude of
a superior? The redactor might have shrunk before the boldness of
the precept, especially in a document destined for public reading.
As a matter of fact, the Gospel pericope evoked here (Mt 18:4) was
never, as far as I know, applied elsewhere to superiors of
coenobia, not even by Basil who dwelt so willingly on the humility
of the *proëstôs.* As for the omission of vss 30-31, the reason is the
same as for the omission of vs 21. It was no doubt intended, like
the latter, to attenuate the absolute nature of the 'equal love' the
abbot owes to everyone.[18]

The third omission bears upon vss 35-38, that is, the conclusion. In this passage, the Master gave the reason for which the abbot shall have to render account for all the souls entrusted to him:

For, so as not to do their own will in the monastery, the

brethren always served his commands in all obedience, and when they are called to account for all they have done they will say to the Lord at the judgment that they did everything in obedience (*per oboedientiam*) by command of the master (*a iussione magistri*). Therefore the master must always see to it that everything he commands, everything he teaches, every correction he gives, is manifestly in accord with the precepts of God, as justice demands, so that he will not be condemned in the judgment to come.[19]

This text manifestly recalls the end of Chapter One (vss 87,90-92). Obedience is propounded in the same starkly realistic fashion as a quasi-substitution of the will of the master for that of the disciple. But whereas Chapter One presented this doctrine to the brethren's view as an incentive to submit to an abbot, Chapter Two draws a lesson from it for the abbot himself. Responsibility for the inferior weighs entirely on the superior. He must see to it that everything he commands, everything he teaches, every correction he gives, is fully in accord with the divine law.

Nothing has been retained of these two passages in RB. Because it is so well delineated, this omission is surely more significant than that from Chapter One, from which the whole of the verses 76-92 have altogether disappeared. Ought we to attribute to the redactor the intention of effacing a doctrine which he thought less sure or less useful? If such was his intention, we can see he did not completely succeed, for this doctrine continues to shine through two words of the introduction which RB preserved: 'The abbot shall be examined by the Lord at the judgment on two things: his doctrine *and the obedience of his disciples.*' We believe that the words here must be understood in this starkly realistic sense. The disciples being presumed obedient, all their actions emanate in some manner from the will of the abbot, and it is he who bears full responsibility.

Such are the three important omissions. We now come to the additions. In number, place, and length, they curiously resemble the omissions.

The first addition comes at vs 18 of RM and amounts to only a verse and a half (RB vss 18b-19). RM has forbidden the abbot to show preference to a freeman over a slave *pro merito nationis*. These last words disappear in RB, which instead inserts 'unless some other reasonable cause exists' - a clause which proposes in explicit form the substance of the reservation implied in the suppressed words. In form, this *nisi* clause recalls the adjoining phrase *nisi quem in bonis actibus inuenerit meliorem.* The rest of the addition shows that the redactor understood *praeponitur* in a rather material sense: with him it was a matter of the rank (*ordo, locus*) occupied by the brethren in community. This application to a particular consideration no doubt circumscribed somewhat the Master's intention, who was thinking of indications of preference in general. The issue of rank is a preoccupation characteristic of RB, whereas RM knows nothing of such things.[20] Studying it from another standpoint, Gradenwitz suspected this passage of being an interpolation. His criticism was based solely on the similarity of the juridical texts.[21] The absence of these lines in RM is a curious counterproof.[22]

The first addition, while it obviously corresponds to the first omission in length, does not exactly correspond with it in place. Though near, it comes a little before it, and in the same development. The second addition, on the contrary, is inserted in exactly the same place as the second omission (RM vss 26-31; RB vss 26-29). Certainly this fact could be explained as a fortuitous coincidence. If one distinguishes two separate stages of RB redaction, as Froger does, one could say the 'annotator' judged it good to insert a comment here without suspecting that the 'abridger' had made a cut at just this spot. The hypothesis that a single hand effected both operations seems, however, to account more naturally for the facts. The addition is, moreover, a little shorter than the omission, which makes plausible its attribution to the abridger himself.

From the standpoint of content, the addition contains two ideas:

1) The speed with which the abbot must correct evil tendencies as soon as they appear (vs 26: *mox ut coeperint oriri*; vs 28: *in ipso initio peccati*). This idea is seen here for the first time; it is missing from RM and does not reappear in RB. The pericope, then, has very much the stamp of an isolated 'note', especially when compared with RM 26-31, which resumes and repeats themes already developed in the first pericope.

2) In this correction, the abbot ought to vary his approach according to character. Here once again we fall in with the theme of diversity of methods appropriate to different temperaments (annexed theme). This theme appears twice in the Master, following the symmetrical law dominating the whole of his plan, each time in contrast with 'equal love' (second theme). Compared with

this well-organized structure, RB looks like a re-worked and less coherent text. In addition to the two passages it shares in common with the Master, RB here adds a *third,* to which, as we shall see, it later adds a *fourth* (RB vs 31c). In each case, there is a new two or three part division of characters, with an indication of the treatment corresponding to each. Thus RB resumes the annexed RM theme no less than four times. And since, on the other hand, it omits repeating the first and second themes in the second pericope, complete disequilibrium ensues. Fourfold repetition of the one theme, with two others, creates that impression of prolixity and confusion experienced by every reader, even the uninitiated, and which is perhaps the most characteristic aspect of the RB text in this chapter.

We would also remark that RB advocates corporal chastisement. This again is a trait peculiar to RB.[23] The whole addition has a severe, even a harsh, tone which contrasts curiously with the humble abasement and universal tenderness recommended to the abbot in the corresponding omission. Does this contrast reflect an express intention on the part of the RB redactor?

The third addition (RB vss 31-36) makes its appearance in vs 25, several lines before the third omission (35-38). This addition, then, was inserted in a way similar to the first. It comes a little before, not precisely in the place left vacant by the omission, but within the same development. One is struck, moreover, by its length, nearly double that of the third omission (five verses as opposed to three).

In content, this addition shows the same traits as the previous one. On the one hand, there are two new themes: the office of governing souls is difficult (RB 31a); spiritual things must be preferred to temporal ones (RB 33-36). On the other hand, the theme of diversity in dealings according to variety of character (RB 31c-32) appears for the fourth time. Innovation and repetition both alter the nature of the section. In the Master there was a simple conclusion corresponding to the introduction and recalling the idea that the abbot ought to take care of his own soul.[24] Here we find ourselves in the presence of new developments, as if the original theme of the Conclusion, the 'account rendering', is not missing in the addition(RB 32cd and 34). The redactor, in order to evoke it, has utilized the proper terms of RM in such a way that RB 34 forms a doublet with RB 37 (= RM 33):

RB 34: *animas suscepit regendas...rationem redditurus est.*

RB 37: *suscepit animas regendas...rationem reddendam.*[25]

The additions and omissions are as follows:

RM 2	RB 2

First Pericope. Second Theme.

(16) non ab eo persona in monasterio discernatur; (17) non unus plus ametur quam alius nisi quem in bonis actibus invenerit meliorem; (18) non convertenti servo pro merito nationis praeponatur ingenuus.

(16) non ab eo persona in monasterio discernatur; (17) non unus plus ametur quam alius nisi quem in bonis actibus aut oboedientia invenerit meliorem; (18) non convertenti ex servitio praeponatur ingenuus
first addition: nisi alia rationabilis causa existat: (19) quod si ita, iustitia dictante, abbati visum fuerit, et de cuiuslibet ordine id faciet; sin alias, propria teneant loca;

(19) Quare? quare? quia servus sive liber omnes Christo unum sumus, et sub uno Dn̄o aequalem servitii militiam baiulamus, quia non est apud Dm̄ personarum acceptio. (20) Solummodo in hac parte apud Dm̄ discernimur, si ab aliis meliores factis inveniamur.

(20) quia sive servus sive liber, omnes in Christo unum sumus, et sub uno Domino aequalem servitutis militiam baiulamus, quia non est apud Deum personarum acceptio. (21) Solummodo in hac parte apud ipsum discernimur, si meliores ab aliis in operibus bonis et humiles inveniamur.

(21) Et tamen ut ostendat Ds̄ circa omnes pietatis suae clementiam pariter, iubet elementa vel terram iustis vel peccatoribus famulari aequaliter.

first omission

(22) Ergo aequalis sit ab eo ab omnibus caritas, una praebeatur in omnibus disciplina.

(22) Ergo aequalis sit ab eo omnibus caritas, una praebeatur secundum merita disciplina.

RM 2   RB 2

Second Pericope. First Theme.

(23) In doctrina namque sua abbas apostolicam debet illam semper formam servare in qua dicit: «argue, obsecra, increpa»; (24) id est miscens temporibus tempora, terroribus blandimenta, dirum magistri, pium patris ostendat affectum; (25) id est indisciplinatos debet et inquietos arguere, oboedientes, mites et patientissimos ut in melius proficiant obsecrare, neglegentes et contemnentes ut increpet admonemus.

(23) In doctrina sua namque abbas apostolicam debet illam semper formam servare in qua dicit: «argue, obsecra, increpa»; (24) id est miscens temporibus tempora, terroribus blandimenta, dirum magistri, pium patris ostendat affectum; (25) id est indisciplinatos et inquietos debet durius arguere, oboedientes autem et mites et patientes ut in melius proficiant obsecrare, neglegentes et contemnentes ut increpet et corripiat admonemus.

(26) Humilitatis vero talem in se eis formam debet ostendere, qualem D̄n̄s contendentibus de gradu fortiori apostolis demonstravit, (27) id est cum adpraehensa manu infantem in medio eorum deduxisset dixit: (28) «qui vult esse inter vos fortior, sit talis». (29) Ideoque quidquid abbas discipulis pro D̄n̄o agendum iniunxerit, indicet factis, et tradens omnia ordinationis suae, protelo sequantur membra qua duxerit caput.

second omission.

Second Theme.

(30) Caritatem vero vel gratiam talem debet circa omnes fratres habere, ut nullum alio praeferens omnibus discipulis vel filiis suis amborum parentum in se nomen exhibeat, (31) matrem eis suam

RM 2

praebens aequaliter caritatem, patrem se eis mensurata pietate ostendat.

RB 2

second addition: (26) Neque dissimulet peccata delinquentium, sed mox ut coeperint oriri radicitus ea ut praevalet amputet, memor periculi Heli sacerdotis de Silo. (27) Et honestiores quidem atque intelligibiles animos prima vel secunda admonitione verbis corripiat; (28) inprobos autem et duros ac superbos vel inoboedientes verberum vel corporis castigatio in ipso initio peccati coerceat, sciens scriptum «Stultus verbis non corrigitur». (29) Et iterum: «Percute filium tuum virga, et liberabis animam eius a morte».

Conclusion.

(32) Meminere debet abbas semper quod est, meminere quod dicitur, et scire quia cui plus creditur; plus ab eo exigitur.

(30) Meminere debet semper abbas quod est, meminere quod dicitur, et scire quia cui plus conmittitur, plus ab eo exigitur.

third addition: (31) Sciatque quam difficilem et arduam rem suscipit, regere animas et multorum servire moribus; et alium quidem blandimentis, alium vero increpationibus, alium suasionibus, (32) et secundum uniuscuiusque qualitatem vel intelligentiam ita se omnibus conformet et aptet, ut non solum detrimenta gregis sibi conmissi non patiatur, verum in augmentatione boni gregis gaudeat. (33)

RM 2   ## RB 2

Ante omnia ne dissimulans aut
parvipendens salutem animarum
sibi conmissarum, plus gerat
sollicitudinem de rebus tran-
sitoriis et terrenis atque caducis;
(34) sed semper cogitet quia
animas suscipit regendas, de
quibus et rationem redditurus
est. (35) Et ne causetur de minori
forte substantia, meminerit scriptum: «Primum quaerite regnum
Dei et iustitiam eius, et haec omnia adicientur vobis», (36) et
iterum: «Nihil deest timentibus
eum».

(33) Et sciat quia qui suscipit
animas regendas, paret se ad rationes reddendas. (34) Et quantum sub sua cura fratrum se
habere scierit numerum,
agnoscat pro certo quia in die
iudicii ipsarum omnium
animarum tantas est redditurus
Dno rationes, sine dubio addita
et sua:

(37)Sciatque quia qui suscipit
animas regendas, paret se ad rationem reddendam. (38) Et
quantum sub cura sua fratrum se
habere scierit numerum,
agnoscat pro certo quia in die
iudicii ipsarum omnium
animarum est redditurus Domino
rationem, sine dubio addita et
suae animae.

(35) quia ut fratres in monasterio
propriam non agerent volun-
tatem, huius semper iussionibus
omni oboedientia militarunt;
(36) quia cum discussi fuerint de
omnibus actibus suis, dicturi sunt
in iudicio Dno omnia facta sua
per oboedientiam a iussione impleta esse magistri. (37) Ideoque
debet semper cautus esse
magister, (38) ut omnia quae im-

third omission.

RM 2

perat, omnia quae docet, omnia quae emendat, de praeceptis Dī, iustitia dictante, monstretur, quod futuro iudicio non condemnetur.

(39) timens semper futuram discussionem pastoris de creditis ovibus, quia et cum de alienis ratiociniis cavet, redditur de suis sollicitus, (40) et cum de monitionibus suis emendationes alliis subministrat, ipse efficitur a vitiis emendatus.

RB 2

(39) Et ita timens semper futuram discussionem pastoris de creditis ovibus, cum de alienis ratiociniis cavet, redditur de suis sollicitus, (40) et cum de monitionibus suis emendationem aliis subministrat, ipse efficitur a vitiis emendatus.

The following table will enable the reader to understand at a glance the placement of the added or omitted pericopes:

RB Additions	RM Omissions
(1) RB 18b-19 (RM 18)	
	(1) RM 21 (RB 21)
(2) RB 26-29 (RM 26)	(2) RM 26-31 (RB 26)
(3) RB 31-36 (RM 32)	(3) RM 35-38 (RB 38)

The coincidence of the second addition with the second omission, as well as their equal length, suggests attributing both operations to' the same hand. Can we, in this hypothesis, account for the other data recorded?

The fact that the first and third additions come a little before their corresponding omissions might be explained thus: the redactor, having felt the need to interject a note into his text while still remaining faithful to his general purpose of abridgment, tried to compensate at the same time for the addition he made by effecting an equivalent deletion. This would explain why the first omission is just as long as the first addition. The effort expended in the second case might be viewed in the same way: the redactor began by writing his additional note and then struck out a section of the same length in the very spot where he inserted his note. In the third case, it would be necessary to admit that his intention remained the same, but that he did not execute it rigorously, having been unwilling to delete as much as he added or having not succeeded in doing so.

It is necessary, finally, to consider certain correspondences between the content of the additions and of the omissions, though matters of this nature are much more delicate to interpret. In the text of the second omission, RM obliged the abbot to humble himself like a little child and to be tender towards everyone like a father or a mother, whereas RB, in its second addition, makes it his duty to correct immediately the first manifestation of sin. One might be led to believe the redactor wanted to replace something that seemed to him too easy-going by an exhortation to severity. In such an hypothesis, the intention of suppressing the passage in question would have preceded and caused the writing of the addition—a factor that would oblige one to modify a little the schema proposed above, which took its start from data of a different sort.

Comparison of the RB redactor's work with that of the E copyist is of some interest. The copyist, of course, inserted no additions. Let us simply survey what he has deleted:

1) the entire first pericope (11-22).
2) The abbot humble-as-a-child-tender-as-a-father-and-mother-toward-everyone section (26-37).
3) the abbot responsible-for-the-actions-of-the-disciples-accomplished-at-his-command section (35-36).

The first of these omissions would confirm our analysis of the RM text: vss 11-22 seemed to form a block-unit between the Introduction and the second pericope. The second omission of E curiously coincides with the second RB omission. Thus the E copyist and the RB redactor both declined to transcribe this passage. Might this be because of its content?[26] E's third omission likewise coincides with the beginning of the third RB omission (the latter omits vss 37-38 as well). Here again, one may wonder if the same sensitivity guided the two abridgers in their selection. The omitted passage underscores the responsibility of the abbot for the disciple's actions performed at his command. The brethren are hypothetically considered perfectly obedient: from that results a transfer of responsibility from disciples to abbot. This naive and somewhat too rigorous logic might have seemed open to censure, inasmuch as it lays a very weighty burden on the abbot and risks being taken as a guarantee of acquittal for the disciples.

THE TRADITION: DIRECTORIES FOR ABBOTS

This was not the first time the superior of a christian community received instructions for his pastoral ministry. Apart from directories for bishops and priests such as those composed by St Ambrose (*De officiis*) and St Gregory (*The Pastoral Office*), cenobitic tradition by the time of St Benedict already counted a good number of writings of this sort designed for abbots. If we are to assess exactly the literary originality and doctrinal content of this chapter, a review of these documents is necessary.

Directories for superiors composed before the end of the sixth century can be roughly classed in three groups:

A. Egypt

We mention first the R Pac, which, when compared to the rest of the rule, contains (*Inst* 18) a passage somewhat unusual both for its length and for its numerous allusions to Scripture. This directory for the head of the house includes a list of some fifty interdictions or negative precepts which terminate with a series of biblical maledictions levied against offenders. The interdictions follow one another without any apparent order. They inveigh against numerous and diverse faults. Among the crimes most often recurring under different forms we may mention desire for money or material goods, oppression of the poor and injustice, dissimulation and false witness, intemperance in food or wine, foolish talk and laughing (especially among boys), transgression of monastic or ecclesiastical rules, and lack of constancy. Quite often these prohibitions are not so singularly appropriate to the superior that they cannot be extended more generally to apply to every monk or every Christian. The scriptural citations are not usually drawn from passages in which the Scriptures are exhorting superiors.

The pachomian milieu has left us another directory for the superior, the *Liber Orsiesii*. This catechesis was meant for the entire Congregation,[27] but some important passages concern superiors alone. First of all, Paragraphs Seven through Twelve put the heads of monasteries and the provosts of houses on guard against several shortcomings: negligence and asperity (7), indifference towards faults committed by their inferiors (8-9), injustices, preferential treatment, culpable indulgence or unjustified aversion (9). The author reminds them that when Christ returns they shall have to give an account for all the souls confided to them. After this general exhortation, each level of the hierarchy receives particular counsels (par 13-18), especially provosts, who are incessantly put on the alert against injustice and are informed of the responsibility they bear and of the solicitude which they should show (15-17). To this long exhortation should be added the brief admonition in Paragraphs Thirty-nine and Forty. The provosts are threatened with punishment if they neglect to give the brethren the necessities provided for in the rule. The heads of monasteries are to remember the lesson in Paragraph Seven: beware of neglecting brothers undergoing punishment; bear with the frailty of the weaker ones.

The directory for superiors in the *Liber Orsiesii* has a quality and significance far surpassing what we find in the pachomian rule. Assuredly, the *Liber* is not, properly speaking, a rule, but a text written in definite circumstances with a particular, temporary situation in view. But the loftiness of views which it bespeaks, the great biblical inspiration behind it, the perfectly appropriate choice of the most meaningful scriptural texts that could be applied to heads of christian communities, place the directory of Orsiesius among the most important bequeathed to us by the cenobitic tradition.

Now we must revert to the pachomian rule, or rather to the two documents derived from it and largely through which it has come to be known in the West. The shorter recension reproduced R Pac Inst 18 without appreciable modification, transferring it to the end of the rule n° 128. R Pac Inst 18 reappears in the *Regula*

Orientalis (n° 17); this time, although the list of interdictions is reproduced, the redactor thought it good to omit the maledictions which end the paragraph. This amputation notwithstanding, the text occupies considerable space in R Or, nearly one-seventh of it. Granted that the author retained only a small number of R Pac paragraphs, often radically abridged, one is struck by the place he gives to this interesting directory for the provost. In the author's view this document apparently held an interest which to some extent escapes us today.

In addition, the R Or harbors another directory, one pertaining to the abbot. This text, with which the R Or opens, is one of the original passages inserted by the Latin redactor in his abridgment of the R Pac (R Or 1). Fairly short, it begins with a list of qualities the abbot ought to possess. The style and even the literary terms obviously recall the Pastoral Letters.[28] The abbot is teacher and father; his authority extends over everyone and everything. The R Or author traces a line of conduct for his judgments: neither preference of persons, nor indulgence, but a right judgment passed on each one 'according to the merits of his daily conduct'. The subsequent words, *admoneat, hortetur, castiget, condemnet,* may well be alluding to 2 Tim 4:2, a text whose presence has already been noted in RB. Finally, the R Or author entrusts the abbot with the decision of admitting postulants and expelling bad religious.

With R Or we conclude our consideration of the principal documents of the pachomian family. Yet before passing to the next category, we would do well to mention R 4 Pat, since it claims Egyptian origin.[29] This small rule discusses twice the subject under consideration. First, in lines thirty-five to fifty six, it propounds 'how the spiritual exercise ought to be fulfilled by superiors'. The position of this passage is significant: it constitutes in some way the second chapter of the rule, preceded by presentation on the unity of the community gathered round a unique superior to whom all owe obedience. After placing the superior before the brethren, the rule turns to instruct him in his duties. This sequence of ideas, remember, is the one which RM presented in its first two chapters. We meet it also, though less obviously, in RB. This is not the only point of contact between R 4 Pat and the other two rules. The theme of example, that of gentleness mingled with severity, and the citation of 2 Tim 4:2 introducing a development on various dealings according to the individuals recall the RM and RB abbatial treatises.

To such similarities may be added several others in the second passage in which R 4 Pat instructs superiors.[30] This second directory, located at the end of the rule (lines 205-225), is introduced by an *ordo excommunicationis* (189-204). Superiors are entreated to correct gently and humbly, in order that offenders persevere in monastic life. There is also an admonition against preference of persons, 'to love all [the brethren] with an equal affection and sincere heart', to observe equity. Another abuse would be negligence in correcting: the abbot would then have to account for the errant brother. Furthermore, mere good words cannot be enough. The example given by the 'teachers' should back up their teaching. R 4 Pat concludes by quoting 1 Thess 5:14, and by promising eternal recompense for all the souls who will be won.

The reader familiar with RM-RB Two will have recognized, incidentally, some rather notable points of contact, in particular the condemnation of preferential treatment, the themes of equal affection and of example, and the insistence on the duty of correction in the light of accountability.

B. Cappadocia

Let us now look at the directories for superiors composed by Basil and Gregory of Nyssa.

Question Fifteen of the *Rules of St Basil* determines what sentiments the superior should have in giving commands. Basil distinguishes two attitudes. Toward God the fundamental sentiment is fear of departing from the divine law which the superior only administers and dispenses. He may add nothing more nor prescribe anything contrary to nor omit any part of it. Toward the brethren the superior ought to be moved by unlimited devotion, 'like a mother nursing her children' (1 Thess 2:7), devotion which should move the abbot to go so far as to lay down his life according to the command and the example of Christ. As we see, the first of these two attitudes holds special interest for the RM-RB commentator. This fear of departing from the divine law is the first and last word of the benedictine directory.

In Question Twenty-Three ('What should be the sentiments of the superior when he is correcting?'), Basil took up the same schema. Once again he distinguished the attitude toward God — motivated by burning zeal for the divine law which the sinner transgresses — from the attitude toward the brother being admonished—which ought to resemble that of a compassionate physician attending his own son. The more bitter the remedy the more 'sympathetic' and merciful ought the correction to be.[31] We note, moreover, that Basil often insisted on the duty to correct and had very strong words about those who neglected this obligation.[32]

Although the West knew only the *Regula Basilii* it is interesting to consider the developments to which the directory for superiors was subjected in later editions of the *Rules*. We constantly meet the image of the physician (or infirmarian) with its lessons. The superior, even when correcting, is but the servant of the brethren. The solicitude he bestows upon each brother as his defects and needs require is inspired by a humble and compassionate charity free from all acrimony and anger (LR 30, 43, 50, 51). In addition, Basil required humility of his superiors, a virtue particularly necessary and difficult for them (LR 30, 43).

This exhortation to humility is inserted in a discourse on the example which the superior's life ought to be for the brethren (LR 43). Is the law of Christianity not the imitation of Christ? Placed as mediator between Christ and the crowd of his disciples, the superior ought to imitate Christ perfectly in order to win the disciples over to the same imitation. Moreover, example is more effective than words. In the example which the superior must give, humility comes foremost. That Christ made himself the servant of his disciples, his creatures, is all the more reason why the superior ought to place himself at the service of brethren who are his equals. These are the considerations Basil developed in the *Long Rules*. We find fairly similar passages in RM. Basil and the Master converge here simply because they are both inspired by the Gospel.

The recent discovery of St Gregory of Nyssa's *De Instituto Christiano* has put us in possession of a new directory for superiors which falls much in line with LR Forty-three of Basil.[33] At the same time, few texts offer more points of contact with Chapter Two of RM-RB. The first theme Gregory developed was humility. Like Basil, Gregory was particularly careful to put superiors on their guard against haughtiness (*phronèma*). Exhortation to humility is a theme reoccuring throughout the whole treatise and applying, of course, to all the brethren; but the superior has special need of encouragement in this virtue because he is first in rank and his charge obliges him to set the example and direct others toward what is good. Gregory began, then, by showing in a series of antitheses that, while excelling in *ascesis* to the point of serving as a model for all the brethren and while outwardly fulfilling his duty to teach, the superior should be inwardly more humble than anybody. If he maintains the equilibrium between authority and humility in this way, he may expect great reward. Without humility, on the other hand, he would be lost while appearing to lead others. Gregory would have him consider the brethren a 'deposit confided to him by God'. This last is noteworthy, as are allusions to the theme of example and the personal salvation of the superior (68:14-69:16).

The 'confided deposit' theme has an important place in the considerations which follow (69:16-70:14). The superior is really like a pedagogue whom the father of the family has charged with the education of his children. Great is the responsibility! While underscoring this idea, Gregory also wanted to inculcate in the superior a sense of adapting himself to the diverse characters of his charges. A good pedagogue distinguishes himself by this flexibility and capacity for adaptation, by which also will be gauged the success of his mission and the recompense accorded by the Master. In adapting himself to different characters and different situations, the superior sometimes uses the rod, sometimes verbal admonition (*nouthesia*), and sometimes praise. This initial division leads to another which seems to be a free citation of 2 Tim 4:2. The superior ought sometimes to admonish, at other times to exhort (70:5-6). Not content with developing this adaptation theme with his own pedagogue image, Gregory took it up again under the physician image familiar to Basil. The physician varies his medication, sometimes gentle, sometimes strong, according to the needs of souls and bodies. Both pedagogue and physician, the superior should place at the service of the brethren an art able to adapt itself to each case. He is guided by neither likes nor dislikes but by the child or patient's interests, that is, the good of the soul he must form to the highest virtue.

This rich development is organized, therefore, around two major themes: the superior should remain humble; he should adapt himself wisely and lovingly to each case. Here we have, as we know, two ideas familiar to the Master. The second of them was particularly developed by RB. A number of subsidiary notations confirm this basic accord. Gregory spoke, as RM and RB would do, of the responsibility of the superior before God, who has 'confided' the brethren to him. He spoke of his duty to set an example

and of the fear he should experience lest he himself be lost while
directing others. He put the superior on his guard against likes
and dislikes and applied 2 Tim 4:2 to him. Yet note that Gregory
and RM-RB do not formulate these common themes in the same
way. The images are also different, although they express a
similar thought. Gregory evokes the pedagogue and physician images. For him, the father is God. RM and RB develop other
metaphors: the vicar of Christ, from whom the superior takes a
sort of delegated fatherhood expressed by the name abbot; the
pastor, a hireling responsible to the owner for the flock. RM also
proposes the image of the child, a symbol of humility (neither
Basil nor Gregory dared propose this), as well as the father and
mother images simultaneously expressive of the universality of
love and of its implications.

3. The Augustinian Family

The *Regula Augustini* relegates its directory for the superior to
the end of the rule. RB produces a second directory for the abbot
in almost the same place Chapter Sixty-four. This is not the only
visible analogy between R Aug Fifteen and RB Sixty-four.
Chapter Two of RM-RB is not so closely related to the augustinian
text. Augustine, after having ordered the brethren to obey the
superior 'like a father' and to respect him as a representative of
God, began his injunction to the superior by making him
guardian of the rule and corrector of all failings.[34] Yet this charge
ought to be exercised in a spirit not of domination but rather of
love and service. Although he precedes the brethren in honor, the
superior, in holy fear before God, ought to reckon himself
beneath everyone's feet.[35] Note how these antitheses recall the
directory of Gregory of Nyssa. Two scriptural quotations follow:
Tit 2:7 (example of good works) and 1 Thess 5:14.[36] Lastly, there
are two new antitheses: while accepting discipline wholeheartedly
for himself, the superior must impose it by making himself feared.
But he ought nevertheless to inspire love even more than fear. The
final words, *semper cogitans Deo se pro uobis redditurum esse rationem,* are (with the exhortation to set the example) the only
point of contact with RM-RB worth mentioning.

This paragraph of the augustinian rule passed, like the others,
into the *Rule for Virgins* of Caesarius of Arles (R Caes V 35), but
all that remains of it are the two scriptural quotations (Tit 2:7 and
1 Thess 5:14) and the final words (*semper cogitantes*), that is
everything constituting a rapprochement with RM-RB.

Elsewhere, R Caes V often addresses the abbess or the entire corps of superiors to recommend especially the observance of the 'holy rule'.[37] These dispersed notations have much less importance than another text which constitutes the most remarkable parallel of all with RM-RB. It is a veritable directory written for an abbess.[38] In it Caesarius develops one by one the three principal themes we have seen in our analysis of RM Two. The abbess ought to set the example; she ought to love all the sisters with an equal love; she ought lastly to correct each as her faults require, in order to save her and thereby merit eternal glory for herself. This arresting parallelism must not be exaggerated. These three are not the only themes Caesarius develops: a preamble discusses how to manage temporal affairs,[39] and an important development at the end of the work is devoted to dealings involving the abbess with seculars.[40] Still more, the three themes mentioned are not developed in all their aspects in the same fashion as they are in RM-RB, nor with the aid of the same scriptural texts. The fact remains, however, that numerous similarities can be seen even in details, particularly when Caesarius treats of 'equal love', the second RM theme.[41]

After this first-class document, the augustinian family offers us only some texts of lesser interest and slightly later than St Benedict. The *Regula Tarnatensis* reproduces R Aug Fifteen integrally, but inserts 'Anyone who listens to you listens to me' (Lk 10:16).[42] The *Rule of Aurelian* is, typically, very cursory on the subject of the abbot. It is content to limit corporal chastisement to thirty-nine blows and to require that the abbot join to this 'just discipline' a tender goodness.[43] Lastly, Feriolus of Uzès, near the end of his Rule, provides a copious and very original abbatial directory made up in large part of scriptural quotations strung together,[44] in which we uncover here and there familiar notations: to set an example, not to condemn unjustly, to fear the loss of those entrusted to him, to adapt himself like a good physician to each case and to provide it with a suitable remedy. Deserving of special notice is the *blandimentum-terror* couplet, a literary parallel to RM-RB, though no dependence can be affirmed.

At the end of this inventory, what can we conclude? The reader will no doubt have felt his patience tried more than once by the continual repetition of the same terms. Analyzing these directories for superiors means encountering an incessant repetition of stereotyped expressions in all the texts. This monotony itself is at least a significant factor and its importance should be underscored. It reveals the fundamental homogeneity of the tradition on the plane of ideas. From one shore of the Mediterranean to the other, the thought scarcely varied during the first two centuries of cenobitic experience. The different directories for superiors spoke unfailingly of the same things: example, humility, adaptation to individual needs, zeal and firmness in correcting, a sense of responsiibility before God, equity in judgments, equal distribution of necessities without preference of persons. These unceasingly recurrent themes are themselves supported by scriptural quotations that hardly vary. The example theme is illusrated by Tit 2:7 or some other passage from the Pastoral Letters; adaptation to individual needs is very often inculcated with the aid of 1 Thess 4:2; zeal for the salvation of all is expressed by 1 Thess 5:14. Holy Scripture was everywhere the sole norm for these legislators. This common source suffices to explain the great homogeneity of the tradition.

And yet, on the other hand, if we leave the plane of ideas for that of concrete expression, we come to observe considerable diversity. Directories for superiors differ, first, according to their length or brevity, and hence by a greater or lesser richness of content. They are also distinguished by very different modes of presentation, extending from the unorganized multiplicity of a catalogue of prohibitions (R Pac Inst 18) to the well thought out and harmonious construction of genuine little treatises such as we find in Basil and Gregory of Nyssa. And when we speak of different modes of presentation, we have in mind a variety which affects not only the form. In fact, form and subject matter can never be dissociated. In passing from the pachomian rule to that of Basil, we pass not merely from one literary genre to another; we pass as well from the culture of a coptic countryman to that of a refined Greek. We pass from a stage in which Scripture is religiously heeded to one in which it is also meditated on within a mental framework able to organize its doctrine around certain principles. What does vary then, along with literary form, is the degree of reflection and orderliness. Though fundamental themes scarcely differ, they do admit of various degrees of penetration and systematization, from which a greater or lesser richness results for the doctrine itself.

One can see from the foregoing how deceptive would be an attempt to set the Fathers of cenobitism in opposition to one another on the plane of their spiritual and social concepts. The role of superior is not conceived differently in Egypt, Cappadocia, Africa, or Gaul during these first two centuries. Common reference to the Gospel inspires the authors of the rules and dictates to them almost identical prescripts. But they express themselves sometimes fleetingly, sometimes at leisure, sometimes by juxtaposed notations and sometimes according to a well-arranged plan. At times they are content to let their scripture-sated memories speak, at times, on the contrary, they make a personal literary contribution, without adding new ideas. In the midst of all these divergencies bearing upon form and, in a sense, as we said, on the subject matter itself, we must recognize a fundamentally homogeneous thought. The cenobitic superior is a person who scarcely changed from St Pachomius to St Benedict. As he is the essential institution of cenobitism, we may presume that the whole of cenobitic thought and life received the same stamp of continuity.

Furthermore, these considerations teach us an important lesson in method. Since the documents of the cenobitic tradition fall into very diverse literary genres and on diverse cultural levels, we ought to put ourselves on guard against subjecting them all to a uniform interrogation. The same questions cannot be addressed to men of different backgrounds and different ages. A sermon and an article in a juridical code cannot be subjected to the same kind of analysis.

How many pretended oppositions of doctrine have been invented by modern historians of cenobitism where the only question was one of different literary styles! For example, analyzing the *Regula Augustini* as if these few elegant antitheses could constitute a doctrine of authority personal to Augustine, and as if one could parallel or even set it in opposition to a pachomian, a basilian, or a benedictine concept, is asking more of a text than it can give.[45] Augustine treated the duties of superiors cursorily, limiting himself to noting in a few felicitous formulas some of the most current principles in christian tradition. What he said and what he did not say are not to be interpreted as an effort at originality or as the mark of a personal conception.

Once one has stopped forcing the texts to express contradictory systems, one finds oneself with formulations more or less developed, more or less complete, more or less elaborate, and fundamentally homogeneous in thought because it is, at its source, pure gospel. Thus good method consists in examining each author to the extent that he is a partial witness to the common thought and not the creator of an original concept. From time to time we shall meet clearly delineated divergencies on certain subjects or in matters of detail which it will be necessary to note.[46] Everywhere else the presumption is that our authors differ one from another on a literary rather than a doctrinal plane.

To such conclusions of a general nature, we may add a certain number of remarks which will situate Chapter Two of RM-RB within the framework of the tradition we have described.

We would remark first that, for Chapter Two, neither RM nor RB have sources properly so-called.[47] In this respect, Chapter Two forms a contrast with the preceding chapter. Although at every moment it presents numerous points of contact with anterior or almost contemporary documents, these coincidences are too many and not sufficiently literal to affirm sure literary dependence. The fact that some of these analogies, and not the least significant of them, are to be found in texts which the Master and St Benedict almost certainly did not read (such as greek Basil and Gregory of Nyssa) ought to put us on guard about other texts. In reality, these similarities can be explained by common reference to Scripture and the fact that they derive from the same background.

In the second place, we note that Cassian is not among the long list of authors who have dealt with this question — not that the author of the *Institutes* did not have gallican abbots in mind when he described the cenobites of Egypt and the East. The first four Books of the *Institutes* were even addressed explicitly to gallican superiors, whose lack of formation Cassian bitterly deplored.[48] But nowhere did he expound what the superior of a *coenobium* ought to be. Independent of Cassian, Chapter Two of RM-RB is therefore in a position altogether different from RM One and Ten (RB 1 and 7).

Basically, neither RM nor RB has a very original directory for superiors. To convince ourselves of this, we need only enumerate the different themes uncovered by our analysis of RM and RB and put them alongside the principal parallel passages of the tradition. We see at the same time how much the *fontes* of Butler can be completed.

1. RM TWO

INTRODUCTION-CONCLUSION. The theme of the responsibility

of the pastor for the flock confided to him is abundantly illustrated by the *Lib Ors* (¶¶ 7, 9, 10, 11, 13, in particular). It
also appears at the end of the R 4 Pat (lines 216-219), in the R
Aug 15.200-201, and in R Caes V 35. R Bas 15, on the other
hand, deals with the conformity of the teaching of the superior to
the divine law of which he is the dispenser.

FIRST THEME (WORDS AND EXAMPLE). This also is in *Lib Ors*
¶¶ 9 and 13, in R Aug 15.196-197, in R Pat, lines 39-40 and
219-222, and above all in the *Letter of Caesarius* (1136d-1137b).
We may further add R Or 1, R Caes V 35, R Fer 37, and finally
the LR 43 of Basil, who specifies that example should be given in
the matter of humility (cf. RM 2:26-29).[49]

ANNEXED THEME (VARIETY OF METHODS CORRESPONDING
TO CHARACTERS). This theme appears, based on the citation of
2 Tim 4:2 (cf. RM 2:23), in R 4 Pat, lines 42-45, and in Gregory
of Nyssa (70. 5-6). Basil develops it in LR 30, 43, and 51. It is also
found in the *Vita Honorati* 17, R Fer 37, and the *Letter of
Caesarius* (1138a).

SECOND THEME (EQUAL LOVE: NO PREFERENCE OF PERSONS)
This harks back to *Lib Ors* 9 and 16, to the *Letter of Caesarius*
(1137c); also to R Pac Inst 18 (60.7-8), to R Or 1, and to R 4 Pat,
lines 208-216.

The care the superior should have for his own sanctification (RM-
RB 2:13-15) is well marked by Gregory of Nyssa (68.14-69.16).
Finally, when RM and RB bring their directories to a close by letting the abbot hope that the very exercise of his function will make
him better, they are voicing an idea much like that articulated by
Cassian (*Conf* 22.1): he who teaches is the first to benefit from his
own teaching. RM comes back to this at the end of its directory for
provosts (RM 11:91-93).

2. RB TWO

In studying the plan of the chapter, we have already indicated the
hypotheses to which the three chief omissions give rise. We shall
here consider only the three corresponding additions and note
parallels, as we did for RM Two.

FIRST ADDITION (RB vss 18b-19). The characteristic element of this addition is the question of *ordines* or *loca,* in other words, rank in community. This question is on the whole rather infrequently treated in ancient rules. R 4 Pat, lines 47-56, may be cited, though it is unfortunately a very obscure text. We shall study this question in Chapter Nine.

SECOND ADDITION (RB vss 26-29). The idea that the abbot must intervene promptly to curtail vice is registered elsewhere only by Justinian (Nou 133.4). The example of Eli is brought in by Basil (R Bas 122 and LR 28) to demonstrate how evil and dangerous it is to let the sins of the brethren go uncorrected.

Physical blows are scarcely ever mentioned in the directories for superiors. Yet R Aur M 41 may be cited in this respect, not to mention here those texts specially devoted to correction.

THIRD ADDITION (RB vss 31-36). The preference to be shown *the spiritual rather than the temporal* is a theme which the *Letter of Caesarius* treats (1136c), but in a somewhat different fashion. Caesarius would have the abbess more willingly occupied in holy reading and prayer; RB would have the abbot concern himself more with the salvation of souls. Except for this parallel, superiors are not put on their guard against temporal cares. The closest thing to this RB addition is surely RM 11:94-106, where the Master develops the same idea with regard to provosts: provosts ought to be treated circumspectly in the amount of work required of them. Manual work must not hinder them from their principal task, surveillance over the brethren of their 'decade'. The Master sets the *causa Dei* (or *causa spiritus*) for which the provosts are responsible in opposition to material profit, which should not under any pretext be preferred to it: *fidem spe sumentes Dominum Deum credamus usibus nostris omnia necessaria ministrare quod minus nobis potuerint manus nostrae perficere.* And like RB, the Master concludes by quoting Mt 6:33: 'Set your hearts on the kingdom of God and his righteousness, and all these other things will be given you as well.'[50]

As an example of an abbot trusting confidently in Providence for the sustenance of his community, we may cite the *Vita Honorati* 20-21. Gregory the Great tells the strange story (*Dial* 1.7) of an abbot who jeopardizes the souls of his monks in order to relieve the material poverty of the monastery. One of the miracles of St Benedict related in the subsequent book of the *Dialogues* illustrates, we remember, the opposite attitude (*Dial* 2.28-29. Cf. 21).

In the tradition we scarcely come across in explicit terms the idea that adaptation to different characters is particularly *difficult*. Yet St Nilus writes: 'The governing of souls is the hardest of all functions.'[51]

The RB additions, to the extent that they do not repeat RM, therefore contain several notations which offer few characteristic contacts with other rules. Let us note, however, that the brevity of these supplemental texts has obliged us, if we are to grasp their content, to examine them more closely than we did the RM themes. On this scale, which lifts detail into sharper relief, the RM itself also offers additional notations, for which we have not been able to make a case and which would probably prove to be as 'original' as our additions.[52] The same would hold true for other rules, so we ought not attach too much importance to the comparative 'originality' of the RB additions.

What we have said about RM-RB sources and parallels may be summed up as follows: the two rules stand, basically, in the great channel of the tradition sprung from Scripture. Their originality is extremely limited and is the same as that of other rules (at least when they do not simply copy pre-existent texts). Compared to texts definitely anterior to St Benedict of which the RM and RB authors must have been aware, Chapter Two of RM-RB presents a good gauge of the current themes and constitutes a complete, though not exhaustive, summary of the tradition. Although having little originality in substance, RM and RB do distinguish themselves for several literary particularities. Firstly, by the amount of attention they pay to the abbatial directory. There is no question here of comparing RM-RB Two with texts as short as R Or One or R Aug Fifteen, or the two successive directories of R 4 Pat. Even the important treatises by Basil and Gregory of Nyssa do not reach the same dimensions. To find texts of equal or superior length, one must resort to the *Letter of Caesarius* and the *Liber Orsiesii*.

Still more remarkable is the organization of ideas in RM Two. We have already shown the plan, rigorous and at the same time supple, by which the Master arranged this treatise. All the abbot's duties surge from a first principle, a clear and profound definition of his mission. This definition is enunciated right from the first verses (1-3), it is recalled at the beginning of the first pericope (11) and at the beginning of the Conclusion (32). The name the abbot bears signifies that he is the lieutenant of Christ. He bears full responsibility therefore for the group. His basic duty is to teach and to govern according to the teachings of Christ (Introduction).

The Master imparts further precision to this duty to instruct and govern in the two pericopes forming the body of the treatise.

First pericope: a) Teaching calls for words, of course, but still more example. In this way the abbot will be sure of reaching all souls, even the simplest. Furthermore, he will avoid discrepancy between words and acts which would lead to his own condemnation.

b) The government of the abbot ought to be alert to avoid preference of persons, surrounding all the brethren with an equal love and imposing the same 'discipline' on them. This is in fact how God deals with men.

Second pericope: a) Reverting to the different categories of souls, the Master would have the tone used which is appropriate to each. The Apostle (2 Tim 4:2) is the model to be followed here. But, repeats the Master, this verbal teaching must be accompanied by example. And example consists above all in humility, according to the model of the child proposed by the Lord himself.

b) However, it must be borne in mind that the diversity of pedagogical procedures should not hinder equal love for everyone. To all his sons, the abbot ought to be like a father and a mother.

The treatise closes by recalling the themes of the introduction. The abbot must never forget his responsibility. Such responsibility extends to all the disciples in his charge, to all the actions they perform in obedience and, finally, to his own soul which must not remain estranged from the work of edification undertaken in others (*Conclusion*).

These themes, taken in themselves, are not very original, but the same cannot be said for their systematic arrangement. The Master's merit consists in having composed a coherent treatise developing a small number of principles in a certain order. It is as far removed as possible from the inorganic multiplicity of R Pac. Among the most developed directories, almost none but those of Basil and Gregory of Nyssa can compare with it. The very remarkable developments of those two authors were probably unknown to him, but like them the Master knew how to fuse the twofold relation of the superior, to God and to the brethren, into a definition and an image which govern all.[53] It is on this level, it seems to us, that the originality of RM in the present chapter lies: it is a literary rather than a doctrinal originality, consisting above all in a labor of synthesis and composition to present with depth, force and clarity the scriptural themes which the tradition had been applying for a long time, but in a dispersed and poorly organized way, to the superiors of *coenobia.*[54]

This merit seems all the greater when one takes account not only of the internal structure of the chapter, as we have done, but also of its place in the whole rule. Materially, other authors had in fact thought of treating of the abbot at the head of their legislation: R Or One is an example of this. In R 4 Pat, we even came across a sort of rough draft of the sequence of ideas of the first two chapters of RM: definition of the monastic community united round a single head who is successively proposed to the faith of the brethren and instructed in his obligations towards them. But aside from this parallel, which is unlikely to have exerted any influence on the Master, no other directory for superiors emphasizes so forcefully, even by the very space allocated to it in the rule, the importance and meaning of the role of the abbot. The mission of the superior is defined with equal depth by Basil, but this definition must be sought in the *Long Rules* among other developments with which it shares no necesary relation. Here, on the contrary, the figure of the abbot stands at the outset of the rule. It explicitly governs all the legislation of the Master, showing clearly the fundamental importance this key piece of cenobitical organization has in his view, as well as that of the whole tradition.

It has been necessary to dwell at some length, as we have done, on the originality of RM in order to acquire an exact appreciation of the originality of RB itself. Since RB, through the combined effect of its omissions and additions, has very much obliterated the orderly character that suffused RM, our conclusions about the literary quality of RB Two are evident. Paradoxical as it may seem, the RB additions, while materially enriching the number of notations of RM, diminish its originality and merit, which consisted above all in its simple and vigorous organization. We have noted how, beginning at the second addition, the RB text became redundant by the tedious repetition of the theme of the 'different approaches depending on different characters'. At this point the reader loses his bearings and can scarcely recognize any thought progression. Even as the conclusion approaches, a new development about temporal concerns breaks in, so that echoes of the introduction, which in RM are meant to usher in the conclusion, become no more than unjustified repetitions.[55] The fact remains, nonetheless, that RB preserved much that is interesting in this chapter of RM, especially the whole sequence of ideas in the introduction and first pericope. For this reason RB Two still belongs, though to a lesser degree than RM Two, among the number of best thought out and arranged directories for superiors which tradition has bequeathed to us.

WHAT IS AN ABBOT?

Having studied the plan of the chapter and its ties with the tradition of directories for superiors, we must now consider the figure of the abbot in his own right, as we find it presented there. Our intention is not to comment one by one on the various regulations of the rule, or to subject to detailed examination the comportment of an abbot 'worthy of the name', as St Benedict says. Others have done this with the competence and authority that only experience can give. Failing those modern commentaries, we could be content with citing the admirable portrait which Hilary of Arles has left us of Honoratus, the first abbot of Lérins,[56] to see in anticipation the image of the benedictine abbot and the perfect realization of principles demanded by the rule. Rather than become involved in the concrete details of the abbot's duties, it seems to us more profitable to investigate the very essence and origin of his power. Given the incomparable importance of the abbot in the cenobitic institution, such an enquiry should also cast abundant light on the meaning of cenobitism.

Our method is dictated to us by the results of the two preceding paragraphs. As we saw, the important considerations which open RB Two and govern the finer points of subsequent regulations come from the Master. The omissions and additions made by RB, though noticeably altering the organization of the chapter, do not touch the definition of the abbot as the Master conceived it. The explanation of what an abbot is must be sought then in RM. Commentary on the first lines of RB Two can only be sought from him who was the first to think through and write these formulations. Without neglecting either in this chapter or in other parts of the rule what is really derived from the RB redactor, we shall mainly scrutinize the texts in which the Master himself explained what he understood by the nature of abbacy. As we may expect after our study of tradition, these texts will not present us with a new concept. It is the traditional idea of abbatial function which RM in fact develops. But for all that, we recognize in the Master an exposition which has seldom been equalled in depth and precision in the West or even in the East.

Before replying with the Master to the question posed, we cannot pass over in silence the attempts made in our own day to explain the abbot by the secular analogy of the roman *paterfamilias*. Today the idea that the benedictine abbot is a transposition of the father of the family of antiquity is readily granted. St Benedict, a sixth century Roman, as everyone knows, would have conceived his *coenobium* on the model of what he had observed at the family hearth in Nursia. Cuthbert Butler had already acknowledged this, and not without some anxiety, he compared the 'fullness of the patriarchal dominion', born of roman law, with our modern ideas of limited monarchy, constitutional government and popular representation, elective functions, boards of directors, and in sum all that is democratic...'.[57] Is the benedictine Order, transposed into modern times, not suffering from incurable anachronism? The Abbot of Downside attempts to dispel this objection by turning the advantages of absolute power, especially in a religious society, to account or by appealing to history and to the success, well attested for fourteen centuries, of abbatial government.

The antithesis noted by Butler was likewise observed by Marie-Dominique Chenu.[58] Instead of laying a claim for the legitimacy of the ancient system, however, he relegated it to the rank of outdated institutions. The twelfth century is Chenu's observation point. At that period of history, when the feudal world began to rock under the force of the new urban civilization, a new spirit appeared among souls avid for perfection. Like corporations and communes, mendicant Orders 'substitute for vertical and paternalistic fidelity a horizontal and fraternal commitment'.[59] 'Abbatial paternalism' had had its day.

Chenu did not try to trace the origin of abbatial power back to the roman *paterfamilias*. He was content to characterize this power in the twelfth century as a replica of the feudal system prevalent in secular society. Collapse of feudalism entails collapse of the abbacy. There is no doubt that for Chenu the events of the twelfth century have had their consequences into our own era and the anachronism of the monastic regime has increased proportionately with the spread of democracy.

Different as their terms of comparison (roman *paterfamilias* or feudal lord) and their final judgment on the validity of the system for our times are, Cuthbert Butler and Marie-Dominique Chenu agree basically in posing the problem in the same terms, terms which are, in the better sense of the word, political.[60] Both of them consider the monastery a sociological reality evolving within the larger framework of temporal society and of the Church. This little society needs to resolve the problem of authority in its own terms. It does so through the conscious or unconscious inspiration of ideas accepted in the surrounding world. Its structures reproduce those of temporal society. They are consequently subject to the same transitory character and threatened by the same aging process. Once the times have passed when the temporal institutions they imitated flourished, they risk being no more than outmoded survivals, institutional and spiritual absurdities.

Let us return to the father of the roman family. Delatte was wise enough to show restraint,[61] but Herwegen fell completely for this explanation of the benedictine abbot. It complies with several dominant tendencies of the abbot of Maria-Laach: with his pronounced taste for parallels with secular institutions,[62] with the special esteem he professed for the roman mentality which he happily exalted at the expense of the oriental, germanic, medieval, or modern mentality. But above all, Herwegen's sense of community seemed to have disposed him to accentuate the analogy between the benedictine abbot and the *paterfamilias* of ancient Rome. The extent to which the author of *Sinn und Geist* was imbued with the primacy of the community over the individual is well known. In his eyes, the historical role of St Benedict consisted precisely in imposing communitarian form on the generous but anarchical effervescence of the *Pneuma*. Monasticism under the discipline of St Benedict lost nothing of its pneumatic richness, but this richness was integrated into a hierarchical order whose keystone was the abbot. This communitarian form which St Benedict gave the monastic *Pneuma* was derived, he believed, from nothing other than the roman family in which he had been reared.

Throughout his commentary on Chapter Two, Herwegen details these similarities. If the abbot has to render account of his disciple's obedience, this is because of his likeness to a *paterfamilias* who bears the responsibility for the faults of his children because he is a *domesticus magistratus* invested with a public charge. If the abbot ought not to command anything *extra praeceptum*, Herwegen believes he sees in these words an expression of roman genius and respect for law. If the abbot can inflict corporal chastisements, it is by virtue of the *domestica potestas,* the right accorded the father of a family, a right which surpasses the power of a bishop over his flock. The abbot thus stands at a crossroad where two major preoccupations of Herwegen intersect. To the charisms of the man of God he joins the juridical powers of the father of a family. Through him is realized the integration of the monastic *Pneuma* within a stable and solid social order, under the control of the hierarchical Church.

Let us stop here. After considering Butler and Herwegen, we have scant need to descend to the general run of writers who repeat this half-truth over and over again. And yet there is little in the texts to authorize our thinking that the roman *paterfamilias* served as a model for St Benedict. Chapter Two of RB like Chapter Two of RM, makes not the slightest allusion to this alleged prototype. Neither in the case of the account to be rendered for his disciple's obedience, nor of the obligation to conform himself strictly to divine law in his teaching, nor of corporal chastisements which he must inflict, is the abbot ever compared to the example of the father of a roman family. Whether one sets in relief the explicit citations upon which the RM-RB prescripts rest, or delves into fine points of wording, or researches the allusions they contain, there is nothing to be found except biblical themes and images. The two rules have taken everything from the Bible contemplated in the light of the Church's tradition. There is not the slightest hint of the roman family.[63]

The term *paterfamilias* does appear once (RM-RB 2:7), but it designates Christ, not the abbot. Moreover, Christ is not considered here as father, but as the owner of a flock of sheep entrusted to a pastor, the abbot. Plainly we have here the great biblical theme of the people of God and their pastors from whom God demands an account of the care bestowed on the flock. Were doubt still possible, two scriptural texts are there to assure us immediately (Ps 40:11; Is 1:2). In the course of the chapter, the word *pater* appears no more than twice in RM, and only once in RB. First is the *pium patris affectum* of RM-RB 2:24: here the father image is only the symbol of an attitude of goodness distinct from the severity of a master. The same affective content recurs in RM 2:31: *patrem se eis mensurata pietate ostendat,* paralleling *matrem eis suam praebens aequaliter caritatem.* If the two rules compare the abbot to a father, then, they do so under the very limited aspect of *pietas,* tenderness. No need to evoke the *pater-familias* and his juridical prerogatives; it is rather the human heart speaking here, the experience of a natural sentiment held in such high esteem by all peoples and occupying a capital place especially in Judeo-Christian revelation.

The image of the roman family therefore is not present in this chapter. It scarcely appears in the rest of the two rules, as we shall observe in going on with this commentary. Once, it is true, RM explicitly compares the *coenobium* to a *familia* (RM 11:6).[64] But the head of this *familia* (also called *domus*) is not the abbot in that passage, any more than in RM 2:7. The abbot is only a subordinate chief, a *vices agens* of the father of the family, who is the Lord himself. Moreover, the *familia* is introduced only as a terrestrial image of the Church and monastery. The abbot is invited to cast a glance at the secular 'family' not in order to copy it in his monastery, but in order to know better the constitution which God gave his Church and which the monastery ought in its turn to imitate.

The *coenobium* is therefore not a society created by the enactment of men and modelled on a secular 'family', but a church organized by God which, like the Church proper presents in its hierarchical structure a striking analogy with the *familia.* 'Churches and monasteries' belong to the same category, the 'divine households'. The 'human household' may serve our understanding of the divine constitution of these societies come down from heaven, but it is not their exemplary cause. Or if it is, it is no more so for the monastery than for the Church. The Master makes no pretentions of having been otherwise inspired by it than were Christ and the apostles in instituting the ecclesiastical hierarchy. Comparison of the monastery to the *familia* tends ultimately not to invest the abbot with the rights of a *paterfamilias,* but, quite the contrary, to confer on him the authority of a steward commissioned by the unique father of the family, who is God. This authority is wholly divine in its origin as well as in its nature. It can only be compared with the authority of the pastors of the people of God: bishops, priests, deacons, and clerics.

Textual silence then is the first objection to comparing the abbot with a roman *paterfamilias.* To that must be added the eminently traditional character of RM-RB teaching. From Basil and Orsiesius to the Master and St Benedict, through all the intermediaries previously enumerated, continuity is so strong that to look outside tradition for the model of the benedictine abbot is unthinkable. Everything indicates that the RM-RB authors drew their conception of the abbot not from secular society, but from the monastic tradition which had its source in Scripture.

To these general objections we might add yet one more remark applicable particularly to the views of Butler and Chenu. These two historians, as we have said, consider the benedictine monastery a society endowed with a certain type of patriarchial government clearly opposed to the democratic and fraternal forms assumed by modern societies. These are observations we would not think of disputing. In our view, no one can insist too strongly on the importance of the vertical relation which unites disciples to master in the *coenobium;* it is the constitutive axis of cenobitism.

But the real issue here is not a system of government arbitrarily chosen to resolve the problem of authority in a given society, but the very essence of that society. The abbatial regime is not justified, as Butler's defence would make one think, by historical circumstances, intrinsic advantages of absolute power, or the test of time and testimony of history. These considerations have in themselves some interest, but they are useless for determining the justification of abbatial government because this government rests on an altogether different and profound basis: the very nature of things. The abbot is not only the crown of the cenobitic edifice; he is also its foundation. He ought not to be set at the end, but at the very beginning. Without him cenobitic society is not even conceivable, because it is he who engenders and assembles it. He is not just *a* solution, even the best possible solution, to the problem of monastic government; he is the *raison d'être* of this society.

In other words, it would be wrong to think first of the monastery and then of the abbot. The abbot, the man of God invested with the charismatic mission of teaching and governing souls, comes first. The *coenobium* is nothing more than the assemblage of his disciples. The monks are there only to benefit from his direction. Consequently, government of the monastery otherwise disposed is unimaginable. The authority problem does not have to be resolved: it is not even raised. The abbot is not the offshoot of a society constituted before him: the society springs from him, both at the time of its birth and at every instant of its existence.

'Abbatial paternalism': we do not reject the term, charged as it is with unpleasant overtones, provided it is quite clear that the monastery is an absolutely original type of society. A purely spiritual need calls for it: the need of a man seeking a guide to go to God. That such a guide might conduct a number of men and at length assemble them around himself in a society is of secondary importance. The primary desire is not the society, but the master of the spiritual life. In the desire to be led to God by the abbot, a desire present in the heart of each disciple, we have the fundamental pact of such a society.[65] From it issue all other social relations. To speak of 'vertical and paternalistic loyalty', consequently, is to define in feudalistic terms a relationship of a purely spiritual order which does not belong in its essentials to the historical context of any epoch. Possibly the monastic order in the twelfth century, the epoch which interests Chenu, was in a state that justified seeing it that way. Possibly the relations between the monks and their abbots scarcely rose above a juridical plane of feudal 'loyalty'. But in any case, one feels how far removed such a petrification is from the living reality of its origins. The abbot may no more be defined a feudal lord than he might, for the Master, be defined as an ancient roman *paterfamilias*. Nor is he to any greater extent what the word 'paternalism' tends to evoke: an absolute monarch or 'master by divine right'. Essentially, in the pure line of the Gospel, he is the good servant whom his master has set over all his household to distribute nourishment to his fellow-servants at opportune times.

We have said enough provisionally to set aside, along with all analogies of a secular type, the roman *paterfamilias*. The field is now free for an objective examination of the concept formed by RM and RB of the nature of the abbatial power. The preceding discussion has, moreover, led us to an essential observation which the present research will but serve to illustrate: the true type of the abbot is the pastor of the people of God such as the Old and New Testaments portray him.

The definition of the abbot is given by our two rules in the introductory paragraph: the abbot holds the place of Christ in the monastery. This definition is so important that it is twice repeated in the chapter, in major articulations of the development. Even more, the RB redactor made it his own to such an extent that he refers to it expressly in a passage unique to him (RB 63:13). What then does *Christi agere uices* mean? The Master expounds on this subject with all the clarity we could wish in three passages.[66] This triple commentary establishes a parallel between monastery and church. Both are divine property. The Lord is represented in each by men to whom he confides the government of souls: in churches these are the bishops, priests, deacons, and clerics; in monasteries, the abbots and provosts (RM 11). This constitution is divinely instituted and can appeal to precise texts. The Master twice cites pauline enumerations of charisms within the bosom of the Church:[67] after the Old Testament prophets come the apostles of the New, and after these the 'pastors and teachers' of Eph 4:11, called more simply 'teacher' in 1 Cor 12:28. These 'pastors and teachers' have been foretold by the prophet Isaiah.[68] They and their respective ministers encompass the double hierarchy, ecclesiastical and monastic, that is, the episcopate on the one hand, the abbacy on the other. To both are addressed the solemn words of Christ: 'Anyone who listens to you listens to me' (Lk 10:16).[69]

To these scriptural 'proofs', the Master annexes also, in Chapter One, the charge given to Peter by the risen Christ, 'Feed my sheep' (Jn 21:17), as well as the dispatch of the apostles on mission, 'Teach them to observe all the commands I gave you. And know that I am with you always, even to the end of time' (Mt 28:20).

The Master boldly applies to the abbot, therefore, the most solemn texts of the New Testament on the mission of the apostles and their successors. He makes them 'pastors and teachers' as well, that is, one of the functions of the Body of Christ defined by St Paul. Ultimately, he sets cenobitic society parallel to that of the church and abbots to bishops. What should we think of all these comparisons?

It seems to me that we ought to guard against two contrary errors in the interpretation of the Master's texts. The first would be to believe that the Master wants to erect, over against ecclesiastical authority, an abbatial authority independent of it and, like it, divinely instituted. The title 'teacher' so insistently attributed to abbots,[70] and the obvious though not explicit reference of this title to the charisms enumerated by St Paul could lead one to believe this.

This is the most glaring interpretation for the modern reader, for we know that St Paul enumerated charisms in order of decreasing importance: 'First of all the apostles, second the prophets, third teachers'. All these functions were exercised *simultaneously* in St Paul's day by different persons in Christ's

Church. Teachers are therefore on a plane different from the apostolate, inferior to it, and their activity is exercised at the same time, but in a different field. Then too, we are accustomed to read these Pauline texts in the context of the Church of our times. To us the apostles are present in the persons of bishop. What then has become of the other functions? Did the Master intend to claim succession to the 'teachers' of whom St Paul speaks for the abbots of his time?

The Master's concept is in fact just the reverse. First, he gives a chronological sense to the pauline enumerations. For him, God instituted 'first the prophets, then the apostles, and finally the teachers'.[71] Notice how he inverts the first two terms of the list. By this inversion he understands the charisms of 1 Cor 12:28 as functions exercised *successively* in the course of the history of the people of God: prophets in the Old Testament, apostles at the time of of Christ, teachers in the post-apostolic Church. For the Master, then, teaching is not a function simultaneous with the apostolate, either in St Paul's time or in our own. It is rather a continuation of the apostolate in the Church today. At this point comes the distinction between churches proper, governed by bishops, and these quasi-churches, the monasteries, called also 'schools of Christ',[72] headed by abbots. Bishops and abbots together constitute the category of 'teachers'.[73] In giving the abbot this title the Master did not mean to claim special authority for him distinct from and independent of the ecclesiastical hierarchy and, like it, divinely instituted. On the contrary, he wanted to set both bishops and abbots in a single, identical category, both pastors of souls in charge of the people of God.

Would the abbot not then be in the Master's eyes a member of the ecclesiastical hierarchy, endowed with some holy order, priesthood for example? This is the second error to be avoided in interpreting these texts. Nothing, in fact, authorizes us to think that the abbot in RM is a priest or cleric. One text seems to affirm that he is a layman.[74] If, like a bishop or priest, he is called 'teacher' and if he is likened to the New Testament pastors of souls and to the members of contemporary ecclesiastical hierarchy, it is not by reason of a holy order with which he is invested.

Having dispelled these two erroneous interpretations, we face the following fact: the Master affirms that the abbot, like the bishop, is a 'teacher' instituted by Christ, a successor and heir to the apostles enjoying the authority conferred on the apostles and their successors by the most solemn texts of the New Testament. Knowing this to be the Master's thought, we are obliged to raise the question of its legitimacy. What is the meaning of this investiture bestowed on the abbot? Has the Master succeeded in basing abbatial authority on a solid scriptural and theological basis?

Let us say first of all that we are dealing with a theme which is thoroughly traditional. The Master is doing no more than making explicit an idea long present in monastic literature. Assimilation of the superiors of the *coenobium* to the pastors of the Old and New Testaments is constantly present from the origins of cenobitism. Elsewhere we called attention to it in the *Liber Orsiesii*[75] and our review of the directories for superiors plainly demonstrated it. Everywhere, scriptural texts referring to the leaders of the people of God are spontaneously and unquestioningly applied to abbots. Even the most solemn of all these texts, the one charging Peter to 'feed my sheep' (Jn 21:17) is employed by others besides the Master, both before and after him.[76]

However traditional it may be, the Master's thought is nonetheless personal. In the first place, he is not content to liken abbots implicitly to the hierarchical pastors by applying to them the scriptural texts pertinent to pastors. With him the assimilation is explicit and deliberate. He utilizes, moreover, pastoral texts of Scripture not only to exhort superiors to fulfill their duty, as is customary in cenobitic literature, but also to define their authority and to provide a foundation for their right to command. Finally, he is also apparently the first who thought of drawing an ordered parallel between abbots and provosts on the one hand, and bishops, priests, deacons, and clerics on the other—that is to say, the *actual* pastors of the people of God and not just, as in the tradition, the pastors *of the apostolic age* of whom the New Testament speaks.

The Master's great originality is apparent here. The three texts under examination are the fruit of reflection never previously attempted, at least not in writings directly destined for cenobites. RM is the only document to have endeavored to define *ex professo* the nature of the fundamental pact which constitutes cenobitism by explicitly comparing it to the hierarchial structure of the Church. The Master was not content with regulating mutual relations between superiors and inferiors, not even with drawing his inspiration from the loftiest principles, as had sometimes been done before him. He wanted to set at the foundation of his legislation an ordered statement of these principles, to provide at the outset a charter for cenobitism in which the nature and cogent authenticity of the institution would clearly appear. This is no mean accomplishment.

What is a monastery then in the Master's eyes? A school essentially. It is distinguished by the relationship of the disciple or inferior with the master or superior. This is conceived in wholly biblical fashion: the prophet, the master of wisdom, and the apostle are all models for the abbot. He is also conceived in a fully ecclesiastic fashion, the equivalent of bishop and priest. But having enumerated these two series of prototypes and inventoried all the images to which the Master explicitly refers, one has still not uncovered the close affinity of his concepts with one of the major themes of ancient thought. If there is one concept profoundly permeating the Fathers, it is surely this necessity for souls to be governed by expert teachers. The great theme of divine pedagogy in Clement of Alexandria comes to mind: in the image of the Logos, the gnostic undertakes to educate perfect souls to virtue. In Origen the theme expands to an even more grandiose vision of the cosmos: in the boundless game in which Providence as teacher and the created liberties are played off against each other from the dawn of history to its close, God rules that superior creatures lead inferiors and restore them to the primordial unity[79] — an hierarchical vision of the spiritual universe which will be continued by Denis.

More modestly, on the level of human *ascesis,* the same notions ground the relations between masters and disciples in monasticism. It is a deep conviction, constantly affirmed by experience, that man as sinner is by himself incapable of practising the divine law and of saving himself. Another man, better than he, must explain the sacred texts to him, must set before his eyes the living realization of it, and discern for him, against the wiles of the devil, the concrete manner of putting it into practice. From that proceeds the general monastic fact of spiritual direction. In its simplest form it is realized in the association of a master and his disciples living together in solitude. But the number of disciples around a single master may multiply, knitting itself into a more or less strict and enduring community. Pachomian cenobitism is but the end result of this process. Pachomius is nothing other than one

of those eremitic spiritual fathers and his *coenobium* a development of the embryonic communities which crystallized around the
first 'abbots'. As the master's activities extended to an indefinite
number of disciples, it took no doubt new forms while the acetical
formation assumed a collective and organized character. But such
a leap forward does not alter its spirit and principles: cenobitism
remains fundamentally an educative enterprise, as in the simplest
association of master and disciple. All the collective organization
of the pachomian 'Congregation' has no other end than to procure
for everyone the benefit of the direction of the man of God. Rule,
subordinate officers, general superiors themselves, all these are
but the extension of the personal action of the 'Father'.
Pachomius' radiating in all directions, through space and time, is
the grace which makes him the savior of all these souls.

This is the perspective in which the Master's texts take their real
meaning. In their own singularly methodical and reflected way
they express this great traditional conviction which we have set in
relief, and on it they ground the entire cenobitic edifice. Nothing
is new in this, as we have seen, save that no one had ever thought
of saying it in such rigorous terms. Too rigorous? Whatever the
value of the scriptural argument, the profound value of the theme
it is intended to illustrate cannot be ignored. Scripture and tradition have provided the Master with this hierarchical and
pedagogical principle which is the general law of providential
economy: on one hand the absolute necessity incumbent upon
weak souls to place themselves under the direction of men filled
with the spirit of God and on the other hand, and corresponding
to that need, the mission given certain men by God to educate and
save their brethren. It is an ecclesial theme of indisputable christian authenticity which furnishes historically the exact meaning of
the cenobitic institution and at the same time connects this institution to the economy of salvation divinely revealed and realized in the Church.

What are we to think of the scriptural presentation of this
theme in the Master's work? At first sight it would seem that, by
wanting to prove too much, he succeeded only in rendering
suspect the abbot's authority. The modern reader feels ill at ease
when he sees applied to the abbot texts which manifestly surpass
him. How could anyone make this layman the beneficiary of
promises addressed by Christ to his apostles and their legitimate
successors, the members of the hierarchy? Should greater

prudence not have dictated using the pastoral texts of Scripture only to inculcate in superiors a sense of duty, as had hitherto been done, and not to proclaim, as here, their divine mission and right of command?

Objections such as these may follow from too narrow a notion of the delegation of authority in the Church. Without anticipating the study of the relations between cenobitism and priesthood which Chapters Sixty and Sixty-two require of us, there is need at least to note here that the mission of teaching and direction exercised by lay monks never underwent serious objection, on principle, in the ancient Church. From Athanasius to Gregory the Great, the most outstanding churchmen willingly acknowledged this charism bestowed by the Spirit apart from all ordination. It is a fact that pastors of souls authentically sent by God were met outside the framework of the hierarchy.[80] It is also a fact that monasticism, and more especially cenobitism, are normally governed in such a charismatic way, independently of holy orders. This certainly does not mean that the abbot escapes hierarchical control,[81] but only that he is not rightfully a member of the hierarchy and does not in the first instance hold his mandate from it.

If this is the doctrine which the Church lived, we hardly need be surprised that the Master expressed himself this way. When he ranks the abbot, though a layman, among the teachers alongside the bishop and priest, he is only explaining the conviction affirmed by the Church's whole atitude towards monasticism. This attitude seems to imply, in effect, that lay pastors given directly by the Spirit to monks inherit within their particular sphere the prerogatives and promises of assistance which Christ accorded the heads of the Church. Yet these lay pastors themselves must belong to the Church, which evidently requires communion with the hierarchical pastors and submission to their authority. The Master never so much as thinks of disputing this point. The texts we have studied stand outside the whole polemic against hierarchical authority, even from any sort of claim against it. The parallel with the priesthood is made only to awaken the monk's faith in the divine character of their abbot's mission.

These considerations are enough to prove the legitimacy of the Master's teaching regarding abbatial authority. We may now turn to the famous opening formula of RM-RB Two which expresses this teaching in concentrated form: *Christi enim agere creditur uices in monasterio.* Now that we know the significance with which it is loaded, we can content ourselves with highlighting the tie which the Master establishes between this definition of the abbacy and the name 'abbot'. Commentators have long been hard put to explain how *abbas* could mean 'representative of Christ', when Christ was considered 'Father' and designated by the words of Rom 8:15, *abba pater*. The difficulty has been removed by studies showing that Christ was readily addressed by the title Father in patristic writings within a tradition warranted by more than one reference to Scripture itself.[82] Moreover, this concept is affirmed throughout the entire RM *Thema*,[83] especially in the commentary on the Lord's prayer which close scrutiny reveals to be addressed not to the first Person of the Trinity, but to Christ. The allusion in Chapter Two to the fatherhood of Christ expresses therefore the ordinary thought process of the Master. In this we have another indication of the homogeneity of the RM text and, in consequence, its anteriority to the RB text.

The name abbot, which means father, therefore refers the person who bears it to Christ himself. The abbot takes his mission from Christ; he represents him. The name abbot in RM and RB evokes less the fatherhood of the superior in relation to his disciples than his capacity of representing in his person the unique *abba* who is Christ. The abbot is father, certainly, but his is only a delegated fatherhood. A consideration of the RM texts as a whole reveals that the author is given to describing the superior not so much as a father but as a servant whom the father of the family has set over his whole household. That is why he never troubled about the apparent discrepancy between monastic terminology and the explicit words of Jesus forbidding his disciples to call anyone on earth 'master' or 'father', since you have only one Father, and he is in heaven... only one Master, Christ'.[84] Already the New Testament attests to a usage quite contrary to this prohibition[85] and, despite Jerome's scruples, monasticism has unanimously followed ecclesiastical usage by calling its own leaders 'fathers'.[86]

These precedents in themselves explain how the name 'father' given to the abbot occasioned no difficulty for the Master. We note, however, that this notion of the abbacy does in fact give a satisfactory solution to this problem. If the abbot is essentially the representative of Christ, if the very name abbot signifies primarily this 'vicarious' role, if the fatherhood of the superior does not appear except within this relationship to Christ, then the words of Jesus are not transgressed save in externals which deceive no one. The abbot, far from being a substitute for the unique father, becomes his most significant evocation.

What we have said about the name abbot is true *a fortiori* of two other names given to the superior in these first lines of Chapter Two. The abbot, as we said at the outset, is a *major* (RM-RB 2:1). The meaning of this term clearly appears in Chapter Eleven of RM where it is a matter of *maiores familiae* or officers established by the master for governing the *familia*. One of these servants invested with the master's authority bore the name *maior-domus* (11:7).[87] In the imagery of this organization, says the Master, 'in the houses of God, namely, churches and monasteries, God has set superiors over subordinates (*minoribus maiores*), the experienced over the inexperienced, the discerning over the simple, and for those who are learning the divine art he has appointed masters' (vs 8). The name *maior*, evidently signifies both authoritative superiority based on a superiority of value, and dependence on the master. By giving the abbot this name, RM and RB emphasize the idea of 'vicarious' power. To be 'superior', *maior*, is to possess authority, but a delegated authority conferred by the master of the household on one of his slaves in recognition of his superior abilities.[88]

The same idea suffuses, without needing explication, the name *pastor* (RM-RB 2:7). This term is too charged with biblical overtones to be ambiguous. Moreover, the rules explicitly describe the intermediate position of this 'pastor', set between the sheep and the owner of the flock, just as the *maior familiae* stands between the slaves and the master of the house. In addition, the image of the pastor evokes more especially the perspective of the account to be rendered, a theme systematically developed by the introduction and conclusion.

We have here before us all the key words defining an abbot.[89] *Doctor, uices agens, maior, abbas, pastor,* all proclaiming one and the same thing, the double relationship a man has to Christ and to his brethren which makes him a mediator of divine grace responsible before God for the salvation of a group of men. This idea, let it be repeated, is essentially biblical and ecclesial.

Although the secular image of the *familia* may serve to illustrate the terms *uices agens* and *maior*, the Scriptures themselves are ultimately the source of such metaphors. The slave placed over his fellow servants to govern them, like the teacher or pastor, is a scriptural theme. While developing the first, the Master no doubt alludes to a secular institution with which his readers were acquainted. But allusions of this sort are only literary techniques for making the traditional image more meaningful. The words alone have a restored value, without any need for speaking of a new inspiration or of an imitation of secular society. Moreover, to the extent that the roman *paterfamilias* is evoked, the abbot appears as 'vicar' of the father of the divine family, not as an autonomous *paterfamilias*.

Everything then brings us back to the idea of a purely spiritual and supernatural mission. This is affirmed lastly by a rigorous parallel with the bishop in which the Master boldly explains a factor which lies latent everywhere in ecclesiastical and monastic tradition.[90] In our rules there is no doubt that monarchical constitution is as essential to cenobitism as it is to the Church itself, and for the same reason.[91] There is scarcely any need to call up political or historical arguments in support of such a regime: it is a matter of divine necessity, a providential law governing the entire economy of salvation. Further talk about 'paternalism' would be to little avail. This epithet is no more applicable to cenobitism than to the Church or to creation or to the divine family itself.

Cenobitism is essentially constituted therefore by the wholly spiritual relationship of each of its members to a man who represents Christ. From this initial relationship springs what unites all the disciples of the same master to one another. Cenobitic society exists therefore primarily between the monk and his abbot, that is to say, between the monk and the God he is seeking. It is the extension of the eremitical experience. It remains fundamentally a life with God alone.

The problem of cenobitic life consists precisely in actualizing this basic relationship as much as possible, in truly living it. On the part of the abbot, first of all, this implies making real the opening words of the present chapter *nomen maioris factis implere*,[92] to fulfil effectively the function of 'superior'. The abbot ought to be superior not only by the power he wields, but by an authentic supernatural value:[93] really in possession of the divine law, capable of teaching and living it beneath the eyes of the brethren, so strong in his faith and love as to enjoin its observation untiringly. Nothing less is demanded of him than that he be so imbued by the Word of God and His Spirit that he be a living Word and dispenser of the Spirit.[94] Otherwise, although the *coenobium* may be a more or less prestigious society in the eyes of men, it will fall short of its true purpose, which is to educate souls in the quest for perfection. The fate of cenobitism depends on this 'superiority' which everyone hopes to find in the abbot, to be guided by him, like members of a body by the head, towards sanctity (RM 2:29).

On the disciple's part, an initial impetus of faith and confidence in the abbot is no less indispensable. This movement upwards, from men who are sinners to the man of God who represents Christ, is required not only at the outset of the cenobitic pact, from the moment one enters the monastery to find salvation. There it ought to continue at every moment, lest the cenobitic society lose its meaning. The mutual relationship uniting brethren to abbot in Christ is the soul of cenobitism. The more clearly this relation appears as the essence of cenobitic life, the more chance will this life have of fulfilling its promises.

SPIRITUAL FATHER AND ADMINISTRATOR

We have defined the abbot, according to the Master and St Benedict, as pastor of the people of God, a 'teacher' imparting knowledge in the name of Christ, a steward set by the Father of the family at the head of his divine household, there to stand in his place and to rule all his servants with the fullness of his authority. These images, as we have seen, are taken from Scripture and they refer the superior of the *coenobium* ultimately not to some sort of secular authority but rather to the head of a church, the bishop. We have stressed the eminently spiritual character of this mediation between God and men which constitutes the essence of the abbacy as well as of the priesthood. In the last analysis cenobitic society seems to us explicable by this fundamental relationship of disciple-sinner to master accredited by God to save him, a vertical relationship, from inferior to superior in Christ, a relation which precedes, engenders, and furnishes the justification for the horizontal relations uniting the brethren. The *coenobium* is essentially a school in which a band of disciples finds itself drawn together only because there is a master to be heeded and obeyed. Each of the monks expects from that master the word which will express for him the divine will he is to carry out in order to be saved. Such expectations suppose that the abbot is indeed a spiritual man, capable of guiding others to the goal because he himself has already arrived there and is at this point so given up to the divine Word and to the Spirit of God that he has become like a living Word and a radiance of the Spirit. Is this not, moreover, what is implied by the title 'teacher' which the Master so resolutely gives him, intending thereby to recognize in him one of the charisms spoken of in the pauline description of the Body of Christ?

This eminently charismatic character of the traditional notion of abbot had to be emphasized before all else. Yet it would be childish to rest at this ideal schema and fail to understand the concrete conditions which go to make up the abbot's task. No doubt he is essentially a spiritual father for each of his disciples by virtue of a master-disciple relationship which, of itself, takes no account of the greater or lesser number of spiritual sons who have assembled to receive the same direction. But one cannot ignore the existence of this group whose head is the abbot, or the problems that the functions of superior, which he is obliged to assume, entail for the spiritual father. If it is true that, according to the texts, the abbot is what we have said, he nevertheless exercises an administrative authority as well, governing a group of men and managing the material goods which assure their livelihood.

Consequently, one cannot avoid asking what influence this social function exerts upon spiritual fatherhood. There is a great difference between the superior of the *coenobium* and the solitary who lives with one or two disciples, notwithstanding the real continuity which, based on history and in the very nature of things, we have been intent until now to underscore. Now we must consider this original modality conferred by cenobitism on the spiritual fatherhood of the monk and make an effort to explain it.

It appears very clearly when one compares the abbot to his ecclesiastical prototype, the bishop. The bishop in effect also governs a christian community and his authority extends not only to the intimate domain of conscience, but also to the collective life of his flock in so far as it constitutes a church. But, for all that, he has no power over the temporal community which his faithful form; in this domain he is not the head. He is not charged with the direction of his sheep in their professional activities, their family life, or the government of their city. These domains pertain to secular authorities distinct from his own, to the father of a family, for example, or to a magistrate or prince. Either in his own right or because he is head of the clergy, the bishop may well have his own ecclesiastical *familia,*[95] but this is not to be confused with his church, nor his servants and the clerics with the christian people whom he has in his keeping. In other words, although he may have a *domus* of his own, his church is the *domus Dei,* not his own. The domestic power he exercises within his household ceases the moment he steps outside of it, and there can be no question of his treating as subjects on the temporal plane the faithful whom he rules in the name of God, with a view to eternal life.[96]

In the face of this very clear distinction made between spiritual authority and temporal power in the church and in its bishop, the case of the abbot takes on the disconcerting appearance of a total merging of the two domains. Here we have a group of men who bind themselves completely to a head at once spiritual and temporal. The human community here coincides exactly with the church, and the spiritual sons of the abbot are at the same time entirely subject to him, in the whole and in every detail of their temporal activity, with no secular domain answerable to a separate power.[97] To say he combines them is not enough, for the bishop also exercises both, though in separate capacities and over different persons. There is here a veritable fusion between pastor and master of the household. The abbot is not, as we have seen, designated as *paterfamilias.* Like the bishop, he is only a steward of God. But it remains no less true that the authority he exercises in the name of the father of the divine family reaches far beyond the limits accorded the bishop, even as far as the entire existence of his flock. In fact, if not by explicit assimilation, he is indeed a *paterfamilias* for the monastery in the fulness of his rights.

It is only right to recognize here the element of truth in the thesis of the abbot-father of the family which we discussed and rejected above. We grounded our criticism, it will be recalled, primarily on the absence of weighty references in the texts, whereas these same texts constantly refer the reader to the biblical and ecclesial type of pastor. We objected also that the benedictine idea of the abbot could not be considered as the fruit of personal experience which Benedict had acquired in the bosom of his own family, nor as the fruit of direct imitation of the juridical institu-

tions of the roman *familia,* since RB falls within an already
centuries-old monastic tradition whose classical and almost
stereotyped portrait of the abbot it reproduces without appreciable modification. Lastly, we brought out the profoundly
spiritual meaning of the abbatial function, which appeared to us
much less a solution to the political problem posed by the community's existence than the *raison d'être* and the generator of this
very community, to which, apart from all historical or political
considerations, it is by the very nature of things bound.

This triple critique manifestly does not exclude the possibility of
a link between the abbot and the *paterfamilias,* a link that can
hardly be doubted if one is attentive to the considerations just
developed. From the fact that the abbot is not only spiritual head
but also, and precisely because of his spiritual function, master of
the entire personal and collective life of the monks, it is manifest
that his temporal situation is analogous to that of the father of a
family. The whole question is to know whether this analogy results
from an extrinsic imitation or whether it is instead imposed by an
inner necessity, an exigency arising from the pedagogical function
of the abbot. In other words, is the domestic power of the abbot,
because contaminated by the profane type of the *paterfamilias,*
subjoined to the religious authority of the pastor, which alone is
accredited by God and grounded in Scripture, or does domestic
power spring instead from the very essence of the spiritual charge
of abbot? Is it an accident attributable to an historical juncture or
a natural development of the 'teacher's' mission which our rule,
and the whole tradition, makes the essence of the abbacy?

It would be a mistake, no doubt, to absolutize this alternative as
if the two members were of necessity mutually exclusive. Nothing
prevents secular institutions from making their influence felt
along with the internal laws of spiritual fatherhood, the one rein-
forcing the other and furnishing it with the juridical framework
which permits it to be realized concretely. All we mean to suggest
by raising these questions is that the temporal aspect of abbatial
authority, though it undeniably resembles the power of the master
of a household, stands primarily in relation to spiritual
fatherhood by reason of its origin and profound finality. Let us
therefore try to shed some light on this necessary relationship
between the domestic power of the abbot and his function as
teacher.

If cenobitic society is essentially constituted by the relationship of the disciple to master, we ought to begin from the disciple's standpoint. As soon as his spiritual needs or what he came to find in the *coenobium* are considered we are facing the basic answer to our problem. The monk is essentially a renunciant. Precisely what he asks of his spiritual master is to learn from him how to realize the renunciation so that no affection for any creature may thereafter interpose itself between his sinful will and that of God. On the other hand, perfect renunciation does not appear only as the object of the teaching of the master, the desired skill which the disciple wants to learn from him. It is also, and from the outset, the necessary condition for authentic relations between master and disciple, relations which have a chance to endure and attain their purpose. Under this double aspect, complete renunciation — object of and condition for spiritual teaching — is proper to the disciple as the characteristic gesture of his conversion, and it consists in resigning into the hands of his master all rights to an autonomous use of the goods of this world. Subjection to an abbot is the efficacious sign of renunciation so that the abbot should, in order to respond to the deepest wish of his spiritual son, agree to assume a full authority from which no facet of his personality and existence are exempt.

What we have traced here may be illustrated by numerous references to the classic texts of monasticism as well as to RM and RB. We will not stress the basic idea that monk is definable by renunciation: this theme of a living death is too clearly set forth by Cassian and Basil for there to be any need to develop it here. We have already had occasion to show, following Cassian, that such renunciation was the necessary condition to establishing the master-disciple relationship. It is useful to recall it here, however.[98] The author of the *Institutes* saw in the giving up of possessions which accompanies the cenobite's entry into community the indispensable guarantee against future temptations to quit. Bridges are burned. The harsh ordeal which perpetual obedience involves demands this precaution: there will surely be occasions a-plenty for looking back with regret towards the world! The postulant had best cast off at the outset the hope of recovering his worldly situation. A man who has no further material security has, moreover, a better chance of giving himself unreservedly to *ascesis,* of proving himself flexible, humble and docile. Still more, this giving-up corresponds to an imperious demand for tranquility of spirit: the brother leaves to his abbot the whole care of seeing to his upkeep. He himself has plenty to do looking after his own salvation, which ought to occupy him completely. Practically speaking, he is dead to the cares of the world and even his life is in the hands of the abbot. He is free to seek the kingdom of God.[99]

In the view of Cassian and of the whole tradition, then, one cannot commit oneself to the disciple's life without being stripped not only of all property but even of the care of providing for one's own maintenance. This condition evidently cannot be realized unless the master on his part assumes charge of his spiritual son even to the extent of looking after his well-being, agreeing to watch over his body as well as his soul.[100] By beginning with the teaching mission of the abbot, then, one inevitably comes up against his administrative power over material goods. The abbot cannot exercise his spiritual fatherhood in an effectual and lasting manner unless the disciple abandons himself to him entirely, turning over to him his possessions and all his rights.

But why entrust temporal administration to the spiritual father rather than to some other officer of the *coenobium?* The very terms of direction given and received enter the picture here. The disciple is asking to learn from the master how to avoid sin and to accomplish the will of God, and to do that not in some who-knows-what intangible kind of universe of 'things of the soul', but in concrete existence, in the use of material things as well as in the intimate thoughts of the heart, in fraternal relations as much as in the encounter with God alone. No sector of human life escapes the need for reformation according to the word of God; there is no domain in which the sinner seeking salvation does not require guidance of the man of God.

Consequently, there can be no question of leaving the least part of the group's or the individual's existence to persons other than the man of God. To erect a distinct administrative power alongside the spiritual authority would be to run counter to the deepest *raison d'être* of a society which proposes nothing else than the subjection of the entire life of its members to the influence of a 'teacher' of life according to God. Meals, work, sleep, reading, trips, alms-giving, relations with the world, everything in this life, beginning with prayer, of course, ought to be under the effective supervision of 'Christ's lieutenant'. He can and must avail himself of the assistance of the competent and trusted officers in specific areas of cenobitic administration. But responsibility for the whole as much as for each detail weighs upon him with a gravity that no collaborator can diminish.

The universal responsibility of the abbot is not only implied by the facts and practice of cenobitism, it is enunciated with the greatest possible clarity by RM. The abbot will have to give account for the actions of all his disciples, presuming that they act in obedience. In some way there is but a single will in the monastery, and consequently but a single responsibility. The disciples are confided to a man who, they hope, is in all circustances capable of making the will of God triumphant over the enticements of the devil and of the flesh. They have placed their will in the abbot's because the will of the abbot is united to the will of God.[101] To withdraw anything from the authority of this master of the christian life would be to frustrate their expectation. No one enters the *coenobium* in order to find there the domination—willed by God surely, but morally ambiguous—of the heads of the terrestrial city. What is sought is precisely the contrary: the authority of a man so holy that the Word and the Spirit may, through his sinful humanity, inform the whole life of his disciples and remodel it according to the new man.

A consideration bordering on what we have just said orients us still in the same line. Turned as he is exclusively towards salvation, the monk aims at a complete break with the present world. In order to follow Christ he renounces all temporal concerns: goods, honor, family. As a result, a society of monks loses, so to speak, the temporal consistency which in the world justifies and requires a distinction between what is Caesar's and what is God's. Because the members of this society have no other interest than the kingdom of God, because they have given up the things of this world and the responsibility for their administration, they can place their entire existence under the direction of a vicar of Christ, a genuine pastor of souls.

From this standpoint, one can see what distinguishes abbot from bishop. The bishop watches over men involved in the present world, the abbot over Christians who have renounced the world. The bishop is not qualified to direct his flock in the things of this world. He must leave that responsibility to authorities of the natural order and limit himself to instructing them on their duties as Christians. The abbot would be in the same situation—obliged to stand aside as soon as it were question of the things of this world—had his disciples not renounced those very worldly values. Between him and them are neither family, property, reputation nor any of those transitory values which come between the bishop and his faithful.

Such a master and such disciples can and must realize a much closer community life than that of an ordinary church. The disciples draw much closer together around the 'teacher' who exercises a complete hold over their lives in order to set them in perfect obedience to divine command. On his part, the master is more committed than a bishop often is (*de facto* if not *de jure*) to christian perfection. Because he was the first to renounce everything and has realized and successfully lived that renunciation, he can now be its effective agent for others in the spiritual fatherhood of the *coenobium*. The authority of the abbot over the community's temporal affairs has its source in the more perfect detachment he has attained. The reason for his authority is the accomplishment of the same detachment in the souls of the disciples subject to him, and the condition for it is the radical renunciation made by everyone, master and disciples alike, of the goods of the present life.

Pursuing this line of thought, we connect with that of Cassian, according to whom the *coenobium* is the continuation during the centuries when fervor had cooled of the primitive and ideal Jerusalem church.[102] The function of this myth here is to focus attention on a biblical precedent by which cenobitism authorizes its audacious fusion of temporal power and spiritual authority. Of the apostles as well as of the abbot it is written, they 'would distribute resources according to the needs of each'.[103] Already in Jerusalem, the faithful's spontaneous giving up the goods of this world in the fervor of eschatological expectation had as a consequence the delivery of administrative power into the hands of the leaders of the church.

This merging of ecclesial community and temporal community imports no harm to the spiritual character of the church and its pastors. On the contrary, it is its highest expression, the sign of the total efficacy of the words of the Gospel. That the apostles, and after them the abbot, had to 'distribute what is necessary', reveals the complete success of their teaching. We will not be forcing Cassian's thought if we say that the abbot is the perfect continuator of the apostles, the ideal bishop. If he combines in his person both temporal authority and pastoral charge, this fact does not constitute a degradation of his pastoral quality but rather the normal extension of that quality, seeing that all his faithful are tending with him toward perfect renunciation. On the other hand, when the bishop with his faithful forms a church distinct from the temporal community and stands in its midst only as one citizen among others, one property owner among others, we see a sign that between them intervenes the weight of this world's things, whose administration does not rightfully pertain to spiritual authority. Thus the primitive episcopal ideal is continued in the abbot and realized only imperfectly, according to Cassian, in the bishop of today,[104] because of the lesser fervor of people with whom in some way he is in fellowship.

But will the abbot, by the sole fact that he is fit to guide souls, meet all the tasks of cenobitic administration? Posed correctly, the question ought to be formulated in terms of charisms. Nothing would run more counter to the ideas of the ancients than to oppose charismatics and administrators, as if administration did not bear witness to a true charism but only to a natural gift for managing affairs. So secularized a notion of administration would do violence not only to the biblical mentality which sees in all 'wisdom', whether of Bezalel, Hiram or Solomon, a particular gift of God,[105] but also to the lofty estimation monks have always had for temporal tasks. They are convinced that great virtue is required to discharge such tasks well, because they are fully conscious of the gravity of the smallest faults of which those obligations are ordinarily the occasion. Even more, the society of monks and its temporal affairs is imbued with a sacred character which increases the peril of misuse.[106] For all these reasons, a high idea is formed of the spiritual qualities which the dean or the cellarer ought to possess,[107] and he should be selected for the degree of virtue he has attained and the gifts of the Spirit which he has received much more than for cleverness which, as we have said, is in other respects considered a sort of charism.

We notice in passing how such a mentality makes the extension of the pastor's spiritual charge into the domain of temporal tasks more readily admissible. Passing from one to the other is not a crossing from the sacred to the profane, from the things of God to those of the world, as our secularized mentality tends to imagine: the perspective remains one of *ascesis* and search for God.

Another question. Can the grace of the spiritual father combine
with the grace of the community head? To give an answer we need
to remember that spiritual fatherhood implies a total authority of
father over his sons. So it was in eremitism: to become the disciple
of an elder meant to become his servant and to live in strict community with him, letting nothing escape his control.[108] But if
cenobitism is none other than a development of such a master-
disciple relationship, the master's hold must necessarily reach to
all the new situations which result from the multiplication of the
disciples' number. Since there is henceforth a society of the
abbot's spiritual sons, how could he effectively direct these souls if
he did not take in hand the society in which their life unfolds? In
the opposite hypothesis, the master's teaching would suffer a
restriction which would be contrary to the totalitarian character
of the moral reform expected from him; the grace of the spiritual
father would cease to radiate over the whole of his disciples' life.
And so, since it is exercised in the heart of a group, the charism
of the teacher involves authority over this same group. To come
fully up to his definition, the spiritual father must be head of the
community.[109]

That this ideal was a reality is proclaimed by every page of the
pachomian *Lives.* The organizational genius of the first
coenobia, the head of veritable armies of monks, was at the same
time and above all else the spiritual father of each and every soul
confided to him. This primordial aspect of the mission of
Pachomius (and of Theodore after him) has been too much
overlooked by modern historians. The administrative role of the
superior of the congregation does not in fact prevent his excelling
in all the gifts of the spiritual father, and his exercising them with
a personal solicitude for any of his children in need of him. The
Lives vie with one another in extolling the Father's ability to read
hearts, the 'maternal' care he took of souls, and that mysterious
gift he had for treating each case according to its true nature and
gravity, disconcerting men's expectations sometimes by his severity and sometimes by his forbearance.[110]

Not all spiritual fathers are fit to govern a *coenobium,* however.
It can happen that someone who knows perfectly how to direct
one or two disciples and to communicate the word of God to all
visitors besieging him has not received the grace to exert the same
teaching activity at the level of a cenobitic society. Hagiography
seems to insinuate this original character of spiritual fatherhood

for the *coenobium* when it places a very special divine call at the beginning of the career of Pachomius, Orsiesius and Apollonius.[111] Alongside these vocations to the abbacy, the successful outcome of which is attributed to a particular grace of God, one can list some more or less unsuccessful examples which also testify to the fact that the gift of ruling a community is not granted everyone, not even every authentic man of God. In the *Life of St Romanus,* the semi-incapacity of the holy man to govern his monasteries in the Jura mountains can easily be divined, whereas at his side his brother Lupicinus proved to be a strong leader and in his own fashion, no less holy.[112] And what should be said of those numerous cases of fleeing abbots which, according to RM, the *Lives of the Fathers* narrate?[113] Such flights are generally attributable to humility, of course:[114] the superior, weary of honors, anxious for his own salvation, tries to get himself received incognito in some other monastery and to return there to the rank of disciple. But in at least one case another motive is acknowledged: when Fulgentius abandoned for the second time the community of which he was abbot, he did so partly to escape administrative concerns and give himself freely to reading and prayer.[115] In this one can recognize a constant trait of his nature: he felt himself made much more for speculation and teaching than for practical tasks and he gladly left the latter to his friend and coadjutor abbot, Felix.[116] Similar aversions for this or that ineluctable aspect of the abbatial charge may well have played their role in other cases of flight. One is always justified in suspecting behind such flights some sort of failure, especially when they are repeated, as in the story of Pinuphius narrated by Cassian.

The vocation to be abbot of a *coenobium* is then a special vocation among the vocations of spiritual father. We may go a step further: even when such a vocation is present, are the two exigencies it involves not so different as to risk harming each other? Irénée Hausherr cited and made his own an impressive page from Smirnov which denounces the harm caused to spiritual fatherhood by the social power of superiors. The reflections of Hausherr in their turn deserve to be quoted at length:

> One has the impression that in the *coenobia* where the *hegumen* takes all powers into his own hands, the ancient manifestation of thoughts becomes more and more a mere confession of sins. ...Instead of a soul to soul relationship,

...there remains only a series of regulated acts and inter-
views of a canonical order.... Spiritual fatherhood congeals
into administrative, official, regimented relations. Where
once the initiative had begun with the disciple going to the
man of the Spirit towards whom his confidence bore him,
codification and control by authority little by little take their
place. The power-wielder easily forgets that he is bound to
encourage what the subjects are obliged to do more by his
entire being than by imposing all the force of his power.
Confidence cannot be commanded—or at least the kind of
confidence that goes no further than strict obedience to
commandment.... The filial laying-open of the soul, which
envisaged especially the healing to come, becomes a painful
accusation regarding little more than the past. The spiritual
father is nothing more than an absolution-giver and
penance-assessor.[117]

These reflections bear directly on manifestation of thoughts.
The abbot, however, is spiritual master not only in these intimate
relationships of direction in which he deals person-to-person with
each disciple about the particular needs of his soul,[118] but also and
primarily by the teaching he gives to the whole community in his
conferences, by the collective direction he impresses on it, by the
rules he establishes or interprets, by the officers he chooses to ally
with himself in directing the brethren. This whole animation of
the community by its head can and should be of a deeply spiritual
nature and it does indeed reach, more or less directly, each of the
souls who have confided themselves to the abbot. So the remarks
of Smirnov and Hausherr, serious as they are, do not imply the in-
compatibility of social power with spiritual fatherhood, at least
with the forms of fatherhood we have discussed.

In addition, these two authors draw their observations from the
oriental tradition. Ancient occidental rules have nothing of any
importance that would permit us either to corroborate or to in-
validate the 'impressions' of Hausherr. In western rules the
manifestation of thoughts often passes unmentioned by reason of
the sketchy nature of such documents, and when it is mentioned
the context is generally a spiritual one from which the regimen-
tary and canonical aspect is almost entirely absent.[119]

Having said this, we must admit that Hausherr puts us on to a
very real and permanent problem of cenobitism. Adding a com-

munitarian dimension to spiritual fatherhood brings the risk of de-naturing it. One runs the danger of an exteriorization of the master-disciple relationship which is transposed to the social plane and emptied of its personal substance. Not to mention the temptation which his social power constitutes for the abbot (Smirnov insists particularly on this), it can happen naturally enough that a head concerns himself mainly with the smooth running of the group and its exterior regularity or even, alas! merely with the success of its works. He will tend then to become a man of the rule or of regimentation, the latter term being understood not so much as a method of personal education and instrument for the salvation of souls, but as a group safeguard, the law of society, and expression of the common good.[120]

The Master himself did not, as we shall see, avoid this sort of peril when he made the abbot the organizer and referee of a contest of virtues instituted among the monks with view to the first place.[121] There again the exaggeration of the social element in *ascesis* brings about a real perversion of the master-disciple relationship: the *ophtalmodoulia* which St Paul mentions comes between them.[122] If the abbot abusively exploits emulation with a view to getting good conduct from his monks, a false appreciation of the abbot's role will inevitably develop, and they will look on him as someone who metes out reward and whose favor is gained by showy acts of virtue.

One could say that the Master's idea is an isolated case in the tradition and that no one else pushed communitarian *ascesis* to absurdity in this way. But apart from the odd virtue contest of RM, there remains in every form of cenobitism a permanent danger of seeing in the abbot first and foremost the wielder of temporal authority, the man who disposes whatever is coveted or feared in social life. And even without descending to schemings for personal interest, one will be led to ask of him primarily shrewd direction of the community and prudent management of its material interests—in brief, the services expected of a good head in any collectivity.

This dangerous impoverishment of the notion of abbacy is moreover the not necessarily fatal but difficult to avoid result of the fact of *abbatial succession*. Here we are touching the thorniest problem, the *Schicksalfrage,* of cenobitism. At a monastery's beginnings is most often found an authentic spiritual father.

Disciples gather around him to benefit from his direction, but after his death the community he engendered lives on. A rule, the reminder of his example, and traditions perpetuate his teaching. But is there among his sons a man of God capable of replacing him as the master of all these disciples?

The serious point is that, even if there is no 'teacher', an abbot will be installed all the same. The group's desire to continue will overlook the lack of an abbot worthy of the name. In the most favorable hypothesis, the successor, even a capable one, will rarely have at the outset the same authority as his predecessor. The spiritual bonds which had spontaneously tied the disciples to their first master must now be re-tied with great effort. It is much more difficult for a disciple to return to his place once a new master who yesterday was standing next to him has entered the chair, especially when he is no longer in the first stages of spiritual growth. Almost necessarily, a diminution of the prestige of the abbot ensues as does the temptation for both him and his monks to be content with the relationship of leader to subordinate on the temporal plane, the sort of relationship required by the necessities of the social life that must be continued.[123]

The problem of succession has two equally formidable aspects: how to find an authentic abbot, a genuine continuator of the spiritual father who was his predecessor; and how to re-enter with the new father the thoroughly filial attitude essential to the cenobitic pact? The very existence of the *coenobium* as a 'school of Christ' is at stake here. Because this school constitutes a temporal society like any other, it can outlive what was its *raison d'être,* the *magisterium* of an authentic teacher. Force of habit, bonds of common life, common patrimony of material goods, all tend to keep the disciples united even though the master is gone and no one is fit to teach in his place. But when, either on the side of the new abbot or on the side of the disciples, the master-disciple relationship ceases to be lived seriously, the school of divine service has perished just as surely as if everyone had scattered.

We shall speak again further on of the abbatial succession. For now it is of interest to us only in so far as it is the critical point where the tendency to dissociate the two components of the abbacy most perilously asserts itself, to see only a temporal head while losing sight of the teacher. We have said enough about this to show the extent to which the remarks of Irénée Hausherr touch the cenobitic abbacy to the quick. Beyond the limited question of manifestation of conscience, beyond the frontiers of Byzantium, lies the most profound and universal problem of cenobitism: how to keep the administrator from swallowing up the spiritual father? The temporal function of the head, which is in origin and by right only a corollary of the mission of teacher, tends under the sheer weight of sinful nature and the 'worldly' reality which the *coenobium* is, to stifle the spiritual relationships which it had been charged to serve.[124]

One particular aspect of the problem is the question of the material cares of the abbot. It deserves special mention here since the RB redactor made it the object of one of the most significant additions to his directory for the superior.[125] RM likes to preach to the monks indifference towards bodily needs, such needs having been taken entirely in charge by divine providence and by the abbot.[126] It supposes, without ever saying so, that the abbot on his part realizes to perfection this commandment of 'not worrying' about nourishment and clothing. On this topic RB did not copy any of the exhortations addressed to the monks by the Master but instead inserted a warning to the abbot on the same theme while appealing to the same basic text,[127] as if it were more afraid the superior than his subjects would have 'worries' about the things of this world. Caesarius had done the same in his directory for an abbess,[128] and we shall see when we study RB Sixty-five how much the history of western monasticism towards the end of antiquity justified such apprehensions.

In fact, it is normal for the abbot to be more exposed than anyone else to cares for the morrow. In order to be entirely free to attend to his salvation, to fulfill the command of Christ, the cenobite surrenders all right and all responsibility for his own maintenance. This complete liberty with regard to material things is one of the fundamental advantages of the *coenobium*, Cassian told us.[129] But it has as its counterpart a servitude which weighs upon the abbot, obliged as he is to bear alone the responsibility of which each of his monks has unburdened himself. He is believed to be so spiritual that his burden will not oppress him and thereby deflect his attention from God. Such strength in faith is expected from him, on the contrary, that material cares become for him and for his sons an occasion for turning to God.[130] Because he is in principle the man of God who alone is able to manage the affairs of this world without committing sin, management of such goods falls on his shoulders. By entrusting to him their power to handle the things of this world, the disciples hope to avoid all sin in this area. Such a sanctified, rectified and fully christian concept of earthly goods and their use will descend on them from the master that, by means of the orders of his vicar, only the will of Christ shall be accomplished in the monastery, and every action performed in obedience will merit recompense.[131]

It is pointless to underscore what such expectations imply in the responsibility, not only material but also and primarily spiritual, shouldered by the abbot. Certainly, he ought not to fail in his duty of assuring sustenance for his sons, but graver still is the obligation to show himself a true spiritual father, an example of detachment and confidence in God for those who are working under his orders, in the very pursuit of that sustenance.[132] Here again the spiritual father's grace ought to impregnate the exercise of administrative authority, even though the bent of sinful nature inclines man to be the less spiritual the more he is immersed in the cares of this world.

The ideal we have traced through RM and RB demands a great deal of the abbot. We understand why RB did not judge it idle to alert him against the temptations his office entails. The conjunction of spiritual fatherhood and temporal responsibility is the very nature of cenobitic abbacy, a necessary conjunction with the resultant perilous tension and the never-ending risk for the abbot of giving in to material preoccupations. In that event, the monk's personal renunciation of preoccupations about the morrow will have been to no purpose. Those same preoccupations will descend upon him once again, multiplied according to the scale of the community.[133]

The successful outcome of the renunciation made by each of the monks depends therefore on the abbot. The renunciation of the disciple will terminate either in a total liberation or in a new bondage, according to the quality of the master and his attitude towards the material plane. Everything ultimately depends on the outcome of the fight waged in the soul of the abbot between the earthly cares of the sinful man, heavily burdened with material responsibilities, and the grace of the spiritual father, in the name of which he has taken on these responsibilities. Will the accidental devour the essential?

For the rest, though the abbot is indeed the pivot of the

cenobitic system and though it depends on him whether this system enslaves or liberates the monks, there are certain factors of the problem which do not depend on his liberty alone, but are imposed on him and condition his attitude. His personal qualities ought to encounter a relatively light task, thanks to the simplicity of the monk's lives: reduction of needs to a minimum by genuine collective poverty, absence of superfluous works, especially those involving relations with the world, a climate of detachment and good will in the subjects in regard to work methods which will cause them to eschew as much as possible the bickering whose arbitration is so wearisome for the superior.

Certainly, it pertains chiefly to the abbot to create or maintain this simple way of life, marked by renunciation and commanded by a clear view of what is essential.[134] Nevertheless, community habits also constitute a real situation with which it is hard not to reckon, even when one remains clear-sighted enough to pass judgment on it. One of the original characteristics of RB, in relation to RM, is exactly this somewhat disillusioned awareness the legislator has of the limits imposed on him by collective customs he can neither sanction nor correct.[135] Once the founder of the monastery is gone, his successors step into a situation more or less mortgaged by acquired habits which rarely tend to the better. From this, in large measure, results that progressive process of temporal encumbrance whereby decadence sets in. Successive abbots find themselves confronted with an administrative task increasingly weighty and complex, confronted with temporal concerns less and less subordinated to the spiritual and apt to serve it. The task reacts on the man who assumes it. The excessively heavy temporal concerns absorb the abbot and weaken in him and in his sons the sense of his true mission.

With these last remarks we have finished laying down the essential points of the problem of the abbatial charism which has occupied us for so long here. Necessarily a complex charism, in which the grace of the spiritual father requires for its full expansion the gifts of head and of administrator, it harbors in its very complexity the threat of corruption. In so far as he is holy and a master of sanctity, the abbot *ought* to be at once spiritual quickener and temporal leader. In so far as he is a sinner, he experiences some very particular temptations because of this administrative task annexed to his spiritual mission, temptations which through him threaten his disciples. But the disciples on their part condition to a large extent the expansion and the fruitfulness of the abbatial charism, not only by the role which is theirs, at least according to RB, of electing the abbot, but even by the attitude they have to take *vis-à-vis* the new abbot, looking on him as real spiritual father and presenting him with an administrative task which ought to be simple, reduced to what is indispensable and clearly ordered to the task of supernatural education it serves.

The step from cenobitic society to what is today called 'clericalism' is apparently a short one. Not that the hierarchy of the *coenobium* is clerical in the ecclesiastical sense of the word; the abbot and his officers are, on the contrary, in principle and often in fact laymen. Clericalism here means only the complete fusion of temporal and spiritual. The religious heads of society are invested, purely by virtue of their religious power, with full authority over the temporal. No distinction however slight exists between what belongs to Caesar and what belongs to God.

The *coenobium* is in truth a unique type of society, a society of renunciants. 'Clericalism' usually conjures up the abuse of a christian pastor pretending to govern temporally when neither he nor his flock have consented to complete renunciation. But from the moment a strong current of fervor propels all the members of the community to total abnegation in an exclusive search for the goods of the next world, it is natural that spiritual authority absorb temporal power. Social authority and material goods cease to be the object of divisive covetousness and become the subject of a unifying renunciation. In such a society, it is necessary that the 'best one', as RM says or, in other words, the one who is most detached and most fit to teach, be the head.[136] His authority over things temporal is legitimate to the measure that he teaches detachment by his word and example.

In addition, a trait largely original to the ancient *coenobium*, as distinguished from more recent forms of religious life, is the lack of distinction within the spiritual authority itself between the internal forum and the external forum, between the religious superior and the spiritual father. The abbot is both. His social authority exercises itself, as we have said, in the extension and to the benefit of the direction accorded to individuals. The greatness of this society is precisely its exclusive ordering to spiritual formation, to the eternal salvation of its members. There is no secondary aim involving a special outwardly-orientated action.[137] Because the society has no other end than the sanctification of its members, the superior does not have to promote a common good to be defined by secondary purpose for the institute or by some fixed work to be achieved.

To the extent that a distinction between the external and the internal fora corresponds to a society's dual aims (sanctification of its members and exterior action), this distinction has no place in the *coenobium*.[138] Blending the attributes of superior and spiritual father into the same person is for cenobitism, on the contrary, the symbol of its simple and exclusive orientiation towards the brethren's spiritual progress. That the abbot is to be inseparably superior of the community and director of souls clearly means that the community has no other end than the promotion of the salvation of souls, and, let it be clearly stated, the souls of those living in the *coenobium*. The absence of any duality of aims in cenobitic life is thereby affirmed: the spiritual life is not just *one* element, even the chief one. It is everything. Even more than a symbol, this fusion of superior and spiritual father in the single abbot is for cenobitic society the safeguard of its true orientation. It maintains the social and economical life of the group in its genuine perspective, which is solely to serve its members' education.

Thus, whether one considers the *coenobium* by relation to the christian community in the world or by relation to more modern religious congregations, its distinctive character in either case is its absolute simplicity. The simplicity of the society is recapitulated in the abbot. If he is to be at once spiritual head and temporal head, superior of the community and father of souls simultaneously, he is so in order to affirm in principle and to maintain in fact that the *coenobium* is meant to be nothing else than a school of God's service. The complexity of his task is the counterpart of the simple and, so to speak, totalitarian character of the life he leads with his disciples. Every disruption of the elements which go to make up the abbatial function is the cause or the effect of an analogous break-down of components of the cenobitic life, a divorce between the life of the group and the personal search for God of each of its members. Although duality is the law of the christian community in the world, and also to some extent of every religious congregation ordered to an external end, it may not be introduced into the *coenobium* except at the cost of deterioration. Either the society and its goods come to figure as an end in themselves or an external aim juxtaposes itself to the education of souls and requires the common effort to take a direction other than that of consciences.

The first of these two aspects of the one evil was no doubt a more constant threat to the cenobitic institution. When the spiritual movement is no longer strong enough to polarize the whole social life, this life takes on an existence in some way distinct and detached from its educational purpose and is erected as an end in itself. Preservation of the society and its temporal possessions becomes a collective preoccupation unconnected with each person's enthusiasm for personal perfection. The goods of this world which, thanks to individual renunciation, had put an end to any justification for distinction between church and terrestrial society, between pastor and temporal head, become the principle for a new distinction within the bosom of cenobitic life itself: the community no longer identifies itself completely with the 'school'; neither is the superior identified with the 'master'.

Not that the *coenobium* is sapped of spiritual life, but its bonds with the hierarchical structure of the monastery are no longer perceived with sufficient clarity. The monastery is seen as a framework within which one seeks perfection but, granted that finality, its maintainance, its administration and its government are treated in the same perspective as in any other collectivity. Thus is lost from sight the profound meaning of the *coenobium,* which is not a mere framework offered to souls, inside which they may advance their search for perfection, but a real structure of relationships between master and disciple at the social level, an extension of spiritual fatherhood into collective dimensions.

The monastery is an educational undertaking; the whole structure as well as each detail of it finds justification within the educational work which is its unique *raison d'être.* In such a 'school' the superior has no other function than to give instruction, to be the 'schoolmaster'. To leave this function to others would be tantamount to admitting that the *coenobium* is not in its very essence a school. And if others besides the abbot are asked to teach, they can do it only in the capacity of collaborators with the unique master and for the purpose of extending his spiritual activity beyond the limits which time, space, the weakness of his nature, and the large number of disciples impose on him.[139] Because spiritual direction is not just one aspect or even the primary aspect of cenobitic life, but its very essence, such direction must necessarily be given hierarchically (which does not mean formally from outside) and the hierarchy formed by the abbot and his deans must be wholly ordered to the task of directing souls.

The abbatial 'monarchy' has therefore appeared to us laden with difficulties and perils, yet for all that indispensable. Cenobitism could not refuse to run the risks involved in such a system without disavowing itself. Now it remains for us to survey the history of religious life in the East and West to see what the fate of this system has been in the practice and legislation of the Church. Everything we have said until now has had only the purpose of illustrating the notion of the abbacy which is affirmed in the ancient documents and particularly in RM and RB. But has such a notion not been subjected to certain repudiations in the experience and wisdom of the Church, repudiations sanctioned by canon law? Is this notion today anything more than a reminiscence, an object of contemplation for the historian?

The byzantine Orient does not seem to have drawn the distinction between 'spiritual father ' and '*hegumen*' as strictly as we sometimes imagine. After reading the pages Hausherr devotes to this question,[140] one receives instead the impression that identification of the two functions was the dominant principle in the greater part of the *Typika,* although concern for safeguarding the freedom and confidence of those being directed did lead to the admission, or even prescription, of some deviations more or less distant from this norm.

This impression is confirmed by recourse to the codification and *fontes* of Placid de Meester.[141] The principle of the 'monarchy' of the *hegumen* is depicted there as the traditional rule.[142] A double series of restrictions came to limit it in the course of the centuries. First, in favor of freedom of conscience, monks were allowed to open their minds and hearts to other spiritual fathers.[143] Then, in a much more recent epoch, the *hegumen's* power to act by himself in administrative affairs was withdrawn: he had to make decisions collegially with the council of elders and the cellarer. This second restriction resulted in an accentuation of the *hegumen's* role in spiritual matters, for only in this domain did he continue to exercise personal ppower, even though other spiritual fathers existed besides himself.[144]

Placid de Meester, moreover, does not try to conceal the anti-

traditional character of this evolution. Withdrawal of administrative authority from the *hegumen* can hardly be considered anything but a corruption. The freedom to make one's
confession (sacramentally or not) to someone besides the *hegumen*
is certainly a right both more ancient and better founded in tradition,[145] but not one which destroys the fundamental principle by
which the functions of superior and spiritual father are essentially
bound to each other. Confession of faults is really just one, admit-
tedly important, element of the spiritual life which the *hegumen*
has as his primary duty to sustain and perfect in his subjects.[146]
Even if the superior himself does not receive these soul-barings, he
remains in large measure the spiritual father of everyone, notably
through the teaching he gives the community.

Still more, it is important to note that even in the matter of
manifestation of conscience the freedom granted monks to confess
to someone other than the superior had been introduced little by
little, in measured steps and various forms, more as a concession
to human weakness than as a constitutive cenobitic norm.
Although the ideal was that of a superior inspiring such full confidence in his subjects that they opened themselves to him without
constraint, the need arose of somehow making allowance for the
possibility of confession to spiritual fathers distinct from the
hegumen, if the weakness of men was to be accounted for and indispensable freedom of souls safeguarded.

This situation, which Hausherr and de Meester agree in
describing, scarcely differs from events occurring in the Occident
under the influence of the same considerations and by an
analogous process. It does not look as though the two hemispheres
of Christianity pursued separate ways in this, at least in the essentials. Both began by considering the abbot as, by right, the sole
spiritual father of the community. Both also came little by little to
recognize the need of leaving the monks free to confide themselves
to others besides the superior, without letting this tolerance efface
the primitive conception, which remained valid in principle and,
to a great extent, in fact.[147]

As for the latin Church, the main features of the evolution of
which we are speaking need not be rehearsed here. The code of
canon law has crystallized the restrictive norms affecting the
superior's power in the internal sacramental forum,[148] but it supposes a clear distinction between sacramental confession and simple manifestations of conscience, a distinction which for many

reasons played almost no role in ancient monasticism. Much more important for us is canon 530, which forbids the superior to exert pressure to obtain a manifestation of conscience from his subjects, and which, although it does recommend that religious spontaneously approach the superior for direction of conscience, adds the significant limitation *si sint sacerdotes*, 'if this superior is a priest', which implies conversely that a superior who is not a priest is not fit to give spiritual direction.

These provisions seem at first glance unfavorable to the traditional concept we have expounded. A few remarks will, however, permit appreciation of this legislation's import. Note first that the code is here sanctioning principles posed by the decree *Quemadmodum* of 1890. This decree had in view specific abuses which had sprung from a rigid interpretation of the Ignatian Constitutions that impose a strict obligation on religious to manifest their consciences to their superior.[149] Such a context is modern, though its links with monastic tradition cannot be denied. In this context the ancient manifestation of thoughts to the superior assumes the appearance of a juridical and moral obligation imposed by the Constitutions, an obligation all the more onerous in that the superior, given the institute's active nature, is responsible not only for the sanctification of the subjects but also for the exterior activity. This fact makes the distinction between the two fora more tangible and their union in one and the same person more delicate.

Certainly, prescripts might be uncovered in ancient cenobitic rules which could serve as points of departure for the abuses the code had in view.[150] Yet the manifestation of thoughts is generally presented in them as an ascetical counsel rather than as a legal obligation, and the exclusive orientation of the *coenobium* towards the education of souls cannot but render the intervention of superiors in this domain all the more natural.[151]

It is also noteworthy that since the time the code was promulgated, the interpretation of this canon has come to mark ever more plainly a concern for safeguarding the traditional notions which seemed called into question. Although it cannot be imposed juridically, union of the two fora appears more and more as normal and desirable.[152] Note that even according to the letter of canon 530, the restriction *si sint sacerdotes* in the second paragraph does not bear upon every kind of direction, but only upon 'doubts and uneasiness of conscience'. It does not, furthermore, prevent canonists from firmly maintaining that the mission of leading religious to perfection (together with the ensuing need of knowing them inside out) springs from the ruling power of superiors and not from the power of holy orders they might have received.[153] 'The religious state, so to speak, urgently demands (*est exigitif de*) a manifestation of the soul to the superiors', even should these be laymen.

To sum up, we can say that there exists at the present time a tendency in the Congregation of Religious to reverse in importance the paragraphs of canon 530 by giving in practice the go-ahead to the positive principle expressed in ¶ 2, and attributing to ¶ 1 only a defensive character bearing upon *juridical* obligation of direction by the superior.[154] This tendency basically accords with the ancient doctrine of cenobitism, if we make allowance for different historical contexts.

Spiritual father and temporal head: the twofold and unique mission of the abbot has set its seal even on his title. The term *abbas* first designated the spiritual quality of the *pater pneumatikos*. Then, and in the West almost exclusively,[155] it came to signify a social function, that of the head of the *coenobium*. From the charismatic sense we passed to the institutional sense. From the time of Sulpitius Severus and Cassian, an 'abbot' was the superior of a 'monastery' (meaning *coenobium*), with no reference to the man's personal sanctity.[156]

This evolution of *abbas* is not a purely latin phenomenon. From the origins of pachomian cenobitism, the synonym *pater* underwent a very similar evolution, passing from the spiritual sense ('our holy Father Pachomius') to the purely formal meaning it has in the rule (*pater monasterii*, or even simply *pater*, meaning 'the superior').[157] In this we have a semantic law which betrays the very law of cenobitism and its deepest problem. For the *coenobium* is in its essence an attempt at organizing spiritual fatherhood. Its purpose is to confer a social dimension upon it and prolong it in time beyond the generation of the first disciples of the first father. But while it gives institutional form to the 'abbacy', cenobitism is not on that account dispensed from possessing in the person of its 'abbots' men who are authentic spiritual fathers. Functional abbacy is meant not to supplant or replace charismatic abbacy, but to insure its extension on the social scale and its continuation in time. This is what the RM and RB redactors felt so deeply when they punctuated their directories for abbots with a threefold appeal to the etymology of the *nomen abbatis.* This testifies to the strictly juridical and institutional meaning the word had in current usage and affirms as well the vital necessity of regaining the spiritual content of the term by directing attention to its original meaning.[158]

In concluding these investigations of the essence of the abbatial function, we might perhaps say that an abbot is the synthesis of three persons: the father of the desert, the head of the christian community, and the *paterfamilias.* The first of these roles remains inscribed in the very name *abbas,* the second is constantly evoked by reference to Scripture, the third is seen especially in legislation and practice. Yet it should be well understood that these are not just three elements assembled haphazardly and juxtaposed without necessary connection. This is a veritable synthesis resulting from the development of a simple principle. The three notions link together according to an appointed order both historical and logical. At the outset is the spiritual father, a person enriched with the qualities of community head and father of a family. The abbot is first and foremost an accomplished monk capable of teaching the perfect life and exercising true spiritual fatherhood. But because this fatherhood is extended to a community, he comes to resemble the head of a church and is likened to a bishop. Finally, since the disciples (like their master) form a community of renunciants of this world and aspirants to the perfect life, the authority of the head extends to the whole temporal and spiritual existence of the individuals as well as of the group, and the abbot takes on the aspect of the father of a family.

In this structuring of the abbacy, the first element gives the other two their meaning. The idea of education to the perfect life commands the whole development of the abbatial function. The abbot is head of a church and father of a family only for the sake of his mission as 'teacher' of the evangelical life in the desert tradition.

APPENDIX: THE ABBOT-TEACHER AND PRISCILLIANISM

Justo Pérez de Urbel thought he could recognize a trace of priscillian vocabulary in the title 'teacher' which RM so often gives to the abbot.[159] We know in fact that the seventh canon of the Council of Zaragoza (380) forbade anyone to 'assume the title of teacher, save those to whom it is conceded, in conformity with the

Scriptures'.[160] This prohibition, certainly aimed at priscillian circles, testifies to a tendency among them to pride themselves on the possession of the charism of *didaskalia* and consequently to arrogate to themselves the mission of teaching independently of the hierarchy.[161]

Recognizing that fact, one must go on to ask whether the canon witnesses to a relationship between the RM author and the priscillian sect. Pérez de Urbel thought so, but he knew where to set limits to the link he suggested. Although other pecularities of the Master, such as his taste for apocryphal literature and the practice of fasting from the seventeenth of December until Christmas, seem to point in the same direction,[162] there are nevertheless certain traits which indicate instead a corrected attitude, an eagerness to conform to the directives of the Church: respect for the clergy, absence of hymns in the divine office, suspension of the fast from Christmas day to Epiphany.[163] The points of contact between the Master and the priscillian sect do not, therefore, warrant our looking upon him as an adherent of this heresy. They suggest rather that the Master belonged to an environment in which certain influences exerted by the sect continued to be felt despite staunch orthodoxy. Pérez de Urbel maintains nothing more. For him it was enough to have uncovered some indications favorable to the localization he proposes for RM, which he sees as originating in Spain during the second half of the sixth century.

We admit immediately that we have some difficulty following Pérez de Urbel when he uses a fourth century council to argue for dating RM in the sixth. The only text he produces, in fact, to attest to the importance of the word *doctor* in the priscillian vocabulary is the seventh canon of the Council of Zaragoza, held in 380. Betweeen that date and the epoch when, according to Pérez de Urbel, RM was written, two centuries elapsed. One might wish that the documents concerned with Priscillianism which punctuate this lengthy period would say something about this question of 'teacher'. Such is not the case.[164] Although certain complaints, such as those of Trinitarian errors and encratism, constantly recur in the condemnations levelled against the sects, one never sees the hierarchy troubled about some erroneous 'teacher' theory. Like other similar sects, priscillianism no doubt gave credence to masters not commissioned by the hierarchy, to directly inspired private 'teachers'.[165] But once the first generation had passed, the issue seems not to have characterized priscillian doctrine. It probably received less attention as more bishops were won over to the heresy and the sect possessed for some time a compete hierarchy which it could oppose to orthodox pastors.[166]

Under such conditions, the disciples of Priscillian never felt obliged to insist on the charism of their 'teachers'. Not only do ecclesiastical documents after 380 not reproach them for it, but the ancient writings of the sect which have come down to us are almost silent on this point. Nothing would prove more disappointing than to peruse the treatises published by Schepss[167] in the hope of hitting upon a theory about 'teachers'. Affirmations of the power to 'prophesy' which all the adherents of this sect were said to have possessed occur again and again, to be sure, but this doctrine is developed without reference to scriptural texts which speak of the 'doctoral' charism.[168] To go no further than the word *doctor* and its synonym *magister,* one notes that these words have no marked importance in this *corpus* of priscillian texts. At most, one may suspect canons thirty-nine and forty-eight (Schepss, pp 126 and 130) of harboring a teaching on the mission of the 'teacher'.[169] The fragments published in *Revue Bénédictine* by de Bruyne[170] and Morin[171] teach us nothing more about the role the sect ascribed to its 'teachers'.

The poverty of the priscillian documents on this question and the silence of the texts relative to Priscillianism after 380 are all the more disturbing inasmuch as there is no lack of references to *doctor* in orthodox monastic literature. The word is one of those not infrequently found to designate the superior of a *coenobium.* Thus Gregory of Nyssa gives his sister Macrina the title *didaskalos,* having in mind the community of virgins she directed.[172] The *Liber Orsiesii* speaks in the same terms of a pachomian house chief.[173] Augustine exalts the *doctores ecclesiarum apostoli* as an example for superiors of monasteries, which implies that those superiors are themselves 'teachers' in their own communities.[174] Eugippius, in his *Vita Seuerini,* calls his hero *doctor humilis, spiritualis doctor, doctor dulcissimus,*[175] titles relevant to his role as monastic superior. The abbot is likewise called *doctor* in the *Regula Consensoria* 5, a document which Pérez de Urbel ascribes to Priscillianism but which seems rather to belong to seventh or eighth century Spain.[176] These examples show that the idea of calling the abbot *doctor* is so familiar to the ancients that recourse to priscillian sources in connection with RM is by no means necessary.

We ought, however, to give closer consideration to our author's

use of this word to designate the abbot. *Doctor* occurs sixteen
times in RM. The incidence of these sixteen occurences is significant. Their enumeration, according to chapters, is as follows:

      Ch. 1:82, 87, 88 (twice), 89, 90.

      Ch. 7:6, 13, 37, 68.

      Ch. 10:51

      Ch. 11:12.

      Ch. 12:6.

      Ch. 14:14.

      Ch. 57:16.

      Ch. 90:40.

From this enumeration we can see that the Master uses *doctor* in
only eight chapters, and that more than half of these cases occur
in two chapters, the first and the seventh. These observations take
on their full meaning when the texts are examined one by one.
Then the following facts come to light.

All six cases in Chapter One belong to the same pericope, the
one in which the Master presents the abbot to the disciples (RM
1:75-92). Mention of *doctor* is introduced by the implicit citations
of I Cor 12:28: 'The Lord has given his Church...three levels of
doctrine — the first that of the prophets, the second that of the
apostles, the third that of the "teachers" '(RM 1:82). Everything
that follows, when *doctor* recurs five times, is controlled by this
scriptural point of departure. The pericope closes with the citation of Lk 10:16: the abbot is one of those teachers to whom the
Lord said 'Whoever listens to you listens to me'! The Lk 10:16 citation is thereafter associated five more times with the mention of
doctores: RM 7:6, 68; 10:51; 12:6; 57:16.

Two other texts employed scriptural citations: RM 11:12 and
14:14, which utilizes Jer 3:15 mixed with Eph 4:11. The first of
these texts follows immediately upon a citation of Lk 10:16 and
explains it (RM 11:11). Both texts present the abbot and his provost as 'pastors and teachers' according to the heart of God, as
'Isaiah' had prophesied.

Although RM 90:40 might appear far removed from Chapter
Seven, the two are closely connected. Mention of the *doctor* occurs
there in the course of a commentary on Ps 66 which we have
previously read in RM 7:61-65, and at the fourth rung of humility
(RM 10:57-58).

All these facts indicate that *doctor* is employed in RM in an extremely specific context. The sixteen occurrences of this term all

belong to the same series of texts, which present the abbot as an authorized master, an authentic 'teacher' accredited by God himself. The point in all these texts is to found the abbatial authority solidly by a thought-out application of the scriptural title of 'teacher'. The basic reference is the list of charisms in I Cor 12:28 (Eph 4:11 being understood, as we have explained above, in a chronological sense unknown to St Paul).[177] If the abbot is a 'teacher', this does not mean that the charism is peculiar to him and distinguishes him from members of the hierarchy, but that, on the contrary, he is associated with the legitimate pastors given by God to the Church since the time of the apostles, and that he, along with those pastors, inherits the promises of assistance made by Christ. Together with the bishop and for a similar reason, the abbot is a *doctor*—each has been commissioned to teach within that portion of the flock, church or monastery, confided to him. For this reason the abbot may appropriate to himself the solemn delegation of authority granted by the Lord in Lk 10:16, a text which flows from the Master's pen no less than eight times to ground abbatial authority.[178]

The word *doctor* is thus charged for the Master with a well-defined theological content. It supports the whole theory of the 'vicarious' power of the abbot,[179] which itself serves as the foundation for the doctrine of obedience, the fundamental pact of cenobitic society. It is not just an ordinary term, a trite administrative tag, an alternate for abbot. It is not employed except deliberately and consciously when the Master wants to affirm that the abbot is entitled to guide his disciples.

This rehearsal of the RM doctrine was necessary to make the reader sensitive to the distance separating it from a theory of individual inspiration such as was found among priscillian adherents. The Master concerned himself exclusively with one certain type of 'teacher', the superior of the *coenobium,* the abbot. This person has a definite place in ecclesial society. From the fifth, and much more from the sixth, century on his authority was recognized by the hierarchy. By forcing himself to render it more precise and to provide it with solid scriptural foundation, the Master only deepened and systematized something already present in the life of the Church. His exposition does not tend to erect a new magisterium over against that of the bishops, but to furnish an explanation for a power recognized by them and even in-

stituted under their control.[180] He is not addressing himself to
clerics, not filing a claim against them to the power of teaching,
but to his monks, in order better to ground their obedience.

In other words, the abbot belongs very much to those 'to whom
it is permitted to assume the title of teacher', as the seventh canon
of Zaragoza put it. The council doubtless did not have in mind
this category of 'teachers', scarcely known in the West at so early a
date, but it is not apparent either how the Master's theory could
run counter to this canon. Between the claims of the Priscillians to
prophesy and the abbatial theory of the Master there is nothing in
common. The first appeals to St Paul's authorization for prophesy
given to every believer,[181] the other constitutes a cenobitic hierarchy which is to imitate and prolong in monasteries the Church's
hierarchical constitution. Far from claiming for the simple
faithful the freedom to teach according to personal inspiration,
our author obdurately pursues the individualistic *ascesis* of
sarabaites and their refusal to subject themselves to duly commissioned 'teachers', which true abbots are.[182] The 'teacher' *par excellence* in the eyes of the Master is the bishop, successor to the
apostles. Like him, the abbot enjoys a teaching charism in this
special kind of church, the cenobitic *schola*.

Pérez de Urbel thought he could read in the conclusion of RM
One a strange theory which would confirm the suspicion of
Priscillianism raised by the use of the word *doctor* in the rule. The
Master, he writes, 'divides the history of humanity into three ages
modeled on the Persons of the Holy Trinity: the age of the Father
which is that of the prophets; the age of the Son which corresponds to the preaching of the apostles; and the age of the Holy
Spirit, animator and inspirer of the teachers who are charged with
regenerating in churches and schools the doctrine of Christ'.[183]

It could be that the inversion of prophets and apostles in this
implicit citation of I Cor 12:28 and the consequent chronological
construction given by the enumeration of charisms do correspond
to the order of persons of the Trinity which is alluded to at the
beginning of the passage. But perhaps the Master had no such
relationship in mind. Merely listing these charisms was enough to
suggest an allusion to the Trinity. We meet such superficial linking up elsewhere, both in RM and in contemporary authors.[184]
Our author, furthermore, tends too readily to develop and explicate symbolical plays on numbers for us to be justified in supposing he has here passed over in silence the profound theory

Pérez de Urbel attributes to him. More probably it did not even enter the Master's head while he was writing these lines.

In any case, and this is the decisive point, the task of the 'teacher' of the post-apostolic age is not to 'regenerate' churches and schools but to 'rule' them, something altogether different. Pérez de Urbel is here the victim of a false reading: instead of *regerentur,* he read *regenerentur.*[185] If the correct reading, given by two of the three manuscripts, is restored, the text says nothing further about 'regeneration' of the Church (which sounds indeed hardly orthodox) but speaks rather of 'direction', of a government assured by legitimate pastors who have succeeded the apostles. If Pérez de Urbel had examined Chapter Eleven, he would have noted that bishops as well as abbots are included in this category of 'pastors' and 'teachers' who rule the people of God in the name of Christ. Whether or not the Holy Spirit is especially at work in these 'teachers', their mission is quite simply to graze their flock in accordance with the discipline of the Church, not to renew it by way of personal revelation.

We called attention above to the fact that *doctor* as a term designating the abbot is not unknown to cenobitic literature. Because the Master very often associates this term with the citation of Lk 10:16, it would be equally interesting to research this citation among monastic authors. By doing so, we would see that the Master's effort to base the doctrine of obedience on this verse is not entirely peculiar to him, and that his views on the abbot-teacher only tend to deepen a theme of monastic tradition. Now there are examples of applying Lk 10:16 in a cenobitic context to the authority of the superior. Basil, Jerome, Faustus of Riez, Caesarius of Arles, and Columban testify century after century to this monastic utilization of the words of Jesus to his disciples.[186]

The Master takes his place, then, within a current traditional among monks. It seems that his insistence on the 'doctorate' of the abbot corresponds to his desire to exploit Lk 10:16 to justify abbatial authority. He must have felt that the application of this text to abbots did not come off without some difficulty. Those words of Christ were addressed to the seventy-two 'disciples' and their successors, who are the members of the hierarchy, and apparently not to abbots, who were often laymen. Hence the need of finding in the Scriptures a hierarchical title which would suit the abbot and authorize the application of Lk 10:16 to him. *Doctor,* one of the pauline charisms, was all the more appropriate for such a purpose in that current monastic terminology was already applying it to the abbot. By styling the abbot thus, the Master was able to make him heir to Jesus' promises to the members of the ec-clesiastical hierarchy. He was also careful as a rule to introduce Lk 10:16 by slipping the word *doctor* into a little phrase. Christ made his statement to abbots, he means to tell us, because they also, with bishops and priests, belong to the category of 'teachers', that is to say, to those who, after the apostles, rule by some right a part of the people of God.

To obtain such a notion of *doctor*, very different from St Paul's, we would emphasize, the Master had only to invert the first two terms of the list in I Cor 12:28 and to understand the adverbs *primum, secundum, tertium* in a temporal sense.[187] Thus this en-tire theology of the abbot-teacher can be explained as a reflection upon two themes of monastic tradition: applying Lk 10:16 to ab-bots, and according them the title *doctor*. The Master was work-ing in line with the monastic theology of obedience, not with a heterodox doctrine of private interpretation. Consequently, the hypothesis of a priscillian influence is groundless save for verbal similarity. It explains nothing and only raises more difficulties than it solves.

NOTES TO CHAPTER TWO

1. Although François Masai had already studied the structure of RM-RB Two in his article 'La règle de s. Benoît et la Regula Magistri', *Latomus* 6 (1947) 220-228, we believe we ought to propose an entirely new analysis. Masai himself has pointed out, moreover, one of the errors he made on the subject of the conclusion of the text in his article, 'Observations sur la langue de s. Benoît et du Maître', *Miscellanea Gessler* (Deurne-Anvers, 1948) II, p 849, n. 31. We have not been able to gain access to the study by Justin McCann, 'The Master's Rule Again', *Downside Review* 57 (1939) 3-22, save through the remarks of Masai ('La règle', p 228, n. 2), and those of Gregory Penco, *Sancti Benedicti Regula* (Florence, 'La Nuova Italia', 1958) p 216. In an unpublished study which he kindly forwarded to us, Jacques Dupont made a comparative analysis of this chapter of RM and RB. Bearing more on details of expression than on the structure of the text, his observa-tions corroborate our own results: the RM text is anterior to the RB text.

2. The second paragraph (Conclusion) subjoins that he shall also have to account for his own soul.

3. Passage from the first to the second pericope is indicated in P by a majuscule at vs 23: *In doctrina....*

4. Although there is a sort of subdividing on the part of the teaching, there is none on that of the disciples: the 'obedient' brethren of the second division correspond very closely to the 'intelligent' ones of the first, the 'undisciplined' and 'negligent' to

the 'hard of heart'. In both sections, the second as much as the first, the whole community is evoked and split in two or three categories. Oral teaching is therefore meant not only for 'intelligent' disciples, as the first pericope would lead one to think. Similarly, example is not directed only to the 'hard of heart'.

5. *Aequalis sit ab eo ab omnibus caritas una prebeatur in omnibus disciplina* (vs 22). The reading *ab omnibus* at first sight raises a difficulty. RB suppressed this inconvenient preposition. But it can be explained pretty well by comparing it with Eccles 32:17: *inebriantem te ab omnibus bonis suis*. There, according to Albert Blaise, *Dictionnaire latin-français des auteurs chrétiens* (Paris: Librairie des Meridiens, 1954), *sub verbo, vi,* there is the matter of a preposition of 'means, instrument, manner'. The meaning would then be: 'that the abbot accord an equal love [testified] by means of all [the goods he disposes of]; that his love be equal *in everything'*. This sense harmonizes well with the divine example proposed above to the abbot: God orders the elements and the earth to serve both just and sinners alike (vs 21). In the same way as God places the goods of the natural order at the service of everyone without distinction, so the abbot ought, in his love, to accord equally to everyone all they need and which he is charged with assuring to them. *Omnibus* in the first member of the sentence therefore designates not disciples but things. This point ascertained, one would be tempted to attribute the same meaning to *omnibus* in the second member. It is noteworthy that the reading *in omnibus* had previously entailed some difficulty for Benno Linderbauer, *S. Benedicti Regula Monachorum* (Metten: Benediktinerstiftes, 1922) p 173. After rejecting the temptation to read merely *omnibus* without a preposition, as do several manuscripts of lesser authority, he understood *in omnibus* to mean: 'in everything', and thought that *omnibus* ('to all the disciples') remained implicitly understood, having been enunciated in the preceding member. The RM text seemed to support his argument: *in omnibus* means 'in every affair, at every turn'. But *omnibus* in the first member does not designate the disciples, who are not explicitly mentioned either in the first or second member. As for *disciplina,* this word designates the firmness of the teacher demanding good behavior of his subjects (cf. below, note 16).

6. *Patrem se eis mensurata pietate ostendat* (vs 31). What is this 'meted' goodness? Is it a goodness *tempered* with severity? This interpretation would nuance the distinction in vs 24, where the goodness of a father (*pium patris affectum*) is opposed to the asperity of a master (*dirum magistri*). One may also understand: a goodness proportioned to the quality of each one, as vs 17 would suggest. In this case, the lucid and firm affection of a father would be in contrast to the non-discriminating tenderness of a mother (*aequaliter,* vs 31).

7. We would moreover call attention to the fact that the second theme alludes to scriptural texts (Gal 3:28, Rom 2:11, Mt 5:45) which constitute so many 'divine precepts'.

8. At the beginning of each pericope appears the characteristic term *doctrina:* vs 11 (*duplex doctrina*) and vs 23 (*in doctrina sua*). This term links each pericope to the Introduction (vss 4-6).

9. *Namque* (vs 23) would set *caritas... disciplina* in opposition to *doctrina.* The first two must be equal and uniform, the third on the contrary must use discrimination according to characters. Opposition disappears in RB because it adds *secundum merita,* thereby nuancing the *una disciplina* preconized by the Master.

10. Verse 34: *sine dubio addita et sua,* and vss 39-40. We must confess that the thought sequence in this paragraph is difficult. This sequence might be better explained without the five words of vs 34 just cited, or by passing from these words to vs 39, skipping vss 35-38 as does RB.

11. Curiously, the treatise on the council of the brethren has eleven verses, making it almost equal in length to the Introduction, to each of the two intermediate pericopes, and to the Conclusion, which have respectively 10, 12, 9 and 9 verses.

On the other hand, we must compare the composition of Chapter Two with that of the preceding chapter. Chapter One presents a very composite make-up, and includes parts as dissimilar as the résumé of Cassian on the different kinds of monks, the interminable satire on gyrovagues, and the theory of cenobitic obedience in the form of an exhortation to the monks. The disparity we detect, then, between the body of Chapter Two and the treatise on the council of the brethren which comes in appendix form should cause no surprise.

RB manifests a similar position in these two chapters: in Chapter One it reduces the plurality of kinds to the unity of a little treatise on the various kinds of monks in which the final pericope disappears, and in which the satire on gyrovagues is so summarized as not to clash with the description of the three preceding types. In Chapter Two, it detaches the appendix in order to make it a separate chapter, thereby conferring on Chapter Two, now occupied from beginning to end by the abbatial treatise, a perfect homogeneity.

12. Ildefons Herwegen, *Sinn und Geist der Benediktinerregel* (Einsiedeln/Cologne: Benziger, 1944) p 78.

13. RB vss 1, 11, 30.

14. Herwegen further divides the second part into three sub-sections: teaching through word and example (RB 11-15); teaching proffered for love of Christ (16-22); teaching which assumes the forms indicated by the apostle (23-29). This division is apparently based on the repetition of *doctrina* at the beginning of each of the two pericopes (see above, n. 8). But the second sub-section (RB-RM 16-22) does not mention *doctrina*. So there is something artificial about the division, and the order which prevails in this part of the schema of Herwegen is only apparent.

15. See above, n. 5. The parallel with *disciplina* suggests seeing in *caritas* less a sentiment than practical behaviour, actions. The first line deals with giving 'everything' (*ab omnibus*) to each monk, imitating God's example (Mt 5:45), without considering whether he is virtuous or not.

16. François Masai, 'La règle de s. Benoît et la RM', p 224, asserts that *disciplina* here means 'doctrine, teaching'. The meaning 'educative rule', current in RM, seems to me more probable, granted the opposition with *caritas*.

17. Verse 23 will give RM editors and translators trouble. But at any rate, whatever the reading of the text there is hardly any doubt as to its general sense: the abbot ought to set the example in everything, drawing the brethren after him as members follow head. The appendix on the council of the brethren picks up the same image again, while applying it this time to the disciple's obligation of obedience to the decisions of the abbot (vs 47).

18. It is important not to forget that abridgment was the set purpose of RB. Hence an omission does not necessarily indicate disagreement between the redactor and his source. Yet his choice of passages to be omitted must have been guided by a feeling that some deserved less esteem. Once the decision to shorten some part of the text had been taken, considerations of this sort must have come into play to suggest omitting one passage rather than another.

19. These last words (vs 38) do not lend themselves easily to translation.

20. See especially RB Chapter Sixty-three and our commentary on that text (Chapter Nine of the present work). Other allusions to rank are RB 29:2 (*in ultimo gradu*); 43:5 (*ultimus omnium*); 60:4, 7 (*locus*); 61:12 (*locus*). Jacques Dupont, who furnished these references, has indicated well the contrast between the first addition and the context in which it is inserted: 'The Master was speaking about the affection of the abbot for his monks. Benedict, possessing the precise and down to earth spirit of a Roman jurist, reduces such affection to an issue of precedence.... He does not legislate for the sentiments of the abbot, but for his acts. For his juridical cast of mind, preference comes across as a concrete advantage: concession of a higher rank.'

21. This is brought out by Jacques Froger in his unpublished study.

22. Note the repetition *Quare? Quare?* in vs 19 of this passage. These two interrogatives do not figure in RB, which in like manner omits *Quomodo?* in vs 12. These are stylistic idiosyncrasies of the Master. Cf. Thema 8 (RB suppressed *Quid?*), 61:4, 92:2, 94:4.

23. RM speaks less often of blows than does RB. It is, moreover, not easy to reconcile what is said here with the procedure indicated in RB Chapter Twenty-three, where the *uindicta corporalis* comes not 'at the outset' but at the end of the admonitions.

24. RM vss 13-15.

25. The expression *animarum... est redditurus domino rationes* (RB: *rationem*) is encountered again in the final lines (RM-RB vs 34). Thus it recurs twice in RM and three times in RB, a repetition made still weightier by that of the words *suscipit regendas* in vss 34 and 37. The RB text is plainly more redundant here than is RM. Worth noting too, in RM vs 33, is a typical case of equal and assonant phrase membering:

> *qui suscipit animas regendas*
> *paret se ad rationes reddendas*

RB, by rendering *rationem reddendam* (vs 37) in the singular, somewhat disturbs the assonance.

26. The remarks made above (n. 18) on the significance of the RB omissions are applicable again here, *mutatis mutandis.* The E copyist must also have been guided in the choice of omitting pericopes by the criterion of textual content.

27. We described the general line of *Lib Ors* in 'Le monastère, Eglise du Christ', *Studia Anselmiana* 42 (1957) 28-29.

28. 1 Tim 3:2-4; 6:11; 2 Tim 2:24; 3:10.

29. In reality, R 4 Pat is the minutes of a synod of abbots in Southern Gaul during the latter half of the fourth century, as Anscari Mundo has demonstrated, 'Les anciens synodes abbatiaux et les Regulae SS. Patrum', *Studia Anselmiana* 44 (1959) 107-125.

30. This second directory does not seem to belong to the primitive text. It is found only in *Par lat 12205* and *Par lat 12634.* See the article by Mundo, p 117, n. 26. This would be a complement annexed when the acts of the synod were transformed into a normal monastic rule.

31. These two epithets appear only in the greek text (Short Rule 99). *Eusplanchnos* turns up again in Long Rule 43:2; *sympatheia* in R Bas 191 (= SR 182).

32. See for example R Bas 17.

33. *De Instituto Christiano* 68:15-70:14. The close affinity between this text and that of Basil confirms the remark of Werner Jaeger: 'Nearly every page of the treatise proves that Gregory had made a serious study of the Rules [of Basil] and knew them practically by heart'. *Two Rediscovered Works of Ancient Literature: Gregory of Nyssa and Macarius* (Leiden: Brill, 1954) p 84, n. 1.

34. The superior is encouraged to confer with a priest in difficult cases exceeding his competence. Authors who later reemployed the R Aug took care to correct this prescript either by suppressing it (R Caes V) or by substituting 'abbot' for 'priest' and understanding *praepositus* not as the superior properly so-called, but as his second (R Tar 23).

35. Cf. *humilitas... auctoritas* (lines 183-184), and further on, *in loco superiore... in periculo majore* (lines 202-203).

36. A text we have already come across in the *Liber Orsiesii* (¶ 15) and in the R 4 Pat (line 222), and which, through the mediation of R Aug, was introduced into the *Rule for Virgins* by Caesarius, as we shall see shortly. Its tenor is: *Corripite inquietos, consolamini pusillanimes, suscipite infirmos, patientes estote ad omnes.*

37. R Caes V 61-63.

38. PL 67:1135-1138. We shall continue to cite this text as the *Letter of Caesarius.*

39. 1136c. We shall develop more precisely the relation between this passage and the third addition of RB Two further below.

40. 1138a-d.

41. Cf. the *fontes* of Butler (RB 2:16-22). Note the reiterated mention of the equitable distribution of material objects. This tends to confirm our interpretation of RM 2:22 (see above, n. 5). When Caesarius or the Master speak of equal charity, they are thinking very concretely of the distribution of necessities.

42. This scriptural text, so important for the Master, will command our full attention when we deal with obedience.

43. R Aur M 41-42. The citation of 1 Thess 2:7 is noteworthy, for it already figures in Basil (R Bas 15, LR 25.2). The same text is cited seven times in the *Coptic Lives.*

44. R Fer 37. Among the scriptural citations, we must single out at least two of them: Jer 3:15, which also figures in *Lib Ors* 47, and is important to the Master, (RM 1:84, 11:12); Jn 21:15, cited likewise by *Lib Ors* 17 and RM 1:85.

45. Something of the same tendency to force the texts is found in Adolar Zumkeller, 'Der klösterliche Gehorsam beim heiligen Augustinus', *Augustinus Magister* (Paris: Etudes Augustiniennes, 1954) I, 265-276. The opposition this author erects between an obedience of a family type (Augustine), military (Pachomius), and servile (Basil), completely lacks foundation. Basil also knew the father image, as we have seen, and this image is at the heart of the pachomian notion of the superior. In reality, the family, military, and servile metaphors are the joint patrimony of all monastic authors. If an author seems to avoid one image while using another, we need to examine whether such absence is not due to the summary nature of the texts. In comparison to pachomian or basilian literature, Augustine wrote little on monasticism.

46. So it is with the different idea which Basil has on the one hand, and the majority of the Fathers on the other, as to the ultimate end of cenobitic life: eremitism or community? See Chapter One of this volume.

47. Butler, with good reason, does not print any of his parallels in boldface type.

48. *Inst* 2.3. In this chapter Cassian sketches a treatise on the formation of future abbots, but says nothing about the behaviour of abbots already in office.

49. The theme of humility, detached from that of example, likewise appears in LR 30. Gregory of Nyssa, who also treats of example and humility in the first part of his directory, has more of a tendency to set the two themes in opposition: example given exteriorly to others easily engenders a sentiment of self-esteem against which one must react by cultivating humility within.

50. This theme of indifference to earthly things often recurs in the Master. Cf. RM 16:1-26; 86:7-13; 82:4-25; 7:53-56. It ties in with the idea that the monk is a spiritual man, a term constantly used to characterize him in contrast to the secular (cf. 85:3), or to designate, within the monastic community, fervent monks in distinction to lax (RM 44:17).

51. Nilus, *De monastica exercitatione* 27; PG 79:756 (cited by Hausherr, *Direction spirituelle*, p 60).

52. It is thus that RM 2:18 (= RB 2:18) protests against any preference for free man over slave (*pro merito nationis*, declares RB precisely). The theme of equal love is, then, particularized in the two rules and especially applied by them to the problem of social conditions. In the *Letter of Caesarius* (1137c) the motives for preference are different: exterior graciousness, obeisance *ad oculum,* flatteries. In no other document, to our knowledge, is social condition given as a potential cause of injustice. The R Aug goes on at some length on the social question (5, 6, 9), but

those considerations, marked by an admirable discretion, tend rather to legitimatize some difference of treatment according to the origins of the monks, and to indicate in what spirit these differences ought to be accepted by everyone. The RM-RB notation is therefore relatively isolated, whereas the theme of equal love is one of the more common.

53. *Christi...uices* (RM-RB 2:2) and further on the image of the pastor. The latter is well known to the *Lib Ors.* Basil talks especially of the physician, an image which well expresses what the superior ought to be for the brethren, but does not indicate the relationship with God. In LR 43, however, he sets out a complete theory of the superior's mediation (*mesiteia*) between God and the brethren. In Gregory the same idea is expressed under the image of the pedagogue, intermediary between the father and his sons.

54. In distinguishing between 'literary' and 'doctrinal', we have been careful not to forget that such a distinction is inadequate; 'doctrinal' is applicable not only to themes but to the effort of reflection and organization whose object they are. In this last sense, there is indeed 'doctrinal originality' in RM.

55. RB 2:30.

56. *Vita Honorati* 17-22.

57. Cuthbert Butler, *Benedictine Monachism* (London: Longmans, 1919; rpt. New York: Barnes and Noble, 1961) 193-194.

58. The expression 'abbatial paternalism' recurs in the writings of Marie-Dominique Chenu every time he tries to characterize monasticism in comparison with the mendicant Orders. See 'Réformes de structure en chrétienté,' *Inspiration religieuse et structures temporelles* (Paris: Editions ouvrières, 1948) p 280; and *Introduction à l'étude de saint Thomas d'Aquin* (Paris: Vrin, 1950) p 15.

59. M.-D. Chenu, *La Théologie au XIIe siècle* (Paris: Vrin, 1957) p 270.

60. The same perspective is reflected in Paul Delatte, *Commentaire sur la Règle de saint Benoît* (Paris, 1913) pp 44-45 (ET: *Commentary on the Rule of St Benedict* [London: Burns, Oates, Washburn, 1921; rpt Latrobe, Penna: Abbey Press, 1950]): 'There is in the government of societies a problem which has still to be resolved in a definitive manner. It is the reconciliation of the two elements: power and freedom.... St Benedict was most circumspect of the constituents....'

61. Delatte, *Commentaire,* p 43: 'The power of the abbot is divine, it is a fatherly power; it is an absolute power, and in that it bears a greater resemblance to the divine fatherhood than to the roman *patria potestas,* familiar to St Benedict'.

62. We encounter the same tendency in the theology of mystery expounded by Odo Casel.

63. At most, one can uncover an allusion contained in the word *maior* (RM-RB 2:1), as we shall see below.

64. This text is quoted in our article 'Le monastère, Eglise du Christ,' p 38.

65. St Jerome and Sulpitius Severus say it in nearly the same words: *prima apud eos confoederatio est, oboedire maioribus et quidquid iusserint facere* (Lr 22:35); *quibus summum ius est, sub abbatis imperio uiuere, nihil arbitrio suo agere, per omnia ad nutum illius potestatemque pendere.... Haec illorum prima uirtus est, parere alieno imperio* (Sulp. Sev., *Dial* 1:10).

66. RM 1:82-92; 11:5-14; 14:13-14. The first of these texts was translated above (Chapter One, p 55).

67. RM 1:82; 14:14. In this latter passage, the third series is called *pastores et disciplinae doctores,* a reading which rather reminds one of Eph 4:11 (*pastores et doctores*). On the contrary, RM 1:82 is inspired more by 1 Cor 12:28, as is demonstrated both by the reading *doctorum* (without *pastorum*) and by the adverbs *primum, secundum, tertium.*

68. Such at least is what RM 1:84 and 11:12 affirm. The text is in fact from Jer 3:15. In 11:12, the Master mixes it with Eph 4:11 by adding *et doctores*.

69. RM 1:89; 11:11. This is an extremely important text for the Master, who cites it constantly: RM 7:6, 68; 12:6; 57:16; 89:20. Most often these citations are introduced by the formula 'The Lord says to our teacher', which recalls the theory we set forth here. It is a precious thing for us that at least once RB did preserve this formula preceding the citation of Lk 10:16 (RB 5:6). We see now the content with which these words *et item dicit doctoribus* are charged; the whole theory of the Master on abbatial power is there. Another citation is RB 5:15. Note in RM 1:89 the introductory formula *dicente ipso Domino discipulis suis doctoribus nostris*. As Augustin Genestout has remarked in his article 'La Règle du Maître et la Règle de s. Benoît', RAM 21 (1940) 81-82, this *discipulis suis* shows that the Master is attentive to the scriptural context of Lk 10:16, a text taken, as we know, from the discourses of Christ to the 'seventy-two' sent on mission. Did the Master intend to take advantage of the fact that this word is addressed not only to the twelve apostles (and to their successors, the bishops), but to a band of disciples among whom it would be easier to find predecessors for the abbot and provosts? RM 11:11 would make one think so: *siue sacerdotibus in ecclesia siue abbatibus uel praepositis in monasterio hoc dixit Deus*. However, the words *discipulis suis* figure only once in introducing the citation. Except in RM 1:89, the Master seems to lose interest in this circumstance, whereas he seldom fails to mention the title 'teacher', the only important thing in his eyes. So it does not seem that his interest in Lk 10:16 can be explained by the fact that those words were addressed to the 'seventy-two'.

70. This is so especially in all the texts enumerated in the preceding note, save for RM 11:11 and 89:20. In RM 11:11, though the allusion to doctors is missing before the citation of Lk 10:16, the allusion to *pastores et doctores* of Eph 4:11 deserves to be noted. It insinuates itself in Jer 3:15; cf. above, n 68. RM 89:20, on the other hand, introduces Lk 10:16 with the formula [*abbas*] *quem mihi, Domine, ad uicem tuam timendum praeponis*, a phrase which evidently refers to the theory of the abbot's 'vicarious' power as it came to be propounded in chapters one, two, and eleven. The Master is extremely consistent throughout his rule. His thought crystallized into interchangeable formulae which are constantly repeated.

71. The temporal sense of *primum, secundum, tertium* in RM 1:82 is already presaged by the fact that the prophets are placed before the apostles, which runs counter to the order followed in the two pauline enumerations. One can hardly doubt this when one reads in RM 14:14: *post prophetas et apostolos posuit et uos pastores et disciplinae doctores*. The E reading in 1:82 (*primum apostolorum, secundum prophetarum*), which represents an emendation of the text to bring it into conformity with 1 Cor 12:28, ought therefore to be rejected. (The E manuscript unfortunately omits 14:14.) As Augustin Genestout has ascertained in his article 'Le plus ancien temoin manuscrit de la Règle du Maître: le Parisinus Latin 12634', *Scriptorium* (Brussels: Editions 'Erasme', 1946-1947) I, p 136 the compiler of E amended the scriptural citations to make them more accurate. We have a striking example here of just that sort of thing. RM Thema 46 furnishes a final confirmation of our exegesis (*per prophetas et apostolos*).

72. RM 1:83.

73. This is the sense in which one should understand what we wrote in 'Le monastère, Eglise du Christ', p 39: 'The abbacy is identified with the charism which immediately follows that of the apostolate in the pauline lists'. Understand that the abbot is not the *sole* beneficiary of the teacher's capacity, but that he shares in it *together with* the bishop and priest.

74. RM 83:9.

75. 'Le monastère, Eglise du Christ', pp 33-34 and 39.

76. *Lib Ors* 17 (120:4) and R Fer 37. Observe in this respect that R Fer 37 cites Jer 3:15 at the same time. So the Master and Feriolus both apply Jer 3:15 and Jn 21:17

to the abbot, and in the same order, though the two citations are separated in R Fer by a text from Ezekiel. No definite literary dependence is implied by this curious fact, however. It shows only that the association of the two scriptural texts was familiar to the mentality of the sixth century. The same two texts were already joined in the *Lib Ors*, but at an interval of several pages (¶¶ 17 and 47).

77. The profound theories of Basil, for example, are found dispersed through the *Asceticon*, without having their position—completely casual—suggest the principal role of the superior in cenobitic *ascesis*. They are, moreover, addressed to the superior to instruct him in his duties rather than to the brethren to set before them the sense of the relations uniting them to superiors. See 'Le monastère, Eglise du Christ', pp 36-37.

78. Taking into account the secondary role played by the secular analogy of the *maior familiae* in RM Eleven.

79. See in particular *De principiis* 2:1.

80. Two passages of the *Dialogues* of St Gregory demonstrate how evident this was in the great pope's view. First there is the story of Aequitius (1:4): this abbot, who was a simple layman and had received no mandate from the hierarchy, began to travel up and down the country, preaching everywhere. An irresistible force prompted him to speak about God after he had been commissioned in a vision to preach, just like an Old Testament prophet. Jealous clerics denounced him to the roman pontiff, who summoned him to appear before him. But God directly intervened to put a stop to the suit. Gregory judged the conduct of the pope, his predecessor, severely: he had given in to 'adulation', that is, he lent a sympathetic ear to the accusations of clerics enticing him to see in the saintly abbot's conduct an encroachment on his episcopal authority. The conclusion is clear: the pope could not but accede to the manifest charism bestowed on a lay monk. No less remarkable is the report in Book Two, Chapter 23, where Benedict excommunicated and reconciled two dead nuns. On this Gregory comments: there is no cause for surprise that a simple mortal had received power to bind and loose souls who have already passed from this life. Was Peter not still living in his mortal flesh when he heard it said, 'Whatever you bind on earth shall also be bound in heaven, and whatever you loose on earth shall be loosed in heaven' (Mt 16:19)? *Cuius nunc uicem et legando et soluendo obtinent, qui locum sancti regiminis fide et moribus tenent.* So, like the Master, Pope Gregory had no fear in applying to Benedict, a simple abbot, words addressed by Christ to the prince of the apostles, and to see in him an authentic successor of the first pastor of the Church. Note how it is by reason of his faith and way of life (*fide et moribus*), not by ordination, that the abbot exercises this 'vicarious' power. Note too that, as in the case of Aequitius, this concerns an authority exercised by the abbot outside his own monastery. *A fortiori* the abbot has power over his own flock. On the 'prophetic' authority acknowledged to 'spiritual fathers' of the fourth century, see Hausherr, *Direction spirituelle*, pp 242ff; 271 (teaching role recognized for women).

81. RM calls upon the bishop to sanction liturgically, by an inscription on diptychs, the nomination of a new abbot by his predecessor (chapter 93). In the case of the sudden death of an abbot the bishop is even asked to designate an acting abbot to make this nomination (chapter 94). For its part, RB calls upon bishops to nullify the election of an unworthy abbot and to proceed to his replacement (chapter 64), and to recall to order a recalcitrant priest (chapter 62). Chapter 65 supposes that the abbot is normally 'ordained', that is to say, installed by bishops and abbots.

82. Basil Steidle, 'Heilige Vaterschaft', *Benediktinische Monatschrift* 14 (1932) 217ff; 'Abba, Vater', ibid. 16 (1934) 89-101. We ourselves have uncovered some facts of this kind in the *Historia Monachorum* (Prol.), in *Vita Honorati* 4, and in the *Monita* of Porcarius of Lérins. This point does not seem to have been well understood by Hausherr, *Direction spirituelle*, p 32, who does at least produce two interesting texts, one by Evagrius Ponticus (Ep 61), the other from the *Liber Graduum* xxix, 19 (that this latter text is touched with 'sabellian modalism' is not

certain). See also Hausherr, p 308. The orthodox and traditional character of this doctrine of the fatherhood of Christ as well as its numerous attestations in RM are facts which greatly weaken the attempt made by Philip Corbett to reconstruct a 'primitive' RM 2 text in which the term *abbas* and the citation of Rom 8:15 would be missing (cf. *The Latin of the Regula Magistri. A Guide to the Establishment of the Text* [Louvain: University Press, 1958] 150-152).

83. RM Th 23ff; Thp 9-10, 17, 21-22, 35-39, 49, etc.

84. Mt 23:9-10.

85. Thus 1 Cor 4:15; Gal 4:19.

86. See the commentary of Jerome on Gal 4:6 (PL 26:374B). Hausherr (*Direction spirituelle*, 17-22) posed this problem of paternity in the Church well. In addition, a discussion of Jerome's texts is found in his book (pp 28-30). Moreover, Jerome corrected himself when commenting on Mt 23:8 (PL 26:169BC).

87. The term, in the sense of chief servant, is already attested in Jerome, Lr 52:5. Gregory the Great, for his part, speaks of a *maior ecclesiasticae familiae*, head of an episcopal household (*Dial.* 4:37).

88. The comparison here between RM 2:1 and RM 11:7 is all the more impressive as *maior* in Chapter Two is glossed by *Christi agere uices*, which in turn recurs in Chapter Eleven: *uicedominum* (vs 7). However, the reservations expressed above on the monastery-*familia* comparison retain their full value here. It is to be remembered that the word *maior* belongs to traditional monastic terminology, in which it signifies 'superior' without any specific allusion to the family of ancient times. One will be convinced of this by examining the *Pachomiana latina*: no other word is employed so often to designate the superior or superiors (*Praec.* 11, 12, 16, 17, 18, 30, 32, 47). The Master ordinarily seems to use it in this technical and purely monastic sense. Cf. RM 7:4, 25, 36, 37, 64, 68; 10:49, 58. It could be that here (RM 2:1) the Master is thinking of nothing more; in that case, *maior* would only indicate in his eyes 'superiority' without reference to the master. But the close proximity of *Christi uices agere* makes the latter at least probable. Note lastly that the notion of vicarious power is itself both secular and ecclesial. Except in RM Eleven, where the secular *familia* is explicitly mentioned, it is difficult to affirm that the *uice Dei* so familiar to the Master (RM 7:64; 89:20; 93:5) clearly evokes the secular image in his mind. The text of Gregory the Great (*Dial.* 2:23) cited above, n. 80, demonstrates quite well how this notion is incorporated into ecclesial thought. To speak of the 'vicariate' suggests to the Christian immediately, and without anything more being said, the spiritual reality of apostolic succession.

89. Other terms more or less familiar to our two rules might be subjoined here, but the analysis of such terms would teach us nothing new. We would mention only *magister* (RM 2:24, 36, 37; 7:13, 16, 17, 20, 43, 58), which is almost synonymous with *doctor*, and also *caput* (RM 2:29, 47). This last term was not retained by the RB redactor; it evokes the famous pauline image of Christ the 'head' of his Church, an image which Hilary of Arles had already applied to Honoratus, 'head' of his community at Lérins (*Vita Honorati* 19). Interesting as this ecclesial metaphor may be, it is noteworthy that its use by the Master is exceptional. RM utilizes it only when calling on the abbot to set an example, drawing after him all the 'members' of the cenobitic body (2:29), or to demand of the 'members', reciprocally, that they rally to the decision of their abbot (2:47).

90. The abbot-bishop comparison is already made by Caesarius of Arles, himself a bishop and former abbot, in a sort of circular addressed to the episcopate (Serm 1, Morin, 18:5): *semper de ouibus dominiciis solliciti simus, timentes illud quod terribiliter dominus de sacerdotibus uel abbatibus clamat...* (Ezek 34:10). But mention of abbots in this exhortation meant for bishops is occasional and fleeting. As it is, it constitutes an interesting counterpart, from a bishop's point of view, to the linking together of abbots and hierarchical pastors made by monastic authors, and a beginning for developments in RM form. See also Faustus, *Hom. de S. Maximo*

in *Bibliotheca Veterum Patrum* (Lyons, 1677) tome 6, p 655g: *Et qui iamdudum in abbate pontificem gesserat, postmodum abbatem in pontifice custodiuit.*

91. See the arguments offered by Jerome (Lr 125:15) to justify the *uiuere debere in monasterio sub unius disciplina Patris.* He remarks: *Singuli ecclesiarum episcopi, singuli archipresbyteri, singuli archidiaconi: et omnis ordo ecclesiasticus suis rectoribus nititur.* It is true that for him this law of monastic government extends to all areas of life, as he tries to show. Exceptions to this monastic law are rare. Scarcely anything can be cited save the *Vita Fulgentii* 8 and 23, and Cassiodorus, *Inst* 32:1. See also below, Chapter Seven, the twelfth canon of the Council of Chalon-sur-Saône (about 650; Mansi, vol. 10, col. 1189): *Ut duo abbates in uno monasterio non sint.*

92. Cf. Jerome, Lr 52:5: *Igitur clericus... interpretetur primo uocabulum suum, et nominis definitione prolata, nitatur esse quod dicitur.*

93. In Chapter Ninety-two, the Master proposes no other conditions for choosing a new abbot than superiority over all the other brethren in observance, good works, and humility (RM 92:7-32, 65: *cum non est dignum ut melior sub deteriore consistet;* 76-82: *meliorem in omni perfectione... uobis omnibus in omni obseruatione mandatorum Dei... melior extitit*). Such a criterion might seem simplistic. Yet the principle proposed by the Master retains its value. It is not enough for the abbot to be a proper religious who knows how to handle men and to command. Something more is required: personal sanctity which will make of this leader a master, someone who will orientate community life towards the search for God.

94. Hausherr has given strong expression to this exigency: 'To consent [to direct others], it was necessary for him to believe that he had arrived where the others would ask to be conducted; to possess the qualities of the spiritual man to such a degree and in such a manner that the disciple, simply by frequenting the master, would, as it were, contract them by contagion', (*Direction spirituelle*, p 61).

95. See Ambrose, *De excessu Satyri* 1.20: *gubernasti fratris domum;* Gregory the Great, *Dial* 4.37 (Moricca, p 288, 1.4: *ecclesiastica familia,* and 1.8: *ecclesiastica domus*).

96. 'Bodies have been entrusted to the king, souls to the priest' (Chrysostom, *Hom.* 4.4.5; PG 56:125). Cf. H.-X. Arquillière, *L'Augustinisme politique* (Paris: Vrin, 1934) p 66.

97. Cf. RM 7:53-56; 89:18-23; RB 33:1-5.

98. See above, Chapter One, p 52.

99. A favorite theme of the Master. See above, n. 50.

100. See above, n. 97. The *Vita Alexandri* ¶7 (PO 6,662) considers it obvious that the cenobiarch has to be on guard to provide his sons with everything necessary. It sees in this a serious inconvenience, moreover, in conformity with messalianistic tendencies which have been brought to light by Stoop in his Introduction.

101. RM 1:82-92; 2:35-36. Cf. n. 97.

102. Cassian, *Inst* 2.5; *Conf* 18.5 and 21.29. Cf. above, Chapter One, p 42.

103. Acts 4:35: *Et ponebant ante pedes Apostolorum. Diuidebatur autem singulis prout cuique opus erat.* This text has been cited and commented upon innumerable times in monastic tradition. Cf. R Aug 5.9; RB 34:1; 55:20.

104. Cassian intimates this when he writes of the abandonment of community of goods by second generation Christians: *non solum hi qui ad fidem Christi confluxerant* (gentile believers), *verum etiam illi qui erant ecclesiae principes ab illa districtione laxati sunt* (*Conf* 18.5). These *ecclesiae principes* are most likely bishops (cf. *Conf* 21.29 and 24.11, where the same expression recurs). Although he says that the abbot is the ideal bishop, it is obvious that he is not considering the sacramental character (the abbot is *de jure* a simple layman), but merely the moral

comportment and example given. The theme of 'the monk, ideal of the priest' has been developed in this sense (cf. below, Chapter Six). St Thomas proposes this parallel between secular prelates and religious superiors in the *Summa Theologica*, II^{a}II^{ae}, qu. 186, art. 5, ad 1: *illi qui in saeculo vivunt, aliquid sibi retinent et aliquid Deo largiuntur: et secundum hoc oboedientiae praelatorum subduntur. Illi vero qui vivunt in religione, totaliter se et sua tribuunt Deo... unde oboedientia eorum est universalis.*

105. This is the sense in which RB requires the cellarer (31:1), guestmaster (53:22), and porter (66:1) to have 'wisdom'.

106. See R 4 Pat 138-150; RB 31:10.

107. Cassian, *Conf* 21.1-10. At Scete the office of deacon was entrusted only to him *quem...fidei atque uirtutem exellentiorem...censuerit*, in the spirit of Acts 6:3-5. Cf. Palladius, HL 58.2: the allocation of alms among the members of a colony of hermits is entrusted by the superior to a brother *gnôstikôtatos* and 'more sagacious'. In the same way, RB 31:8 applies to the cellarer 1 Tim 3:13: *qui bene ministrauerit, gradum bonum sibi adquirit*, a text concerning the ecclesiastical offices of deacon. RB has greatly developed the directory for the cellarer and the qualities demanded for this office (compare R 4 Pat 138; RM 16:62-66; and RB 31). These qualities are very nearly those required of the abbot (Chapter Sixty-four; see our commentary). On Caesarius the cellarer, see *Vita Caesarii* 1.6 (*sancta discretio*).

108. See *Vies Coptes de saint Pachôme et de ses premiers successeurs*, tr. into F r e n c h by L. Th. Lefort (Louvain: University Press, 1943) pp 60-61 (Pachomius and Palamon); Palladius, HL 22.1-8 (Paul the Simple and Anthony). Jacques Dupont has brought out this necessity for close community living between disciple and his master in his article, 'Le nom d'abbé chez les solitaires d'Egypte', *Vie Spirituelle* 77 (1947) p 217, while still, with good reason, stressing the freedom characterizing such relations in eremitism as distinct from cenobitism. As correct as this last remark is, one should not mistake the fact that the disciple's absolute obedience to his master is often presented as the norm for hermits as well as cenobites. Cf. VP 5.14: *De oboedientia* (PL 73:947-953).

109. However, see Hausherr, *Direction spirituelle*, pp 119-120 (The case of a private director in the life of Simeon the New Theologian). We have come across nothing comparable to this in ancient western tradition.

110. On Pachomius' gift for reading hearts, see the Index of *Vies Coptes*, p 423. The tenderness of a mother for her children which the superior ought to possess is expressed in the citation of 1 Thess 2:7: 'Like a mother feeding and looking after her own children' (see Index, p 415); unexpected rigor: *Vies Coptes*, pp 138, 139, 140, 176; disconcerting longanimity, pp 111-112.

111. Palladius, LH 32 (Pachomius, HM 2 (Hor) and 7 (Apollonius). In these last two cases, it is a matter of *coenobia* in the wide sense, perhaps simple colonies of hermits.

112. Notwithstanding divergencies of detail in their accounts, Gregory of Tours and the author of the *Vitae Patrum Jurensium* agree in characterizing Romanus by his goodness and Lupicinus by his severity. It is Lupicinus who saves the situation in the episode about the revolt of the brethren narrated by Gregory in VP 1.3 and by *Vita Romani* 13. Romanus, through excessive indulgence, had let himself be overrun (AS 6:750).

113. RM 92:57.

114. Thus in the case of Pinuphius (Cassian, *Inst* 4.30-31), and of John of Réomé (see below, Chapter Seven).

115. *Vita Fulgentii* 29. Compare this with the case of Hilarion (*Vita Hilarionis* 29), itself dependent on that of Anthony (*Vita Antonii* 49). Anthony wanted to escape both from the cares of the world and from spiritual pride.

116. *Vita Fulgentii* 16, 30, 57.

117. Hausherr, *Direction spirituelle,* 227-228.

118. See below, n. 151.

119. Cassian, *Inst* 4.9 and 39. For RM and RB, see below, n. 151. Confession does not take on an official aspect except in R Fruc II 13, where there is a sort of weekly chapter of faults. Note too the inquisition by the provosts in RM 15:14-16.

120. It is generally known that the concept of a rule actually changed in this way in the thirteenth century. Cf. M. H. Vicaire OP, *Histoire de saint Dominique,* 2 vol. (Paris: Cerf, 1953) II:209. Instead of appearing as the expression of the will of God as transmitted by a prestigious legislator, the rule appeared foremost as a creation of the community in view of the common good.

121. RM 92 and 93. See below, Chapter Seven.

122. Eph 6:6.

123. Ancient cenobitism very soon came to know successorial crises which led to threats of secession. Cf. the revolt of the Pachomians against Orsiesius, and of the monks of the Jura against Eugendus (*Vita Eugendi* 10; AS OSB 1:555). RM seems to have foreseen such contradictions: *Videte, fratres, ne quis hanc ordinationem animo malo suscipiat et Christum contemnat, cuius uices in monasterio uobis iste acturus est* (RM 93:4-5).

124. This problem will be illustrated with concrete examples taken from tradition when we study Chapter 65 (below, Chapter Eight).

125. RB 2:33-36 (third addition).

126. See above, n. 50.

127. Mt 6:25-33.

128. See PL 67:1136c.

129. *Conf* 19.6-8. On the other hand, see the *Vita Alexandri* ¶ 7 (cf. above, n. 100). The author of this *Vita* is of the opinion that cenobites do not practise evangelical *aktèmosunè* since their superior has to provide for the needs of each. This seems diametricaly opposed to Cassian, who makes *aktèmosunè* the privilege of the cenobite, rather than of the hermit (*Conf* 16.9). In reality, Cassian was thinking of the absence of property and cares for the individual, whereas the author of the *Vita* attacks collective wealth and worries. The two viewpoints are different, and mutually correct each other. Moreover, the messalianistic tendencies of this *Vita* are to be kept in mind.

130. Thus it was with St Benedict in Gregory the Great, *Dial.* 2.21 and 28-29, whereas the abbot of Soracte allowed himself to be dominated by fear of poverty (*Dial.* 1.7; Moricca, pp 46-47). Another example of an abbot taking advantage of material difficulties to plunge both himself and his monks into prayer occurs in Greg Tur, VP 18.2 (Ursus).

131. RM 1:90-92; 7:53-56.

132. In particular, he ought never to prefer material advantage to the good of souls (RB 57:2-3), and the rest of the chapter, which is inspired by RM 85.

133. Such is, it seems, the profound sense of the *Vita Alexandri* ¶ 7 (cf. above, n. 125).

134. Notice how Lupicinus led the monks of the Jura back to frugality (cf. above, n. 112).

135. RB 40 and 65 (cf. 18:23-25). The author of RM shows himself more peremptory, surer of his authority, not so much pulled between the inevitable present and the impossible past. But notice the latitude the Master leaves fervent monks in matters of obedience (7), silence (8), sleep (44:15-19), fasting (53), and the quantity of food and drink (27:47-51). This latitude makes up part of a resolutely applied

pedagogical system; it is seldom accompanied by reserve and nostalgia for the past, as in RB.

136. See RM 92:28-29, 72, 76, 82. Cf. RM 2:1.

137. See 'Le monastère, Eglise du Christ', p 26.

138. In speaking this way, we remain aware that the distinction between the two fora does not correspond solely, even primarily, to the dual purpose of an active religious institute. The need to preserve freedom of conscience may require it even when no such dual purpose exists. Again, to look upon the superior merely as the organizer of community action would limit excessively the role of the external forum. In every religious institute, active or not, the external forum has as its primary duty to watch over—from without—the sanctification of the religious. These remarks made, it remains true that the distinction between the two fora is related both historically and by the very nature of things to the dual purpose introduced into the religious life by the existence of 'active' orders.

139. This appears clearly in RM 11 with regard to the institution of provosts. See also *Vies Coptes*, pp 96-97 (Boharic 26 and parallels), and RB 21.

140. Hausherr, *Direction spirituelle*, 110-122.

141. Placid de Meester, *De Monachico Statu iuxta Disciplinam Byzantinam* (Vatican City: Polyglot Press, 1942) Art. 30.1; 31.3; 39.3-4; 50; and the *fontes*.

142. Art. 30.1 and pp 204-205.

143. Pp 246-248. It is even stated here and there that only spiritual fathers distinct from the *hegumen* are able to hear confessions. It is insisted, furthermore, as in the latin Church later, that the *hegumen* must not oblige the brethren to make their confessions to himself.

144. Art. 31.3.3 and pp 209-210.

145. De Meester and Hausherr agree in uncovering the first evidence for this in the *typika* of the eleventh and twelfth centuries. It might even go back as far as St Basil (LR 23 and SR 227) according to Pierre Humbertclaude, *La doctrine ascétique de S. Basile* (Paris: Beauchesne, 1932) p 127, n. 2, and p 165, whom Hausherr follows.

146. See de Meester, *De Monachico Statu*, 246-248.

147. These highly schematic remarks, based on assumptions on which both Hausherr and de Meester agree, evidently demand completing and adjusting. We restrict ourselves to mentioning what Herwegen pointed out (*Sinn und Geist*, pp 115-116 and n. 4): 'Teaching given by masters other than the abbot...was not something unheard of in communities of oriental monks. In a more recent epoch, 'starzism' underwent a great development, especially in russian monasticism, conferring upon the monk who had the gift of the Spirit a position of teacher and guide alongside and above the abbot'. See also Jean Leclercq, *The Love of Learning and the Desire for God*, trans. by Catherine Misrahi (New York: Fordham University Press, 1961) pp 207-208. Here it is always by the abbot's delegation that another gives instruction.

148. Canons 518 (superior) and 891 (novice master).

149. See Fr Gabriel of St Mary Magdalene, 'Direction', *Dictionnaire de Spiritualité* (Paris: Beauchesne, 1957) III: cols. 1197-1199.

150. RM 15:14-18 (provosts ought to question the brethren to obtain avowal of their thoughts); R Fruc II 13 (see above, n. 119).

151. RB does not present the laying-open of conscience except in an ascetical context devoid of all juridical obligations: RB 4:50 (an addition); 7:44 (= RM 10:61, cf. Cassian, *Inst* 4.39); 46:5-6 (note *aut spiritalibus senioribus;* this probably means the deans). Compare this with 49:9, where *pater spiritalis* seems very likely to be the abbot in person.

152. See the study by A. Gutiérrez, 'De manifestatione conscientiae et directione spirituali in religione', *Commentarium pro Religiosis* 36 (1955) 153-174.

153. This is contrary to the thesis held by Fr Gabriel of St Mary Magdalene in his article 'Direction', cols. 1180-1185. To make the commission to direct depend on the power of holy orders seems to us a thesis untenable from the standpoint of tradition. See the article by Gutiérrez cited in the previous note.

154. This defense of the juridical obligation also includes the defense of a moral obligation in the strict sense.

155. *Abbas* was not understood in the formal sense in the East except under latin influence and in a small number of documents. On this subject, see the remarks of Pargoire cited by Hausherr, *Direction Spirituelle*, 35-38.

156. Sulp. Sev., *Dial.* 1.10; Cassian, *Inst* 4.15; 2.3; 4.128; *Conf* 4.20. In Cassian, however, the purely spiritual meaning of the term is also present (notice the title of *abbas* given to all the great hermits of the *Conferences;* when this title is applied to a novice like Germanus, it shows the tendency to make it a simple mark of respect analogous to our 'Reverend Father'). This spiritual meaning did not entirely disappear in the West, despite the general use of the institutional meaning. Thus the *Vitae Patrum, liber V,* translated at the height of the sixth century, calls all the Fathers of the desert *abbas* in oriental fashion. This seems to be nothing more than a literary feature dictated by the original Greek, apparently without any relationship to a living usage in the Latin spoken at that period.

157. See *Pachomiana Latina*, Index, under *Pater;* likewise Jerome, Lr 22.35: *quem patrem uocant* (the superior), and Aug., *De mortibus ecclesiae.* 1.31.67. Observe that *pater* in this formal sense occurs alongside *abbas,* though much more rarely, in western texts. Cf. Caesarius, *Serm.,* pp 885.14 and 887.1, and the texts cited by de Meester, p 302, notably those of RB.

158. Jacques Dupont has brought out well the distance separating the two senses—spiritual and institutional—of *abbas,* as well as their continuity, in his article 'Le nom d'Abbé chez les solitaires d'Egypte', *Vie Spirituelle* 77 (1947) 216-230.

159. Pérez de Urbel, 'La Règle du Maître', RHE 34 (1938) p 720. The priscillianist hypothesis is still in favor at the present time. See especially François Masai, *Il monachesimo nell'alto medioevo* (Spoleto: Centro italiano di studi sull'alto medioevo, 1957) p 459; Philip Corbett, 'The *Regula Magistri* and some of its Problems', *Studia Patristica* (Berlin: Akademie Verlag, 1957) I, pp 85 and 89, and in *The Latin of the Regula Magistri* (Louvain, 1958), *passim.*

160. Mansi, III, col. 633.

161. See canon 1, which especially concerns women.

162. Cf. canon 4 and RM 45:4-7. The priscillian practice of fasting from the seventeenth of December until Epiphany is likewise attested in the letter published by Germain Morin, 'Pages inédites de deux pseudo-Jérôme des environs de l'an 400', *Rev Ben* 40 (1928) p 303.

163. RM 45:2-3. To these traits of orthodoxy which Pérez de Urbel pointed out may be added the prescripts concerning the use of meat (RM 53:27).

164. Nothing on this subject exists in the *Commonitorium* of Orosius, in Lr 237 *or De Haeres.,* n. 70, of Augustine, in the acts of the Council of Toledo in 400, or Lr 15 of St Leo, or the Council of Braga in 563.

165. Cf. the *Liber Apologeticus* published by Georgius Schepss in CSEL 18, pp 32-33. Charles Babut has stressed this point in his *Priscillien* (Paris: Champion, 1909) pp 128-132 and 164-166.

166. At the sect's beginning there were three bishops heading it: Instantius, Salvian, and Priscillian himself. At the Council of Toledo (400) ten gallican bishops accused of Priscillianism appeared, four of whom were deposed and six admitted

to repentance. In his letter to Turribius (PL 54: 667-692), which reflects the preoccupations of his correspondent, St Leo reverts several times to the uneasiness caused by untrustworthy bishops (cf. 680b, 688b, 689c, 691a). These bishops, and not lay 'teachers' were the center of attention. They caused the Pope to exclaim: *quales illic erunt discipuli, ubi tales docebant magistri* (691a). The same thing appears in Turribius' letter to his colleagues (PL 54:693-695).

For the period following Leo's intervention (447), Gustave Bardy observes: 'The gallican bishops who signed the formula were not all in good health. Thus Priscillianism took its toll even among members of the episcopacy'. (Fliche Martin, *Histoire de l'Eglise* [Paris: Bloud & Gay, 1937] IV, p 263).

167. CSEL 18. See the Index, under *Doctor* and *Magister*.

168. See above, n. 165.

169. Canon 39 (Schepss, p 126): *quia opus doctoris lectio sit atque euangelii preadicatio, in quibus nocte ac die operabatur apostolus.* Can. 48 (Schepss, p 130): *quia in ordinibus ecclesiae elegerit Deus primo apostolos, secundo prophetas, tertio magistros.* (This last text utilizes 1 Cor 12:28; later on we shall have occasion to emphasize how the Master uses this text in an altogether different way in RM 1:82 and 14:14). Babut, *Priscillien,* p 132, n. 1, and pp 164-166, has exposed all possible aspects of these two canons, in which he uncovers with some likelihood a vindication for the power of the 'teachers' of the sect to teach.

170. Donatien de Bruyne, 'Fragments retrouvés d'apocryphes priscillianistes', *Rev Ben* 24 (1907) 318-337; 'Epistula Titi, discipuli Pauli, de dispositione sanctimonii', *Rev Ben* 37 (1925) 47-72. The first of these two series, fragment no. 6 (pp 331-334), speaks of *doctores* (1.84) and of *magistri* (1.85-86; 136; 142) with no discernible sectarian intent.

171. Morin, 'Pages inédites de deux pseudo-Jérôme', pp 293-302. The monk Bachiarius, who seems indeed to have had a hand in the redaction of these two letters, was also the author of a *professio fidei* (PL 20) in which he exonerated himself of errors imputed to the sect. *Doctor* is used as a synonym for *sacerdos* (¶ 7,col 1035) and for *episcopus* (¶ 8, col. 1036b). There is no more an allusion here than elsewhere to a theory of the magisterium of 'teacher'.

172. *Vita S. Macrinae* (Jaeger, 400, 6).

173. *Lib Ors* 25 (Amand Boon, *Pachomiana Latina,* 126, 9): *doctorem et monitorem suum.*

174. *De correptione et gratia* 3.5.

175. *Vita Seuerini* 44; 47; 51. See also R 4 Pat 219; superiors, like true 'doctors', ought to preach by example.

176. *Clavis Patrum Latinorum* in *Sacris Eruditi,* n. 3 (Steenbrugge: Abbatia S. Petri, 1951) n. 1872. The *Consensoria* is here envisaging especially the doctrinal role of the abbot. Cf. R Fruc II 10: the 'fourth duty' of abbots is to arm both themselves and their subjects against heresies.

177. See above, pp 105f.

178. See above, n. 70.

179. RM 2:2; 11:6-10; 14:13; 89:20.

180. Cf. RM 93 and 94.

181. Cf. the *Liber Apologeticus,* CSEL 18, pp 32-33.

182. See in particular RM 7:37.

183. 'La Règle du Maître', p 720.

184. See above, Chapter One, p 55.

185. RM 1:83: P alone has *regenerentur,* E and A accord on *regerentur.* Holste and Migne correctly reproduce the A reading. So it seems de Urbel has been led

astray by P. The agreement of A with P seems decisive in favor of *regerentur:* the two mss belong to different recensions. The P reading can only be a mistake.

186. R Bas 70. Jerome, *De Oboedientia* (Morin, *Anecdota Mareds.* 3.2, p 398). R Caes V 63 (note however that Caesarius is both bishop and monastic legislator at the same time) R Col M 1 (G.S.M. Walker, *Sancti Columbani Opera* (Dublin: Institute for Advanced Studies, 1957) p 122, l. 18; note the reminiscences close to R Bas: Columban is probably inspired by R Bas 70 when he cites Lk 10:16). To these texts may be added *Vies Coptes,* p 340, 6, which combines Lk 10:16 with Mt 10:40 to legitimatize the cult of Pachomius.

187. This alternation of 1 Cor 12:28 by our author (RM 1:82; 14:14) and the definition of *doctor* which results from it are not attested in priscillian literature. Canon 48 of Priscillian (Schepss, p 130) on the contrary reproduces the enumeration such as St Paul gives it. The Master's attempt recalls rather the efforts of the Ambrosiaster, Pelagius, and St Jerome to give this title of *doctor* an acceptable meaning in the fourth and fifth centuries (see 'Le monastère, Eglise du Christ', p 39, n. 62). The meaning at which the Master arrives (*doctor* = every pastor actually in charge in the Church) is not unlike the interpretation which Jerome proposes in his commentary on Eph 4:11 (*pastor et magister = praeses ecclesiae*).

COMPLEMENTARY NOTE

In speaking of monarchical constitution and of abbatial 'monarchy' we have borrowed the expression of Gregory of Tours, VP 1.2 (PL 71: 1013a): *Lupicinus tamen abbas super eos obtinuit monarchiam.* Gregory wanted to indicate that, although they were brothers and co-founders of the Jura foundation, Romanus and Lupicinus did not stand on an equal footing, but Lupicinus held the supreme authority. It goes without saying that term must be entirely purified of the ideological and emotional connotations with which it might be charged for the modern reader.

Chapter Three

THE COUNCIL OF THE BRETHREN (RB 3)

T HE STUDY OF THE PRECEDING CHAPTER has already provided us an occasion for indicating the relationship between Chapter Three and Chapter Two.[1] The two chapters were but one in RM, the treatise on the council of the brethren being no more than an appendix to the abbatial treatise. Precisely because it stood in appendix fashion, however, RB detached it from the chapter on the abbot to make a separate chapter of it. Characteristics distinguishing the treatise on the council of brethren from that on the abbot in RM are really quite obvious. First, because of the very structure of the abbatial treatise: by framing it between a symmetrical introduction and conclusion, RM makes everything following the conclusion necessarily appear adventitious. Furthermore, its content is in part heterogeneous to a directory for the abbot: no longer addressed to the superior alone but to all the brethren, it stipulates certain attitudes for them. The higher plane of the abbot's pastoral function is abandoned for the particular and humbler sphere constituted by the community's interests. So there was no lack of reasons for detaching the council treatise from that on the abbot and erecting it into a separate chapter, as RB did.

The institution of the council of the brethren as it is described in RM and RB in itself poses for the historian a problem which until now has been only imperfectly resolved. What is the origin of this council? Can this origin and its development be traced in monastic tradition before St Benedict? Or should we not attribute to him the merit of having created an institution almost unknown to his predecessors? And if this is the case, what sort of extra-monastic institution could have served to inspire St Benedict?

On this point we find that each commentator has his own characteristic trend. Herwegen notes that 'neither the ec-

161

clesiastical discipline of the first centuries nor pre-benedictine monasticism knew such a council of the whole community'. And, referring to roman familial law, he observes that St Benedict transposed the 'family council' of ancient Rome into his community. Steidle, on the contrary, tries to locate the beginnings of the council of the brethren in monastic tradition. He recalls the two annual 'general chapters' of the Pachomians, the meetings of basilian superiors at fixed intervals (Basil, LR Fifty-four), the assemblies of desert solitaries, and the election of the abbot of Lérins by 'the whole community of laymen'. Steidle is compelled to admit, however, that no rule before RB had enunciated such an idea so clearly, and he seeks a prototype of the monks' council in that of the priests assembled around their bishop, mentioned by so early a writer as Ignatius of Antioch.[2]

What should we think of such 'sources'? In truth, none of those produced by Steidle fully meets our expectations. The general meetings of the Pachomians, even that of harvest-time which had economic and disciplinary purposes, did not amount to real councils so far as we know. During them the bursars rendered accounts to the general bursar, the superior of the congregation nominated men to every post, and remission for public and private grievances was made. But in all this we do not see the superior taking counsel with his subordinates. Basil's LR Fifty-four furnishes no truly relevant clue, for it concerns a meeting of local superiors, not an assembly of brethren belonging to the same fraternity. As for the text of the Third Council of Arles concerning the Lérins community, it deals only with the specific case of an abbot's election.

The most interesting of Steidle's parallels is surely the assembly of hermits held for deciding disciplinary questions or for inflicting punishments.[3] Here we do indeed have an institution which rather clearly prefigures the council prescribed by RB. Yet this is an eremitical institution witnessed in Cassian's day in the solitude of Scete. In the interval between so distant a source and the legislation of the Master and St Benedict, it is rather surprising that no intermediate milestones turn up. Cenobitic literature, the rules especially, ought to have furnished us with such signposts, whose absence would indeed oblige us to conclude with Herwegen that RB presents us with an almost new element in the history of cenobitism.

Before examining this issue, we would note that in this chapter RB distinguishes two sorts of council: a council of all the brethren, which the abbot convokes only for important affairs, and a council of the elders for routine affairs. RM, on the contrary, knows only a single council, the whole community, and the abbot is bound to summon it 'whenever he wishes to do anything that concerns the monastery'. The Master makes no distinction between affairs of primary and secondary importance. Here as elsewhere, RB legislation waxes more complex than RM. With good reason this greater complexity is looked upon as an indication of the more recent composition of RB. In any case, we are here obliged to study separately the two councils described by RB: the council of all the brethren, an institution taken over from RM, and the council of the elders, which is peculiar to RB.

Of these two councils, that of the elders is certainly the best attested. We find it both in pachomian monasticism and in Basil. Several passages of the *Coptic Lives* show us the superior general convening the 'great' or 'elders' of the congregation either to ask them to designate his successor,[4] or to tell them his decision on the appointment of brethren to various offices,[5] or to disclose to them the sad state of some particular brother and with them to visit the unfortunate man before expelling him.[6] Actually, in the last two cases, the elders do not seem to have been invited to offer their opinion: the superior convokes them only to notify them of his decisions or to make them witnesses to a particularly weighty act. Only the first case, designation of a new superior, involves consultation of the brethren, who in fact excuse themselves and leave the superior himself, at their request, to name his successor. We are still quite a way from the institution which RB is setting up.

The basilian rules, on the contrary, provide a perfect parallel which commentators, surprisingly, have not pointed out. First, LR Forty-eight, after forbidding the brethren to busy themselves about the administration of the superior, adds the restriction: 'save for those who are nearer the superior in rank and wisdom'. The superior must invite the collaboration of these brethren in his deliberations and examination of affairs of common interest, heeding the words of Holy Scripture: 'Do everything with counsel' (Prov 31:4 LXX version). SR 104 states the general principle: 'In absolutely every affair the superior should remember the words of Holy Scripture: "Do everything with counsel".' Here again we are dealing with a limited council for only men 'capable of judging' are asembled. The occasion which prompted Basil to speak of it was the appointment of brethren to charges.[7] While the procedure

of this council is not indicated in any detail, certain expressions
make one think they did more than merely offer advice. Appoint-
ments were settled upon 'with their consent' (*meta dokimasias
autôn*), and they cast their vote (*tôn adelphôn psèphizomenôn*).

The connection between these texts and RB Three is obvious.
In both, the superior is obliged to summon around himself at
regular intervals a council formed of capable brethren or 'elders'.
In both, too, support is drawn from the same scriptural text (Prov
31:4 LXX). Basil did not however trouble, as RB does, to reserve
the right of decision expressly to the superior, and quite possibly
the council had for Basil a deliberative, and not simply con-
sultative, voice.[8] Moreover, the council of elders does not appear
as an institution complementing the council of all the brethren.
Basil says not one word about the latter. On the contrary,
everything indicates that he was hostile to it.[9] On the other hand
RB only mentions the council of elders as an afterthought to the
development on the council of all the brethren, which should be
convoked 'whenever a matter of major importance arises'.[10]

We shall have to seek the origin of the plenary council elsewhere
then. RM provides us with several useful indications. We have
already noted that the expressions *pro utilitate monasterii* (RM
2:41), *de utilitate monasterii* (2:42), *communi utilitati* (2;45),
pointed towards the temporal administration of the goods of the
community.[11] This stands out all the more clearly in vss 48-50 of
RM:

> So we have said that all the brethren are to be called to the
> deliberation, according to the monastic maxim (*sententia
> monasterii*) that the monastery's affairs are the concern of
> all and not of one person. Of all, because the brethren ex-
> pect to go on replacing one another in the monastery in the
> course of time. Of no one person, because there is nothing in
> the monastery that any of the brethren can claim exclusively
> as his own, and no one determines or does anything by his
> own authority, but all live under the command of the abbot.

The *res monasterii* which the Master tells us belong to everybody
and not to any one person are the worldly goods of the monastery:
vessels, tools which change hands each week or each day, perhaps
also the instruments of the craftsmen and the materials confided
to the custody of the cellarer and the custodian for an undeter-
mined time. All these things circulate among the brethren at
various rates, and in the 'progressing', either in the regular course

of time or by increase in experience, know-how, and virtue, all the brethren may expect sooner or later to use or administer them.[12] Consequently, the goods of the monastery belong to everyone. At the same time they are the property of no one person in particular, individual ownership being excluded along with any right to dispose of an object or perform any action on one's own initiative. The authority of the abbot over all the brethren and over all their activities entails a radical disappropriation.[13] He alone is in some measure 'owner' of the community's temporalities,[14] which he bequeaths by testament to his successor.[15]

The prescripts of the Master on the subject of the council of the brethren take on their full meaning within this context, which is simultaneously juridical and spiritual. Since material possessions belong to no one person, nothing may be withdrawn from the general deliberation under the pretext of personal right and ultimately the abbot is completely free to dispose of each object, as well as of each person, in accordance with his own judgment, enlightened by the counsel of the brethren.

This context of temporal administration had to be stressed, for it allows us to compare the council of the brethren as ordered by RM with indications furnished by several other cenobitic documents. The rule of Aurelian, developing a point in that of Caesarius, had already authorized monks to rebel against an abbot who 'would give away or sell the goods of the monastery': the brethren were to stage their resistence *sancto consilio et uno consensu.*[16] The rule of Feriolus is still more interesting, for it presents a theory of monastic property comparable to the Master's, though in many respects it differs. The abbot cannot set a slave of the monastery free *absque consensu omnium monachorum, quia non potest multorum seruus, unius ad ingenuitatem remissione transire, nec libertus fieri quem omnes unanimiter non absoluunt, cum manifestum sit illum tot dominos habere quot monachos.*[17] Isidore of Seville in his turn forbids either abbot or monk to set a slave free: 'He who has nothing of his own cannot grant freedom to what is *res aliena.* Even secular law forbids it: *non potest alienari possessio nisi a proprio domino.*'[18]

We have seen on three occasions in the course of the latter half of the sixth century and the first quarter of the seventh the tendency to concede to all the brethren a certain right over the management of the monastic patrimony. In the last two cases, this right was shored up by juridical principle and it was affirmed that each monk was co-owner of everything belonging to the monastery. It is evident that we are very close to RM: the abbot surrounded by the council of the brethren, deliberating on the subject of a temporal affair of interest to everyone because everyone shares in community property. Reference in both these texts to *sententia* of a juridical nature further accentuates this resemblance.

A certain number of important differences still exist between RM and these parallel documents. First of all, the others deal with only certain well-defined cases such as alienation of goods or emancipation of a slave, whereas RM legislates very generally: 'whenever the abbot wishes to do anything which concerns the good of the monastery...'. Second, according to Aurelian, Feriolus and Isidore, the abbot is no more owner than the other monks. It is in order to forestall any attempt which the abbot as master might make to dispose of the goods of the monastery that these rules broach the question, and the R Fer orders the convening of a council of all the brethren. In RM, however, the abbot acts with full freedom after having listened to the counsel of each (vss 47, 50). Furthermore, we know from other passages of RM that the Master considered the abbot a sort of owner of all the monastery's worldly possessions. Continuity of property is guaranteed by the will the abbot drafts, each abbot bequeathing all the goods of the community to his successor.

Nothing, then, is more contrary to the Master's thought than the insurrection preached by Aurelian and the restrictions imposed on the power of the abbot by Feriolus and Isidore. In the R Aur, the brethren assemble to confront the abbot; in the R Fer, to exercise control over him, but in RM, only to offer him their light on an issue, without in any way diminishing his complete independence.

We would remark finally that although RM expresses itself in almost the same terms as Feriolus, *res monasterii omnium est,* it adds at once a negative counterpart missing in R Fer, *et nullius est.* Thus it affirms that the monks are not really co-owners of the cenobitic patrimony, as Feriolus would like. Closer consideration reveals that the first member of the phrase (*omnium est*) does not bespeak a right of ownership, but refers solely to the use of the monastic goods which the monks have by turns.[19]

If a similarity in the context of temporal administration obliges a comparison between the RM council and that which Feriolus mentions, this comparison only serves to manifest the almost diametrical opposition existing between the two rules. Feriolus, like Aurelian before and Isidore after him, maintained a juridical perspective which was that of Justinian's legislation: Justinian, as we know, required the concurrence of all the monks,[20] or of the majority of them,[21] for every act of alienation or rental of community goods. To this very limited and juridical perspective, in which the superior is but one among other co-owners of common property, that of the Master is opposed, for it encompasses the entire temporal existence of the monastery and tries to arrange it wisely by procuring for the abbot all the brethren's insights without in any way subtracting from his absolute authority. The Master seems aware of the necessity of giving the community some share in the administration of its property, according to a right recognized by imperial legislation and very clearly affirmed in rules from the mid-sixth century onwards. But at the same time he means to maintain intact the traditional authority of the abbot and leave him sole master of goods as well as of persons.[22]

It seems, then, that the RM plenary council reflects the antagonistic tendencies of a transition period, in the midst of which the Master strikes an equilibrium. The solution he adopted conforms much more basically with the traditional order than with views which prevail in Aurelian, Feriolus, and Isidore. Here, as in the rest of RM, fidelity to the fundamental cenobitic idea is preserved; the monk is entirely relieved of all temporal preoccupation, the abbot assumes full charge of both his temporal and spiritual existence.[23] We remember how insistently Cassian made himself the theorist of such total abdication of self-concern into the abbot's hands: thereafter the abbot alone is responsible for the life and material lot of his subjects.[24] Such is also the Master's thought affirmed many times in the course of his rule. On the juridical plane it betrays itself in the concepts we have mentioned. The goods of the monastery are the possessions of the abbot, who bequeaths them to his successor. Yet within this framework of very classical ideas and institutions, he has a tendency to give the community a share in the management of temporalities. This tendency—we know its development through later rules—remains here fully integrated within the traditional order of things. Brethren limit themselves to an expression of their views, the abbot alone makes the decisions. Though RM concedes that the *res monasterii* belong to everyone, this is not by reason of a co-ownership right, but only because everyone takes turns using those goods.

Fundamentally, therefore, RM stands much nearer the first cenobitic generations than the mentality of the sixth and seventh centuries already reflected in the legislation of Justinian. But the institution of the council of the brethren as presented in RM looks less towards the past, in our opinion, than towards the future. It ought to be interpreted less in the light of the 'sources', whose insignificance we have seen, than in the light of contemporary or later institutions. Divergent as such institutions may be, they furnish the *Sitz im Leben* which allows us to understand the plenary council of RM. We readily admit with Herwegen that 'neither the ecclesiastical discipline of the first centuries nor pre-benedictine monasticism knows such a council of the whole community'. Rather than seek the model for this institution in the 'family council' of ancient Rome, we prefer to see in it signs of the concerns of an epoch moving towards a modified concept of cenobitic property and of the abbot's rights over the temporalities of his monastery. This RM text is better explicated within the ecclesial and monastic tradition[25] with no need of recourse to the hypothesis of secular influence. The independence of the abbot in making the decisions, after taking the brethren's advice, can indeed recall the similar independence of the *paterfamilias* and the family council, but it recalls most of all the sovereign authority of supernatural origin which ancient cenobitism accorded its superiors.

After thus situating the 'council of elders' and the 'council of the brethren' within the monastic tradition, we are left to consider the RB text more closely by comparing it with the RM text from which it issued. Let us begin with a rapid inspection of the RM text. After describing the institution for the first time (RM 2:41-43), the Master justifies it by two successive developments, the parallelism of which is underscored by an almost identical introductory formula:

>   *nam ideo omnium quaeratur consilium quia...* (vs 44).
> *ideo omnes fratres diximus ad consilium debere uocari...* (vs 48).

The first of these developments (vss 44-47) justifies summoning everyone together by the usefulness of the brethren's counsel to the abbot: 'Perhaps the best advice may well be given all at once by one from whom it was least expected, and this may redound most to the common good; and then when one hears many opinions it is easy to find the right course of action.'

The second development (vss 48-50) justifies calling everyone

together by some quasi-juridical considerations of which we have
spoken: 'according to the *sententia monasterii* the affairs of the
monastery are the concern of all and not of any one person', and
so on.

So the council treatise is divided into three small, almost equal
paragraphs (three, four, and three verses respectively): an introduction and two parallel developments. The conclusion (vss
51-52) is more linked to what follows than to what preceded: it introduces the *ars sancta* theme which is developed in the following
chapters. What is more, it is set off from the council treatise by
the spiritual character of its object, which reminds one more of
the treatise on the abbot. It acts as a pivot between chapters Two
and Three rather than as a conclusion to the council treatise.

Putting the absence of a true conclusion on one side, we can see
that this little treatise is composed according to a plan very
reminiscent of the outline of the abbatial directory. In both, the
same law of symmetry is strengthened by juxtaposing parallel
developments which form the body of the treatise. This
parallelism also affects the internal structure of each paragraph,
as the following schema shows:

	Introduction	First Development	Second Development
Role of the community	41-42	44-46	48-49
Right of the abbot	43	47	50

This treble balance confirms what we suggested above about
the problem the Master was seeking to resolve in these lines. His
thought vacillates continually from community to abbot, from the
role played by the brethren to the exclusive right of the superior.
No sooner does he say one thing about the rights of the plenary
council and the services that may be expected from it than he im-

mediately reverts to the fact that everything remains in the abbot's power, whether it is the convocation of the council (Introduction) or the decision resulting from it (Developments). Perhaps this movement of his thought reflects the head-on encounter and subsequent jostling of two tendencies, one conservative, the other innovative, which one can detect in RM on this question. The accent is put on the second swing of the pendulum, that is, on the abbot's traditional role.

Because the structure of the RM treatise is so very simple, the RB text is striking (as was also true for the abbatial treatise) for its more complex and less orderly character. Distinction is made between two councils: of all the brethren and of the elders only, each of them set in relation to some category of affairs to be treated (*praecipua, minora*). An element not mentioned by the Master is introduced: the sovereign authority of the rule, which exercises its dominion not only over the brethren (vss 7-10), but over the abbot himself (11). Once the utility of the plenary council has been indicated (3), it is not enough to recall to the brethren their entire subjection to the abbot (4-5); the abbot in turn receives his share of admonition: dispose everything with foresight and justice (6), do everything in the fear of God and observation of the rule (11). A brother who argues hotly with his abbot either inside or outside the monastery is threatened with the discipline of the rule (9-10). Such are the chief elements of the RB text, which comparison with RM reveals as additions. They disrupt the orderliness which the treatise had in RM and give it a somewhat complex appearance — one hesitates to outline its plan. It seems in any case that the simple RM rhythm (role of the community, right of the abbot) has been complicated by a supplemental element (the duty of the abbot in making decisions).[26]

But for all that, the fundamental principles remain identical. RB holds as firmly as RM to the complete independence of the abbot's decisions. It has even indicated with sharper precision the abbatial prerogatives in convening the council, presenting the question (*dicat ipse unde agitur*), deliberating (*tractet apud se*),[27] and reaching decisions (*quod utilius iudicauerit faciat*). The clarity with which, even from the opening words, this procedure is described both in overview and in detail, seems to reflect a more mature experience than the Master's, but an experience in perfect continuity with the Master's views.

There are, however, two points where RB diverges notably from its source. In its first development, RM justifies the plenary council by a common-sense consideration based on the saying *quot homines tot sententiae*. The abbot, amid a number of various counsels, has a chance of discovering which has greatest value, and this may perhaps be given by a brother from whom nothing of the sort was expected. Instead of these very human, common-sense considerations, RB substitutes a more supernatural viewpoint, 'God often reveals to an inferior what is best' (3). We are reminded of an analogous remark in RB (63:6), 'Samuel and Daniel, though mere boys, passed judgment upon elders'.[28]

On the other hand, RB purely and simply suppresses the second RM development, that is, the *sententia monasterii*, 'The possessions of the monastery belong to all and to no one', along with the commentary on it.[29] From this fact, the *Sitz im Leben* of the council of brethren and its relationship to the administration of community goods in RB, appears less distinctly. One can hardly conclude from this that the *Sitz im Leben* has changed.[30] The motive behind this suppression is not obvious. Perhaps the RB redactor felt uncomfortable about ending with the affirmation *res monasterii omnium est* this chapter where a limited council is introduced which does not bring together 'all' the brethren, but only the elders.

In conclusion, we may say that the council of brethren assembled around the superior is an institution as old as cenobitism itself, to say nothing of colonies of hermits. The first generations, it is true, do not seem to have known real councils, that is, meetings where each expressed his view, save in the restricted form of the *council of elders*. This institution functions on special occasions among pachomians (to designate the superior general, for example), and regularly among basilian fraternities, where the superior seems bound not only to seek the counsel of the elders, but also to take account of it in making his decisions. The motive Basil gives is the command to 'do everything with counsel' (Prov 31:4 LXX). It is therefore a matter of human wisdom corroborated by revelation and seeking to secure to the superior's various decisions the benefit of the insights of experienced and prudent brethren.

This sort of limited council is scarcely attested in later documents. Western rules say nothing about it,[31] though we cannot thereby assert that latin monasticism did not practise it until the time of St Benedict. In any case, it reappears in RB with the same frequency and based on the same scriptural command as it does in Basil, but appended to a treatise on the council of all the brethren and as a simple complement of it. Because any dependence of RB on Basil in *Greek* seems out of the question, this can surely be only a coincidence which underscores once again the spontaneous harmony among the legislators of cenobitism due to their common reference to Scripture.

The institution of a plenary council, if by that is meant a real council as we defined it above, is never encountered in the most ancient documents of cenobitism. The legislation of Justinian and the rule of Feriolus, in return, show us the abbot obligatorily surrounded by a council of all the monks for certain temporal administrative transactions. This regulation is grounded on a right of co-ownership imputed to each community member. Feriolus states this explicitly, and his viewpoint is shared by Isidore and before that, it seems, by Aurelian. It is in just such an economic context, and with reference to a *sententia* of juridical tone regarding how the goods of the monastery belong to all the monks, that RM legislates on the plenary council.

It seems, consequently, that the key to the institution as RM-RB present it is to be sought in the late texts of the sixth and seventh centuries. Possibly the plenary council of our two rules answers a need to allot the community some share in the administration of its goods, a need which primitive cenobitism apparently did not experience, but which arose in the contemporary documents we mentioned. Yet whatever its relationship to such innovative tendencies, the institution is conceived by our two rules in the most traditional spirit, with no attack on the abbot's absolute sovereignty. And then too, this council is not restricted to a very limited number of affairs (selling, renting, emancipation) as in imperial legislation and the rule of Feriolus. It covers all affairs involving the good of the community (RM), or at least all important affairs (RB). This wide competence falls in line with the ordinary, regularly-convoked council envisaged by Basil: one must 'do everything with counsel'. The RM-RB plenary council is not a juridical act meant to satisfy the monk's right over what is theirs by co-ownership; it is, like the basilian council, a pooling of everyone's insights for the enlightenment of the superior, a jointly conducted search for the will of God.

So the institution described by our two rules appears simultaneously as an innovation linked up with non-primitive tendencies and as bearing the authentic mark of the most traditional cenobitism. It might be reckoned an enlargement of the council of elders known by the first generations.[32]

In all that we have said about RM and RB, what is unique to RB? Its treatise on the council of the brethren, when compared with the Master's, appears more complex, more subtle, richer in subsidiary notations, and having a literary structure which is much harder to identify. These characteristics suggest that RB is indeed a recension of RM. The institution itself is more developed than in RM, having two kinds of council instead of one and taking remarkable care to ensure precision in describing the procedure right from the very first sentence of the chapter. These further perfections no doubt imply greater experience, perhaps also a larger community.[33]

Nothing essential has been changed, however, and RB appears to stand in complete continuity with the Master in the spirit of the institution. Only RB's careful reference in explaining motives, to more 'supernatural' reasons than the principles of common-sense and equity invoked by RM, turns up as something new. Thus, RB speaks of revelations frequently granted by God to inferiors, and cites Prov 31:4 (LXX) in support of the council of elders. We note lastly that the role accorded the elders by RB in matters of counsel is only one particular instance of the tendency affirmed many times in the course of the rule. The 'elders' reappear in several roles (deans, *senpectas*, spiritual seniors, roundsmen, master of novices). The term, and sometimes the function itself, does not derive from RM, but from the experience peculiar to the RB redactor, a witness to more developed institutions in which the greater recognition was given to the abbot's need to rely on approved collaborators, indeed specialists, in the many and overwhelming tasks of his charge.

NOTES TO CHAPTER THREE

1. See above, Chapter Two, p 69.

2. Basil Steidle, *Die Regel*, p 94, n. 1 [ET: *The Rule of St Benedict, a Commentary*, trans. by Urban Schnitzhofer (Canon City: Holy Cross Abbey, 1967).]

3. See for example Cassian, *Conf* 18.15; VP 5.9.4; 5.16.2 etc. These assemblies were held in the church of Scete or of Cellia, usually upon completion of the weekly liturgy. A priest, as head of the community, presided. He was the one to make the decisions; no known text leads us to think the brethren had a deliberative vote.

4. *Les Vies Coptes de saint Pachôme et de ses premiers successeurs*, trans. into French by L. Th. Lefort (Louvain: Bureaux du Muséon, 1943) p 48 (Pachomius designates Petronius); p 325 (Orsiesius appoints Theodore).

5. Ibid., p 331.

6. Ibid., p 259.

7. Same context in RB 65:15: the abbot chooses his provost *cum consilio fratrum timentium Deum*. Note that this is not a matter 'of lesser importance' for which, according to RB 3, only the council of elders is convoked, but a major affair which would justify (in our eyes at least) convoking all the brethren in council. The very gravity of the question and the qualities of wisdom it required, not its 'lesser importance', led to its being reserved to the council of elders. The community (*congregatio*) did not intervene save by 'humbly petitioning' the abbot to name the provost of his choice. The specific case of nominating a 'second' to substitute for the superior in case of his absence is envisaged by Basil in LR 45. There also the nomination is made by the superior '*and by the other [brethren] capable* of making a good choice'.

8. Besides the expressions of SR 104, to which we called attention above, see LR 27: the brethren, at least those who are 'first in age and in intelligence', have the duty of reprimanding the superior when they perceive he is in the wrong. Such an eventuality is never envisaged by either RM or RB.

9. LR 27 and 48 deny brethren the right either to exert control over the administrative function of the superior or to criticize him unless they belong to the number of the elders (cf. SR 27 reproving disparagement against the superior). 'The fraternity must not assume a democratic demeanor'. This is one of the reasons why LR 45 prescribes appointing a 'second' capable of substituting for the superior in his absence. It is evident that Basil admits only the council of elders. This limited council does not *complement* a plenary council, as it will in RB, but substitutes for and eliminates it.

10. Apart from these divergencies, the reader ought to bear in mind an important fact: none of the basilian texts cited above (with the exception of SR 27) belongs to the initial redaction of the Rules, to that *Regula Basilii* which alone was accessible to the latin public. Consequently, as arresting as the rapprochement between Basil and RB may be, it ought not to be looked upon *a priori* as anything more than coincidence. RB does not depend on Basil here; it simply squares with him. See below, Chapter Seven, n. 40.

11. See above, Chapter Two, p 69. The expression *pro utilitate monasterii* occurs again in RM 50:74 to designate urgent garden work or an errand that cannot wait. Likewise in Gregory the Great the expression is applied to an affair which obliges the provost to go out of the monastery (*Dial.* 1.2; Moricca, 20, 16; 22, 8; 24, 6 and 22. Cf. 22:8: *pro causa monasterii*). Cassian had already spoken of the *monasterii utilitas* in connection with works performed in the monastery (*Inst* 7.9).

12. Notwithstanding some similarities of expression, the issue here is not one of abbatial succession, but of the place of the abbot's 'second', a place to which all the brethren 'aspire' and which is offered to everyone according to their progress in virtue (RM 22:9-12; 92).

13. This bond between obedience and non-ownership is constantly affirmed by Cassian (*Inst* 2.3; *Conf* 18.7; 24.23). It is found again in RB (33:4-5; 58:24-25.).

14. The abbot's dominion over the possessions of the monastery seems affirmed by RM 16:58-61, a passage which contains again the *sententia monasterii* which occupies our attention here: *De omnibus uero, quae sunt in monasterio, extra abbate nullus sibi aliquid uelut suum, siue quod attulit, siue quod inuenit, siue quod laborauit uel adquisiuit, nullus aliquid peculiare uindicet aut defendat, quia regulae sententia haec est: res monasterii omnium est et nullius est.* This text is the best commentary on the council of the brethren. It plainly shows in what economic

context the Master envisaged the council. Chapter 16 deals with the cellarer: he receives in trust, and each day distributes, the *usitilia* of the monastery. The important restriction *extra abbate* should be noted: no one may claim right of ownership over any object, *save for the abbot*. Of course, one might understand these words in another sense, i.e. without the authorization of the abbot. But the interpretation we propose seems more probable, and is confirmed by the fact that the abbot draws up a will (cf. n. 15). The *sentena monasterii* of RM 2:48 is here (16:61) called *regulae sententia*. Another *regulae sententia* is expressed in RM 90:95, which likewise concerns things belonging to the monastery.

15. RM 89:31-35; 93:13. The first of these texts shows that the monk is bound not only by a pact with the community (*stabilitas monasterii*) but also by a personal relationship with the abbot (*fides abbatis*). The latter entails for the abbot the obligation of making a will so that after his death no monk may reclaim what he brought to the monastery and the abbot received in his own name. So the abbot, by means of his will, guarantees the conservation of the monastic patrimony. By appointing his successor, he makes him his heir as well, solemnly handing over to him on the day of his installation the inventory of all the goods of the monastery.

16. R Aur M 43. Cf. R Caes V 64. The council of Agde in 506 had already forbidden abbots to sell anything whatsoever unless they had their bishop's consent (canon 56 in *Concilia*, ed. Labbeus-Cossartius [Paris, 1671-1672] tome 4, col. 1392; cf. canon 22 on selling done by clerics). The text goes on to forbid abbots to emancipate serfs who belong to the monastery: *mancipia uero monachis donata ab abbatibus non liceat manumitti. Iniustum enim putamus ut monachis quotidianum rurale opus facientibus serui eorum libertatis otio potiantur.* This text throws a great deal of light on those of Feriolus and Isidore which we cite further on. In reading it, one divines the complaints monks made about the reservation of slave's manumission to the community council. Yet the Council of Agde limited itself to curtailing the abbot's administrative power, without instituting a council of brethren competent in this matter. The right of co-ownership by monks remained unknown.

17. R Fer 36. This theory of co-ownership was already set forth by ¶ 35 in terms singularly reminiscent of those of RM. In this paragraph, a monk eats a piece of fruit apart from the common meal. He is punished by being excluded from community meals and shall have to implore the pardon of *everyone* in order to be readmitted there, *quia justum est ut cunctorum indulgentiam postulet qui omnibus quod erat commune subtraxit... ne communem omnibus cibum gustu sibi ipse furetur... quapropter erit congregationi semper una proprietas ita ut cuncta omnium et omnia sint cunctorum.* The case of fruit found in the fields is handled in the same way by Cassian (*Inst* 4.18), but in his writings the concept of common property does not yet have the same clarity of expression. This rule dates back to Pachomius himself (R Pac Praec 73-77).

18. R Is 18. The text goes on to treat of the revenue and expenditures of the monastery. An officer, the *custos sacrarii*, is in charge of it. Money may not be spent except by order of the abbot and *sub testimonio praepositi uel seniorum.* Once again, in everyday administrative transactions, a tendency to control the abbot's administrative function is perceptible.

19. Note too that *omnium est* seems directed above all against particularist pretentions. The Master forestalls the objection, 'why should something of which I alone have charge be subject to the council of all the brethren?' Thus, the first part of the sentence is meant not so much to grant the brethren a right to be consulted by the abbot as rather to combat certain monks' spirit of private property. It is aimed less at the abbot than at individualistic tendencies of the brethren.

20. *Codex iuris civilis, Lib*. I, *tit*. 2, ¶ 17. —Nov. 123, 6.

21. Nov. 120, 6-7.

22. This second element is surely more important. The first (recognition of the

community's right to be consulted) cannot be discerned in RM with full certainty. See above, n. 1.

23. RM 82; 89:21-22 etc.

24. *Inst* 4.5; 7 *passim;* 12.25; *Conf* 18.7; 19.6-9. A significant passage is found in *Inst* 4.14: each monk of Tabenna considers himself an owner of all the monastery's material possessions (*ut omnium dominus*) as regards the carefulness with which he treats such things, but as a boarder and servant of the monastery with no right to the least object (*potius... quam dominum rei cuiuscumque*) as regards the ownership of them. This theory, which the *sententia* of the Master approaches, contrasts with the *tot dominos quot monachos* of Feriolus for whom a right of each monk to co-ownership exists over everything belonging to the monastery, the abbot in this respect finding himself on an equal footing with the brethren. The idea that the abbot is in some way the owner of monastery goods seems implied by a retort narrated by Cassian (*Inst* 7.12). *Si tu habes plurimos unde sustentes, me similiter habere cur prohibes?* says a 'possessive' monk to an abbot. This situation, an abbot holding the temporalities of the monastery in his hands, recurs in *Conf* 4.20, where Cassian laments that the idea of founding a community (of which he plans to be abbot) becomes a pretext for a monk to hoard part of his wealth. This same passage again affirms the necessity of a monk's beginning his monastic life by abdicating all his cares, not only about others, but even about his own material lot: *ut curam non modo aliorum nullam sed ne sui cuidem gererent.*

25. We say 'ecclesiastical', for it seems, from reading the legislation of Justinian, that it is by virtue of their assimilation to hospices, churches and other ecclesiastical establishments that monasteries were obliged to subject themselves to the general regulations about renting or alienation, and that the agreement of community members was required for these transactions to be valid. See above, nn. 20, 21.

26. The phrase *sicut discipulos conuenit oboedire magistro, ita et ipsum prouide ac iuste condecet cuncta disponere* appears charged with meaning when it is compared with RB 61:4 and 65:14-15. The three passages are proper to RB and reveal the same preoccupation with having the abbot pay heed to the advice given by his inferiors. This concern is far from being present to the mind of the Master; apart from the treatise on the council which we have studied, he never reverts to this obligation of the abbot. Indeed, as we have seen, his major preoccupation here is more to ensure the obedience of the brethren than to invite the abbot to take counsel. So we have here a trait characteristic of RB, one which, when compared with the Master, indicates a certain evolution in the direction of a less absolute reliance on the abbot. *Prouide* recalls RB 64:17; *iuste cuncta disponere* is repeated in negative form by RB 63:2, where the abbot is lectured again.

One final remark will serve to bring out the full import of this phrase and of the warning it directs to abbots. RB 3:6 is modeled on RB 6:6:

> nam loqui et docere magistrum condecet,
> tacere et audire discipulum conuenit.

In both, 'master and disciple' are set in opposition. The vocabulary is identical: *condecet* for the master, *conuenit* for the disciple. Whereas RB 3:6 follows a disciples-master order, RB 6:6 inverts the two: first master, then disciple. In both, the accent weighs upon the second member: RB 3 means to lecture the abbot while RB 6 gives the monk a lesson. Now if one observes that RB 6:6 is taken over literally from the Master (RM 8:37), it seems more than probable that the redactor of RB 3 repeated more or less consciously a type of phrase which he had read in the Master and had perhaps already transcribed into his rule (*conuenit* recurs only in RB 5:2, which is taken over from RM 7:2; *condecet* occurs nowhere else in RB). But in taking over this whole phrase from the Master, the redactor inverted its terms and reversed its meaning. No longer is it an afirmation of the abbot's right to teach (*condecet docere*), but the proclamation of the abbot's obligation to govern prudently and justly (*condecet prouide et iuste cuncta disponere*). Nothing is more significant than this reversal of thought underlying the apparent identity of expression. RB, as we shall see many times, is preoccupied with certain abbatial failings which the Master never envisages. Abbatial prestige is somewhat diminished in RB, where one might say that the figure of the abbot is more human and closer to his subject's weakness.

27. These words contrast with RM: *tractetur communiter* (vs 42).

28. Note that *iunior* designates not so much one who is 'younger' in age as one who is 'inferior' in rank. The idea that God can make use of anyone to voice his will occurs again in RB 61:4. On the value of inferior's advice, cf. Cassian, *Conf* 16.12.

29. This is all the more remarkable as the RB introductory formula, *ideo autem omnes ad concilium uocari diximus* (vs 3), bears greater resemblance to the second RM development (vs 48) than to the first (vs 44; see above, p 168). So RB took over the formula of the second development. This is of some importance, for it enables us to affirm that the RB redactor read RM 2:48-50; if he did not reproduce this passage, it is because he deliberately omitted it. Nothing authorizes us to suppose that these lines are a late interpolation which has not yet been incorporated into the text utilized by RB.

30. The expression *in monasterii utilitatibus*, of which we have mentioned the significance in Cassian, the Master and St Gregory, reappears in RB 3:12, a passage by the hand of the redactor himself. *Utilitas* occurs again, in both the singular and the plural, to designate any occupation dispensing religious from kitchen service (RB 35:1, 5). In 65:12 the *monasterii utilitas* is the general running of the community, anything falling within the province of the subaltern officers, deans or provosts. This last passage suggests a very broad meaning of the term, implying spiritual responsibilities (cf. 21:2). Possibly the expression had the same breadth in 3:12.

31. At most, one may cite R Or (¶ 21) which, basing itself on the pachomian rule, prescribes deferring disputes which might arise between a brother and his provost to a tribunal composed of elders. This tribunal seems to function even when the abbot is present. But this is not an instance of a real council of the abbot. For the sake of completeness, we would also mention the 'testimonial of the elders' required by Isidore (R Is 18) whenever the abbot orders the depositary to make an expenditure.

32. Gregorius Holzherr, 'Die Regula Ferioli, das älteste literarische Zeugnis der Benediktinerregel', *Studia Anselmiana* 42 (1957) p 227, thinks the RB council represents an expansion of the council which R Aur and R Fer sketch roughly. The negative consensus of R Aur preceded the positive consensus of R Fer, which, having in view only the particular case of the slave to be freed, would in its turn be outstripped by RB which prescribes obligatory council for all important affairs. These observations are correct, but incomplete. We have seen how the spirit of the institution is different in RM-RB and in R Fer. Consequently, the chronological schema proposed by Holzherr does not command acceptance. We believe on the contrary that RM and RB both pertain to a period earlier than R Fer.

33. The council of all the brethren must have been readily assembled and quickly heard in a community as small in number as the Master's seems to have been. It apparently amounted to no more than two dozen monks. In a more numerous community one could hardly imagine the abbot having recourse to a long capitular session for *every* affair. The idea of reserving plenary sessions for *important* affairs might have been conceived in a community more numerous than the Master's.

Chapter Four

OBEDIENCE (RB 5 AND 7)

TEXTS AND SOURCES[1]

WE NOW PROPOSE to study the treatise on obedience (RB Five = RM Seven). But as soon as one broaches a commentary on this chapter one becomes aware of the close links, both literary and doctrinal, between it and the next two (RB Six-Seven = RM Eight-Ten). This affinity, particularly evident in RM, makes it necessary to expand the commentary and to consider the treatises *De oboedientia, De taciturnitate,* and *De humilitate* which form a whole. Without losing sight of the purpose of our research, which is to elucidate the doctrine of the two rules on obedience, we shall examine this ample section composed of RB Five-Seven and RM Seven-Ten.

An over-all view here at the outset may prove of some assistance. In the table below, we present RM Ten and the corresponding passages of RM Seven-Nine. We will thus be able to see at a glance the nature of RM Ten, which is a veritable recapitulation of the three preceding chapters.

RM 10 (*De humilitate*)	RM 7 (*De oboedientia*) RM 8-9 (*De taciturnitate*)
First rung:	
thoughts, tongue, hands, feet ...	8:24-37; 9:30, 39
self-will, carnal desires	7:39-46
Second rung: Jn 6:38	7:51
Third rung: Prov 16:25; Ps 14:1	7:39-40
Ps 18:45; Lk 10:16	7:5-6, 68-69
Fourth rung: Ps 44:22; Ps 66:10-12 ...	7:60-63

Fifth rung
Sixth rung
Seventh rung

Eighth rung

Ninth rung: Prov 10:19 ....8:35; 9:34
Tenth rung
Eleventh rung: Sentences of Sextus ...9:31 (cf. 9:43)
Twelfth rung: 9:19-24

Summary though it is, this table shows clearly enough the progression pursued by the Master through this cluster of chapters. Having dealt successively with obedience (RM Seven) and silence (RM Eight-Nine), he takes up these two treatises again in a full chapter devoted to humility (RM Ten). The doctrine of the treatise on obedience is reproduced in the first four 'rungs of humility', and that of the treatise on silence in the last four. So the Master has used the same method, moving from obedience to silence, in both the expositions he provided on this pair of virtues. The order observed in RM Seven-Nine repeats itself in RM Ten.

These summary statements must be complemented by two observations, however. First, at the 'first rung of humility', before taking up the series of developments which parallel RM Seven, the Master propounds a theory on custody of the thoughts, of the tongue, and of the hands and feet, which corresponds not with RM Seven but with RM Eight-Nine and consequently anticipates the last rungs. And furthermore, rungs 5-8, coming between rungs 1-4 and 9-12, form a medial section without parallel in the treatises on obedience and silence.

The 'twelve rungs of humility' are largely copied, however, from the 'marks of humility' expounded by Cassian in *Institutes* 4.39, as has been known for some time. We may, then, draw up a comparative table of Cassian's 'marks' and the Master's 'rungs', in order to examine the arrangement of the latter, the order in which they are enumerated. If this systematization for rungs 1-4 and 9-12 corresponds to that of Cassian, we will be justified in thinking that the 'obedience-silence' sequence observed in RM Seven-Nine and in RM Ten owes its origin to the author of the *Institutes*.

So let us attempt a comparison between 'marks' and 'rungs'. Others have done this before us, but, it seems to me, without drawing all possible parallels by methodically comparing the two texts.[2] To do this, we must reckon not only with word for word correspondence such as Butler indicated in bold type in his *fontes,* but also with certain similarities of thought at times confirmed by the use of the same word;[3] we shall indicate in parentheses such less obvious but sufficiently certain *rapprochements.* We need above all to co-ordinate the 'first rung' of RM with those lines where Cassian, before enumerating the 'marks of humility', declares that the starting point for salvation (*principium nostrae salutis*) is fear of the Lord, because this cleanses man from every vice. Manifestly the Master had this preamble of Cassian in mind when he composed his 'first rung': *timorem Dei sibi ante oculos semper ponens* (RM 10:10). This introduction of the subject corresponds, in the Master as in Cassian, with the goal of the ascent, the love which casts out fear. So within the 'rungs of humility' the Master has incorporated at the first rung this fear of the Lord which Cassian had previously placed at the starting point of the journey towards God but had put as a preamble outside the scheme of the 'marks of humility'.

With the benefit of these remarks let us see how Cassian's 'marks' relate to the 'rungs' of the Master:

RM 10	CASSIAN (Inst 4.39)
First rung (fear)	(*Principium nostrae salutis...*)
Second rung	(Mark 1)
Third rung	(Mark 3)
Fourth rung	(Mark 4-5)
Fifth rung	(Mark 2)
Sixth rung	(Mark 7)
Seventh rung	(Mark 8)
Eighth rung	(Mark 6)
Ninth rung	(Mark 9a)
Tenth rung	(Mark 10)
Eleventh rung	(Mark 9b)
Twelfth rung	(lacking)
Conclusion (love)	(*confestim te ad caritatem...*)

Careful consideration of this table reveals that the first four rungs of the Master regularly follow Cassian's arrangement. RM deletes two pericopes: (1) between fear of God and the first mark, a sentence describing *contemptus rerum* (Petschenig, p 75, ll.10-13). The Master makes no allusion to it, reserving this question for his treatise on the administration of postulants; (2) between marks 1 and 3, the Master deletes mark 2, but takes it up later at his fifth rung. The RM method of composition is therefore clear in these first four rungs: RM follows the text of Cassian but omits certain passages.

At rungs 5-8, on the contrary, Cassian's sequence is no longer observable. Although it is true that at the center of this section rungs 6-7 form a core which exactly corresponds to marks 7-8, the fifth rung is derived from the preceding section (mark 2). It has forced mark 6 from its original place to a position at the end of the group, at the eighth rung.

With the three following rungs (9-11) we resume Cassian's order, save that the ninth mark has been partitioned, the second half constituting a new rung (11). Finally, the conclusion matches Cassian's.

It goes without saying that so schematic a table is far from suggesting all the relationships between RM Ten and Cassian. But it does at least show clearly enough what we wanted to learn. By tallying it with the preceding table, in which parallel passages of RM Seven-Nine and RM Ten were arranged opposite one another, we see that rungs 1-4 correspond, by means of some omissions, both with the treatise on obedience (RM Seven) and to a Cassian sequence. The beginning of Cassian's text, followed *grosso modo* for the first four rungs of RM Ten, finds an echo at the beginning of the large section formed by RM Seven-Nine. Likewise, the end of the Cassian text, from the ninth mark onwards, reappears at the last rung of RM Ten and finds its echo in RM Eight-Nine, which form the end of the section constituted by RM Seven-Nine.

Let us assemble these results in a new table which will draw together all that we have ascertained in the two previous tables:

CASSIAN	RM 10	RM 7-9
Fear; marks 1-3-4-5	Rungs 1-4	RM 7 (obedience)
Marks 2-7-8-6	Rungs 5-8	— — — —
Marks 9a-10-9b	Rungs 9-11	RM 8-9 (silence)
— — — —	Rung 12	RM 9
Love	Conclusion	— — — —

The 'obedience-silence' sequence which constitutes the ground plan of RM Seven-Nine and is found again in the enlarged plan of RM Ten derives ultimately from the 'marks' of Cassian. That the Master was inspired by Cassian when composing his chapter on humility is obvious. No less interesting, though less apparent, is the knowledge that RM Seven-Nine allies itself through the medium of RM Ten with this great text of the *Institutes*. The common origin of RM Seven-Nine and RM Ten seems to have been meditation on *Institutes* 4.39, in which the Master discovered, or believed he had discovered, the subject matter and order of his two great treatises *De oboedientia* and *De taciturnitate*, synthesized in the 'ladder of humility'.

These preliminaries were necessary to enable us to answer the first question that arises when one broaches the chapter on obedience (RB Five = RM Seven). What place does it hold in the rule? Why do we find it in this spot?

This chapter is patently the first of a series which closes with RM Ten. From the first sentence we are oriented towards humility. The RM Seven-Ten block which opens this way, connects easily with what has preceded if one does no more than look at the themes treated. After the *ars sancta,* the teaching of the abbot, the subject seems to change to the disciple's attitude, compounded in humility of silence and obedience.

Several literary facts square poorly with this analysis, however. For one thing, the RM Seven-Ten section is hardly symmetrical with the *ars sancta* treatise: no allusion is made to the 'artisan' metaphor constantly developed in RM Three-Six. The style is very different. Instead of enumerating 'good works', virtues and vices, the author gives an extended description of certain great monastic virtues in what is really treatise form. One would, moreover, seek in vain a link uniting RM Seven to the preceding chapter: the subject changes by an exordium *ex abrupto*, without any transition, from the *officina diuinae artis* to the treatise on obedience. Nor is there, either before the *ars sancta* or at the end of the chapter on humility, a résumé which declares or recapitulates the order of subjects by drawing a distinction between the abbot's teaching and the disciple's attitude.[4] Noteworthy finally is that most of the attitudes recommended in RM Seven-Ten have already been sketched out in RM Three-Six, sometimes in literally identical sentences,[5] and that each section describes the joys of paradise.[6]

From all appearances then one is led to believe that the Master

merely juxtaposed these two sections without originally having
foreseen their juncture and without even having taken the trouble
to establish between them some rapport to explain their sequence.
This would come only *post factum*. Consequently, it does not
seem that RM Seven-Ten would match RM Three-Six in the sense
that the first of the sections set forth what the abbot's teaching or
the second what the disciple's attitude ought to be. The doublets
we have marked out suggest rather that RM Seven-Ten develops
in a new form the themes of obedience and silence which had been
no more than sketched in RM Three-Six, and that this second
presentation is distinguished from the first above all by its literary
characteristics. Basically we, along with Froger, could at most
distinguish between the teaching of the abbot 'in so far as given by
him' (RM Three-Six) and 'in so far as received by the disciples'
(RM Seven-Ten), but not without noting that this distinction
scarcely holds except for the rather extrinsic framework of the *ars
sancta* and for the artisan's role there accorded the abbot (RM
2:51).

Among the parallels which lead us to see in the *ars sancta* a sort
of preamble to, or first version of, RM Seven-Ten rather than a
treatise clearly differentiated and forming an antithesis, there are
two very significant texts worth mentioning. First, in the *fer-
ramenta spiritualia* enumeration we read *humilitas, oboedientia,
taciturnitas* (RM 4:3), to which the inverse series in the subsequent chapter corresponds: *primo superbia, deinde inoboedien-
tia, multiloquium* (RM 5:2). This shows us that the *ars sancta*
redactor had the sequence of material found in RM Seven-Nine in
mind: obedience and silence. But he did not relegate humility to
third place, in the way the *De humilitate* chapter takes third place
in the RM Seven-Ten section. Humility comes first in the series of
the three virtues; it is ranked before obedience, a little as in the
first sentence of Chapter Seven (*Primus humilitatis gradus est
oboedientia*). It presupposes obedience, which constitutes its first
manifestation, its 'first rung'. Likewise in Chapter Ten humility
comes well before obedience which here amounts to no more than
one of the rungs, not even the first one.

These facts cast some light upon the meaning we should give
the order of chapters in RM Seven-Ten. The sequence, obedience
+ silence, should correspond to a well-defined plan, because it
dominates the internal structure of RM Ten in similar fashion and
recurs in RM 4:3 and 5:2. From all appearances, the Master drew
it from his meditation of *Institutes* 4.39. The obedience-silence +

humility sequence (RM Seven-Nine + RM Ten), on the contrary, corresponds neither to the internal structure of RM Ten,[7] nor to the enumeration of RM 4:3 and 5:2, nor to the first sentence of RM Seven. All these texts rank humility before the other two virtues, or at least presuppose it to them.

One may suspect then that RM Ten is not in its original place, which might well have been at the head of the section, before the chapters on obedience and silence. The treatise on humility would thus have served as an introduction to these chapters, whose teaching it proposes in a more concise form, midway between the fleeting notations of the *ars sancta* and the extensive developments of RM Seven-Nine. The RB Seven *exordium,* referring to the 'rungs of humility' which seem to have been known already, could be explained quite easily by this hypothesis.

We must now approach directly the first sentence of RM Seven, *Primus humilitatis gradus est oboedientia sine mora.* How to reconcile these words with the presentation of 'rungs' in RM Ten (= RB Seven) is one of the classic difficulties of benedictine exegesis. People generally extricate themselves by speculating on the connection of the three virtues at issue, humility, obedience and the fear of God. Depending on the viewpoint they adopt, they say it is legitimate to see either in obedience or in fear the 'first' step of humility. Abstract mental gymnastics, for which every reader of the *Summa Theologica* is well-prepared, then permits us to resolve the contradiction.

One cannot object *a priori* to solutions of this sort, for the ancients, and especially Cassian, were already well enough acquainted with such speculations to have proposed various schematizations of virtues which are justified by various points of view. But in the present case such justification is wholly wanting. The Master furnishes us with no explication on the manner of harmonizing these two assertions: the first rung of humility is obedience; the first rung of humility is fear (and the third obedience). The two propositions, downright contradictory, betray inconsistency.

Better to concede this blunder and try to account for it by an avatar in the redaction. Leander Bopp thought this when he conjectured that Benedict, in writing the chapter on obedience, had had no more than a summary idea of the 'twelve rungs of humility' and of the place obedience held among them.[8] This trail has every chance of being right. The Master, writing Chapter Seven, seems to have had in mind a 'ladder of humility' different from the one he formulated in Chapter Ten. No doubt he had the text of Cassian in mind and was already thinking of converting the 'marks' into 'rungs'. But it had not occurred to him so far to integrate 'fear of the Lord' within the series of marks-rungs. He remained with Cassian's scheme, in which 'fear' precedes humility,[9] and in which the initial 'marks of humility', up to the fourth, are indeed manifestations of obedience.

Perhaps in writing Chapter Seven, the Master was thinking not only of composing a later treatise on humility in which obedience would be, as with Cassian, the 'first rung', but also of locating this *De humilitate* at the beginning of the section, in front of *De oboedientia*. The *ex abrupto exordium* of Chapter Seven might thus be explained, presupposing as it does that an exposition of the rungs of humility is already known. In this way too the order of enumeration *humilitas, oboedientia, taciturnitas* of RM 4:3 and 5:2 could be explained. In any case it is very likely that Chapter Seven was written before Chapter Ten since the ladder of humility which it presupposes involves a first rung of obedience, just as with Cassian.

When the Master undertook the composition of his treatise on humility and looked more closely at Cassian's text, he would have felt a desire to preserve along with the 'indications of humility' the 'fear to love' transition which serves to frame it. Because the chapter was to be *De humilitate,* humility could fittingly envelop all the material treated, including the initial 'fear' which for this reason became integrated into the 'rungs of humility'. Hence the shuffle which caused 'fear' to be dislodged from its preliminary and extra-schematic position to that of the 'first rung', while obedience was relegated to the subsequent rungs. In doing this, the Master did not bother to emend the first sentence of Chapter Seven, which attests to the primitive order, the order of Cassian. The location of *De humilitate* at the end of the series, after *De oboedientia* and *De taciturnitate,* results possibly from the fact that this chapter was composed after the other two. It would have assumed the place in the rule its date of composition assigned it, even though the author's original intention had been rather to prefix it to the treatise on obedience.

The first sentence of RM Seven still requires a word of explanation on the term *gradus humilitatis* which appears there for the first time. The writer was obviously thinking of a 'ladder of humility' which would recapture in more graphic form the exposition of 'marks' found in *Institutes* 4.39. Actually, the relish for metaphors so pronounced in RM would in itself explain this transformation, inasmuch as the ladder of Jacob was a commonplace endlessly exploited in the patristic age.[10] But no one has pointed out forcefully enough that Cassian himself suggested this spatial figuration. In *Inst* 4.38, he announces the way of perfection in these words: *his gradibus atque hoc ordine....* Similarly, he concluded his description by passing from humility to charity, *gradu excelsiore.* The Master found in Cassian himself then a double incentive for setting up his 'rungs'.

Beyond these suggestions of the immediate context, the whole of Cassian's works offered him more than one example of 'gradation'.[11] Particularly worth mentioning is *Inst* 12.29-30, where the 'marks' of carnal pride, the inverse image of the 'marks of humility', are called *decessuum gradus,* descending rungs. The Master surely knew this text, parallel to *Inst* 4.39, and he could have culled from it the idea of presenting the 'marks' in the form of 'rungs', The very term he used, *humilitatis gradus,* figures textually in another passage of the *Institutes,* in the course of a sentence which could have served as a résumé of the treatise on humility.[12] Lastly, *Conf* 12.7 offered the Master the model of the literary device he used in Chapter Ten from beginning to end. There Cassian describes six 'rungs of modesty' which he introduces with a stereotyped formula: *primus itaque pudicitiae gradus est ne... secundus ne... sextus castimoniae gradus est ne...*[13]. The extent to which a reader of Cassian such as the Master would have been disposed to develop the ascensional metaphor in RM Ten and to employ for that purpose the very terms we read in this chapter is evident. It is really only a small step, once one is familiar with the thought and language of Cassian, to pass from 'marks' to 'rungs'.

According to this first sentence of RM Seven, then, obedience is the first rung of humility. We have seen how this conception of obedience as the *first* manifestation of humility is derived from *Inst* 4.39. We ought to enlarge this literary reference by considering the place such a doctrine holds in the works of Cassian and in the monastic tradition. When Cassian posits as the first indication of humility 'to keep all the movements of one's will mortified', he is only summing up what he was professing throughout *Inst* 4.8, the *eruditio principalis,* the first formation which the provost gives the young monk to teach him to 'acquire dominion over the movements of his will'.

The 'primordial' character (*primitus*) of this *ascesis* is clearly indicated by Cassian: any success in the subsequent fight against vices is impossible if this foundation has not been laid. But this theory of Cassian is itself no more than the development of a statement which St Jerome and Sulpitius Severus recorded in almost identical terms. *Prima apud eos confoederatio est oboedire maioribus et quidquid iusserint facere,* wrote Jerome as early as 384.[14] And Sulpitius wrote: *haec illorum prima uirtus est parere alieno imperio;*[15] *cum prima ei lex oboedientiae poneretur.*[16] For Jerome, Severus and Cassian, obedience is therefore a 'first thing' in cenobitic life. Feriolus of Uzès expressed the same thought at the outset of his rule in a sentence obviously inspired by Cassian: *Primum ut monachus, quem proprie manet multas in se uirtutes aedificare, oboedientiae in se collocet fundamentum.*[17] Thus the exordium of RM Seven plunges us directly into the most traditional doctrine there is — the 'primacy' of obedience in the formation of the cenobite.

We encounter no further difficulty in identifying the source for what follows. This obedience, says the Master, is immediate, *sine mora.* He goes on to depict for us in picturesque and edifying terms the promptness of the obedient monk (RM 7:1-9 = RB 5:1-10). Once again we find ourselves in Cassian's company. In *Inst* 4.12, Cassian portrays the cenobites of Egypt issuing forth from their cells at the first summons, without the least regard for the work they had in hand: *In eodem puncto quo ad aures eius sonitus pulsantis aduenerit, summa uelocitate prosiliens ne tantum quidem morae interponat, quantum coepti apicis consummet effigiem, sed imperfectas litterae lineas derelinquens....* No doubt Cassian had a particular case of obedience in view, not the execution of the verbal order of the superior, but what we today call 'obedience to the bell'. Apart from this difference, however, the idea and even the vocabulary are identical.[18]

In the middle of this edifying little scene inspired by Cassian, however, the Master introduces two citations entirely his own: Ps 18:45 (*ab auditu auris abaudiuit mihi*), and Lk 10:16 (*qui uos audit me audit*). These scriptural texts not only do not figure in the corresponding development of Cassian, they are also not found anywhere in the *Institutes* or *Conferences*. The fact is particularly significant as regards Lk 10:16. We shall have occasion to stress this point further below.

Still another element to be reckoned a personal contribution of the Master in this initial pericope is the restriction in vs two, *sed haec forma paucis conuenit et perfectis.* This restriction no doubt reflects clearly the intention of Cassian who, in Book Four of the *Institutes,* presents the ideal picture of cenobitic obedience realized among the monks of Egypt without concealing how far short of that ideal the monks of Gaul fell. The Master, on the contrary, accepted human weakness. Immediate obedience was restricted to the 'small number of the perfect'. After describing it, he turned towards 'the weak and the lazy' to adapt obedience in proportion to their infirmity.

This involves a pericope of the same length as the preceding one (RM 7:10-15, 20-21), a pericope in which the Master urges the abbot to repeat his orders when the first injunction has not been obeyed. The disciple is not considered 'contumacious' unless the superior is obliged to repeat his command a third time. In the midst of this pericope a long parenthesis omitted by E (RM 7:16-19) introduces an analogous case to this repetition of commands: when the abbot questions his disciple, the latter may maintain his silence and await a second interrogation. Seeming repugnance to speaking is regarded as virtuous; such behavior is seen as a mark of 'taciturnity'. This odd parenthesis announces the next chapter, in which it is however worth noting that this particular case of the repeated interrogation is not envisaged.

Sources are lacking for the pericope just considered. Cassian, as we said, was not aware of such jurisprudence for the weak. The Master's personal relish for casuistry, of which RM offers many an example,[19] is perceptible here. Everything must be forseen in detail, in order that a precise directive of the rule may respond to each concrete situation in which the abbot and monk find themselves. In addition, this passage introduces a distinction between two categories of disciples: the perfect and the imperfect. We shall come across this again in Chapter Nine. There as well, the Master indicates for silence two norms of conduct corresponding to the diversity of graces and the measure of faith (RM 9:46-50).

These first two pericopes form a single unit (RM 7:1-21). The same theme is developed in these two parts: obedience *sine mora* and obedience *cum mora.* From beginning to end the issue is the manner of implementing obedience, whether perfectly or im-

perfectly. But with vs 22, we launch into an entirely new development which occupies three fifths of the chapter (RM 7:22-66).
This is an exposition of the 'two ways' which, somewhat curiously,
either recalls or announces other RM passages. The Master
himself does not conceal its relationship with the Prologue: *Nam
et illud de duabus uiis congrue hic et conuenienter taxandum est*
(RM 7:22). By his own admission, then, we shall witness a resumption of the theme of the two ways already introduced in Prol
10-14, a theme to which the *Thema* made more than one allusion.
But the theme is made more precise this time by its special application to obedience in the strict and cenobitic sense of the
word.

Furthermore, it will be combined with the description of the
different kinds of monks (RM One), and more precisely with the
description of sarabaites and gyrovagues. These latter two, like
seculars, travel the 'broad way', while the cenobites alone advance
along the 'narrow way'. Obedience is what distinguishes one way
from the other and divides the two categories of monks:
sarabaites-gyrovagues and cenobites.

The category of evil monks[20] is described first (RM 7:24-46).
Actually, the twenty-three verses devoted to them make up two
pericopes quite distinct in their nature as well as in their affinities.
There is first the description properly so-called (RM 7:24-38),
which employs the satiric style already used in Chapter One to
ridicule the gyrovagues. Now it is directed against the sarabaites.
This description allows us a glimpse of several of the traits which
make up the encomium of cenobites: the name abbot which these
independents arrogate to themselves (7:30; cf. 7:50), fretting
about their livelihood, about clothing and footwear (7:35; cf.
7:53) and spiritual security (7:36; cf. 7:54).

From verse thirty-nine on, we have a new piece of work. The
satiric description yields to a scripturally-grounded critique
(7:39-46). True, a lengthy descriptive sentence which prolongs the
preceding theme recurs in the midst of this scriptural development (RM 7:41-44; cf. 7:30), but the series of *testimonia* at the
beginning and end vests this passage with its characteristic aspect.
With this series we enter upon the section where RM Seven corresponds very closely to RM Ten, as we indicated summarily in
our first table. At this point a more diligent comparison between
RM Seven and RM Ten becomes indispensable. It becomes obvious at a single glance that we have before us two parallel redac-

tions of the same treatise. Can we discern more lucidly the ties between these two redactions, discover the chronological order according to which they were composed, and interpret their convergencies and divergencies?

Here first of all is how the two texts match up when schematized laterally:

RM 7	RM 10	
criticism of sarabaites:	*first rung: self-will and carnal desires*	
39: Ps 14:1	30: Qo 18:30b	(31: Mt 6:10)
40: Prov 16:25	32: Prov 16:25	
45: *Acta Sebast.* 14	33: Ps 14:1	(34: Ps 38:10)
	35: *Acta Sebast.* 14	(37: Prov 15:3;
46: Qo 18:30ab		Ps 14:2)
	36: Qo 18:30a	(41: Ps 50:21)
encomium of cenobites:	*second rung:*	
51: Jn 6:38	43: Jn 6:38	(*Passio Anastasiae* 17)
	third rung:	
	46: Prov 16:25	
	47: Ps 14:1	(48: 1 Cor 6:12)
		(49: Phil 2:8)
	50: Ps 18:45	
	51: Lk 10:16	
martyr of obedience:	*fourth rung:*	(53: Mt 10:22)
60: Ps 44:22	55: Ps 44:22	(54: Ps 27:14)
61-63: Ps 66:10-12a	57: Ps 66:10-12a	(56: Rom 8:37)
65: Ps 66:12b		(59: Mt 5:39-41;
		2 Cor 11:26;
		1 Cor 4:12)

This table yields the following information:

1. In addition to the citations common to both chapters, RM Ten has an almost equal number of its own citations (indicated within parentheses on the right of the table).

2. Also proper to RM Ten is the third rung, to which nothing

in RM Seven corresponds. Yet four of the texts cited in the third rung do occur elsewhere in RM Seven, the first two in the 'criticism of the sarabaites', and the last two in the description of 'immediate' obedience (RM 7:4-6, 68-69).

3. From the third rung on, if we take account of some inversions in the citations of the first rung, RM Ten follows the same order as RM Seven in citing scriptural texts.

This last fact is particularly remarkable and poses the problem clearly. The Master has patently utilized the same citation material to illustrate the same network of ideas in two apparently very different pericopes: one an exposition of the 'two ways' (sarabaites and cenobites), the other a 'ladder of humility'. One of these two pericopes should represent an effort at original thought, while the other is content with re-using a ready-made series of citations. How can we discern the first redaction from its doublet?

Several indications suggest *the anteriority of RM Seven*. This hypothesis has, it seems, previously furnished us with the most credible explanation for the opening words of the chapter as well as for their contradiction with the 'first rung' of RM Ten. And now note how the two texts cite Qo 18:30. RM 7:46 gives the full, unaltered citation according to the scriptural lection:

a) *Post concupiscentias tuas non eas*
b) *Et a uoluntatibus tuis auertere*

In RM Ten, on the contrary, the two members of the verse are detached and placed at opposite ends of the pericope (RM 10:30, 36). What is more, the first member (a) is cited last, while the second member (b) comes first. This inversion can be explained by the fact that RM Ten, in the pericope we are here considering, successively attacks two kinds of impulsions: 'self-will' and 'desires of the flesh'. Member (b), since it speaks of 'volitions', has been incorporated within the development of 'self-will', and member (a) has been reserved to illustrate the criticism levelled against 'desires', a term closely corresponding to *concupiscentias*. In RM Ten we detect then the mark of an effort at classification exercised on this particular scriptural passage which occurs in its untampered state in RM 7:46.

Furthermore, the artificial character of RM Ten's double development on 'self-will' and 'desires of the flesh' deserves attention. A careful consideration of the 'first rung' in its entirety quickly reveals that it has two heterogeneous and rather poorly knit parts: the first (RM 10:14-28) is allied with RM Eight-Nine, as shown in our first table. Just as in the corresponding enumerations of RM Eight, the order here goes from interior to exterior: *cogitationum, linguae, manuum, peduum;*[21] the theme is that of the divine presence, announced by four formulae which scarcely vary.[22]

The second part of the 'first rung' (RM 10:30-36) is allied on the contrary with RM Seven. It expresses movement towards the interior by treating *uoluntates et desideria* contrarily to the order followed in the first part. Moreover, the redactor could not locate a scriptural citation to illustrate the theme of the divine presence in our wills, and as a result he had to modify the introductory formula in which the words *praesente Domino* witness rather awkwardly to a determination on the Master's part to link this textual segment to the preceding.[23]

Everything leads us to conclude therefore that this second part was joined to the first without any previous intention of doing so. The Master apparently wanted to round out his 'first rung' by a development on 'self-will and desires', the substance of which he found in RM Seven. Utilizing RM Seven, he sought to enrich its scriptural illustration and became engrossed in a work of classification which ended in a distinction between two kinds of spiritual motions: self-will and desires.

This classification brings the development of RM Seven into harmony with the genre of RM Ten, which necessitates the sharpest possible distinctions among the various sectors of man's activity in order to render more impressive the recall to God's presence of each of these faculties. The *uoluntates et desideria* sequence, moreover, was well known to Cassian.[24] Note that it is found again at the 'second rung':

> *si propriam non amans uoluntatem,*
> *desideria sua non delectetur implere* (RM 10:42)

This repetition points once again to the tacked-on character we identified in the 'self-will and desires' development of the first rung. In the redaction as it presently exists, the second rung repeats the first without any perceptible progression, save for the scriptural illustration. It is probable that the second rung originally followed a first rung in which the 'self-will and desires' development did not figure. This would have been added later, thereby depriving of its *raison d'être* the second rung it anticipates.[25] Everything then suggests that the 'first rung' of RM Ten has been rounded out by the tirade against 'self-will' previously vented in the 'criticism of the sarabaites' in RM Seven.

A third indication of the anteriority of RM Seven is furnished by a comparison of RM 7:60-66 with RM 10:55-58. These two texts press into service the same series of *testimonia:* Ps 44:22 + Ps 66:10-12a. RM Seven arranges these two psalm citations in chronological order: *first, in the monastery,* the brethren say to the Lord, 'For your sake we are daily put to death....' (Ps 44:22); *then at the judgment,* they say to the Lord: 'You tested us, God...' (Ps 66:10-12a). Not content with spinning this little story, the Master prolonged it still further by citing Ps 66:12b, which the brethren shall pronounce after the judgment, *in illo iam saeculo:* 'Now the ordeal by fire and water is over, and you allow us once more to draw breath'. This ingenious paraphrase is missing in the corresponding passage of RM Ten. The two psalm citations suc- ceed one another (separated by Rom 8:37) with no connective save a banal *et item in alio loco* (RM 10:57). Nothing recalls the chronological arrangement of RM Seven. Ps 66:12b, which RM Seven puts in the mouths of the blessed *in illo saeculo,* does not even come up.

Which of these two redactions is likely to be more ancient? We would be hard pressed to explain how it could be RM Ten. How could the Master have noted that Ps 44:22 and Ps 66:10-12a, first assembled without regard for chronological order, did in fact in- volve such an order and that this order was even prolonged, as if by magic, by adding vs 12b to the Ps 66 citation? Everything ap- pears, on the contrary, as if the author had carefully assembled these texts for the first time in RM Seven and then reproduced them in the same order in RM Ten, but without remembering or bothering himself with the conductor wire which had bound them together.

In this new and much more summary arrangement, the eschatological perspective created by Ps 66:12b is probably inten- tionally avoided. We are only at the 'fourth rung' of the ladder; we must await the summit of the ascent to discover the *refrigerium.* In the place of this reposeful perspective Rom 8:37, introduced quite naturally by Ps 44:22 (= Rom 8:36), puts in the mouths of the suffering a cry of hope in keeping with their present tribulations.[26]

Several indications exist then for the anteriority of RM Seven to RM Ten. The Master seems to have adapted to his ladder of humility all the citations he had assembled for his chapter on obedience. We must begin from the chapter on obedience to understand the sequence of ideas common to both chapters: criticism of self-will (sarabaites), an encomium of obedience according to the example of Christ (cenobites), martyrdom through obedience.

We should not fail, however, to recognize the probable influence a prior reading of Cassian exercised on the composition of RM Seven. Meditating on *Inst* 4.39, the Master could have conceived the idea of presenting successively a criticism of self-will (cf. first mark), an exposition of obedience (marks 2-3), and a description of the tests of heroic obedience (marks 4-5). This would explain the fact that he was so easily able to make his treatise on obedience coincide with the ladder of humility and could lend to this second treatise its scriptural illustration. This dovetails with the observation we made on the subject of the first sentence of RM Seven, which presupposes that the author already has a 'ladder of humility' in view, and therefore that he has *Inst* 4.39 in mind and draws inspiration from it.

Probably anterior to RM Ten, the RM Seven text ought not necessarily be considered a 'source' in the strict sense of the word for the first rungs of humility. There is no need to imagine the Master as a scrivener laboring over a written document and on the basis of RM Seven elaborating the parallel RM Ten text. Much more likely we are dealing with a *theme of oral preaching set to writing on two different occasions*. In the first instance the Master was freer to develop thoughts familiar to him because the framework of the 'two ways' left him full latitude. In the second instance, he was subject to the constriction of the very exacting framework of the 'twelve rungs', and the redaction became more methodical (distinction between 'self-will' and 'desires') and the meditative attention which bound certain citations together was lost (fourth rung).[27]

Having finished the study of its relations to RM Ten, we ought now to take up from another point of view the examination of this section of RM Seven. If we concede that RM Seven does not depend on RM Ten, but is instead an original composition, a first setting-to-paper, we should ask whether the Master might not have been inspired by exemplars outside his own work and, in particular, to what extent he is here tributary to Cassian.

Of the four *testimonia* invoked in the criticism of the sarabaites (RM 7:38-46), only Prov 16:25 is cited in the works of Cassian, and then in a slightly different form.[28] In *Conf* 20.9.5, it is cited in a context having nothing in common with the Master's,[29] but in *Conf* 1.20.8 it does illustrate a theme almost identical with ours: in his choice of works (of *ascesis*), the monk must not pursue his personal views, which are susceptible to illusion, but adhere to traditional teaching and to the advice of elders. These alone are legitimate interpreters of Scripture in its application to the monastic life. Closer still to RM—because placed in a cenobitic context—is the use of Prov 16:25 in a sermon of Faustus of Riez.[30] The issue in this case concerns a cenobite who lacked docility towards his superiors and threatened to walk out. In this very lifelike portrayal we recognize an abbot who, like the Master, put his monks on guard against their own will with the aid of this text from Proverbs.

The encomium of cenobites (RM 7:47-66) first exploits two scriptural citations, Jn 6:38 (RM 7:51) and Mt 16:24 (RM 7:52), the second being more a kind of reminiscence. In proposing to cenobites the imitation of Christ who said 'I have not come to do my own will, but the will of him who sent me' (Jn 6:38), the Master appropriates a veritable commonplace in monastic literature. Basil, Cassian, Faustus of Riez, the *Historia monachorum*, and the R 4 Pat all vie in using this saying of the Lord.[31] The reading *non ueni* (instead of *descendi de coelo*), common to all these authors and to the Master, vouches for the traditional character of this citation.[32] The use of Mt 16:24 is less clearly attested outside RM. The expression *abnegans uoluntates*, found in Cassian,[33] is an evident allusion to this text, but Cassian cites explicitly only the Lucan parallel, 9:23, with the characteristic addition of the word *quotidie*, and he does so without having the monk's obedience especially in view.[34] The application the Master is making here of Mt 16:24 to the cenobite who renounces his own will (*abnegantes semetipsos*) and obeys God through the abbot (*sequuntur Deum quocumque abbatis praeceptio duxerit*) is therefore relatively original by comparison with Cassian.[35]

In verse 53, after this reminiscence of Mt 16:24, the Master interrupts himself brusquely to interject an extensive parenthesis on the 'security' which the obedient cenobite enjoys (RM 7:53-56). That this really is a parenthesis becomes apparent to us by the resumption in vs 57 of the theme initiated with Mt 16:24: obedience is a 'narrow way' which leads to a true 'martyrdom' for Christ.

This parenthesis of the 'security' of obedience for both soul and body does not lack precedent in Cassian. With him we find the notion that the cenobite is exempt from all material care,[36] and also the notion that direction by an elder provides spiritual security.[37] But still the two themes in Cassian are not mutually related. It was the Master, it seems, who conceived the idea of pairing off the spiritual security of the person directed with the absence of temporal care which the monk under obedience enjoys.

At the same time, RM modifies Cassian's teaching a little. As Cassian sees it, the security of the disciple's soul is insured because the elders are reliable guides, armed with a rule of traditional discernment and, so to speak, infallible. One may therefore be sure that by obeying them one is following a perfectly approved objective norm and is not deluding oneself. The Master, on the contrary, makes the security consist in the real transfer of responsibility. The disciple need no longer answer for his actions; let him but obey and leave to his superior the concern for rendering account for an issued order.[38]

This doctrine pushes to the extreme the principle established by Cassian according to which the disciple must not argue over the example received, but must follow it without personally assessing its worth.[39] But what was with Cassian no more than a counsel of prudence given to some apprentice-hermits becomes in RM the fundamental law of cenobitism. Furthermore, the author of the *Conferences* had not gone so far as to raise the question of the responsiblity assumed by the master of asceticism in the event his instructions are unsound. So RM goes much further than Cassian by professing that the disciple is entirely discharged by the abbot of any responsibility for his actions. At most, such a doctrine is implied in certain examples Cassian gives of obedience to some extravagant orders.[40] Here, as in the teaching on the abbot, the Master deepens with special stringency a factor already present in monastic tradition. The problem of obedience is posed in all its acuity and the solution leaves nothing to be desired in strength and clarity.

If the Master here surpasses Cassian's thought, this does not mean that this doctrine stands isolated from tradition. Basil, to be sure, in principle posited conformity of the order with divine law as the indispensable condition for obeying.[41] But that reservation, which has become classical in the modern theory of obedience,[42] is not generally mentioned by ancient legislators. It called into question the competence of the superior as a master and interpreter of divine law and opened the door to discussion and personal judgment, thereby unsettling the fundamental scheme of cenobitic life by which the subordinate, by the fact that he is a disciple, is by definition not qualified to judge in spiritual matters.

Not only did ancient authors not think of imposing this restriction on obedience, but it sometimes occured to them, as to the Master here, boldly to envisage the case of an order which raises doubts of conscience and to settle the issue with an unconditional affirmation of the duty to obey, *si habet quis in aliquo fidem, et tradit se ei ad subjectionem, non debet attendere in mandatis Dei, sed patri suo spiritali omnem uoluntatem suam committere, quia illi per omnia oboediens, non incurret peccatum apud Deum.*[43] More explicit still is the development St Columban gave this idea:[44] the security of the obedient monk is complete because there is a transfer of his responsibility to the one who is the guide, *cui alieni ponderis imponitur moles et totum portat quod suscipit periculum....* Even were the director to abuse his authority, 'the faith of the believer and the labor of the obedient one do not expose themselves to deception, and he who has asked for guidance shall not be deprived of his recompense. If, instead of seeking guidance, he weighs the matter by himself, everything is lost: he has been deceived since he has dared to judge, whereas his duty was to submit himself to judgement. Even if his own judgement were correct, it would still be reckoned evil, since he has erred simply by doing the judging himself. His duty consists solely in obeying; consequently, one is never right in judging'. This categorical declaration squares exactly with RM teaching.

We have had to research the parallels of this doctrine carefully because it occupies a considerable position in the thought of the Master. In this respect, the 'parenthesis' constituted in Chapter Seven by the pericope we have studied ought not to be regarded, in spite of appearances, as a passage of secondary importance. One should re-read the parallel text at the end of the directory for the abbot,[45] where the Master depicts the disciples' defense address at the final judgement: 'When they are called to account for all they have done they will say to the Lord at the judgement that they did everything in obedience by command of the master', *omnia facta sua per oboedientiam a iussione impleta esse magistri.* Without being so explicit, several other RM passages similarly suppose a veritable substitution of the abbot's will for that of his subjects,[46] of his responsibility for theirs.

That parenthesis closed, the Master reverts to the theme of the 'narrow way' and of the *sequela Christi.* That this way leads nowhere but to martyrdom now looms starkly into view. The word itself is uttered in vs 59, *uelut in martyrio patienter.* Except for this preciseness, the passage is identical with the 'fourth rung of humility' in RM Ten. In RM 90:12-59 the theme of martyrdom is profusely developed.

Here the Master depended again on a commonplace of ascetical literature which is notably present in the writings of Cassian. In antiquity the idea that ascetics had taken the place of martyrs won currency. In drawing this parallel between the victims of persecution and the 'peacetime martyrs', ancient writers usually thought of all the harsh observances and the fights against the devil which the latter martyrs had to suffer.[47] Sometimes, however, the martyr theme was applied specifically to the monk's obedience.[48] There are several examples of this representation in Cassian.[49]

The Master was once again following a traditional stream when he likened obedience to martyrdom. More personally his, apparently, is the use of Ps 44:22 and Ps 66:10-12 to illustrate this theme, above all in the careful application it assumes here with a chronological arrangement, the ingeniousness of which we have already pointed out. Of the psalm verses employed by the Master here, only 66:12 is used by Cassian, and even that occurs in a very general context of 'virtues and vices' in which obedience is not particularly envisaged.[50]

Obedience is a martyrdom, for the superior deliberately selects the opposite of what the subject would like, purposely enjoining 'harsh' things on him and 'testing' him pitilessly (RM 7:57-59). Our modern sensibilities revolt so much against this manner of conceiving the exercise of authority that a reminder of its authentically traditional nature will not be futile. Cassian would have the provost 'expressly command the young monk whatever he will have noticed he does not want', and the examples of impossible or absurd commands proffered a little further on illustrate this recommendation.[51] The same idea, sometimes accompanied by the same anecdotal illustration, is repeated often in the literature of ancient monasticism.[52]

With this passage on martyrdom through obedience we have reached the end of the lengthy section of RM Seven which parallels the first four rungs of RM Ten (RM 7:38-66). The end of the chapter (RM 7:67-74) has apparently only a rather loose connection with this section. It brings us back, by means of a method previously implemented in the abbot's directory, to the introduction of the chapter (RM 7:1-9), with which it forms a sort of doublet.

Here, as in Chapter Two, however, the conclusion does not purely and simply revert to the introduction, but enriches it with new elements. If he speaks anew of the qualities which obedience should manifest, his purpose is not only to bar any hesitation,[53] but to spell out other perils to be avoided—fear, indifference, murmuring, back talk. Stress is laid on one quality which sums up all the others: obedience ought to be 'good-hearted', *cum bono animo*. By that is meant an interiorization to the very heart of the disciple. The external act is not enough, the will itself, which only God can see, should be handed over to him with joy. 'God loves a cheerful giver' (2 Cor 9:7). If this fundamental good will is lacking, the material performance of the prescribed act remains without recompense.

This conclusion, then, echoes the beginning of the chapter, but that echo reverberates to depths hitherto unsuspected. The two citations (Lk 10:16 and Ps 18:45), repetitions of the first paragraph, underline the continuity linking the two extremities of the chapter,[54] but a concern for interiorization impels the Master to distinguish between the attitude observed before the superior and the attitude which only God can see. The tone is exigent, no longer enthusiastically descriptive. From the panegyric on the obedient 'perfect' monk, one passes to the consideration not only of external faults, but even of intimate and secret ones which could pervert the action.

Another distinguishing trait of the conclusion is that Cassian did not know such an 'interiorized' problematic, at least as regards obedience. Nowhere is he preoccupied with a possible discord between the external punctuality of obedience and interior murmuring.[55] The Master is no longer in Cassian's company here then. Even the scriptural texts to which he makes allusion Qo 35:10 and 2 Cor 9:7) do not seem to figure in either the *Institutes* or the *Conferences*,[56] any more than does the theme of 'murmuring'.

However, the warning against 'murmuring' in matters of obedience is a leitmotiv of the cenobitic rules.[57] They sometimes go so far as to demand that the monk obey *cum laetitia*, making this quality the requisite condition if the act is to be pleasing to God, *acceptabilis Domino*.[58] But one may suspect that some of those texts depend on one or the other of our two rules.

Having arrived at the end of our analysis of the chapter, let us recapitulate the data it has given us. RM Seven is composed of two series of quite distinct texts: the first, at both extremities of the chapter (vss 1-21 and 67-74), deals with the qualities of obedience, in conformity with the title of the chapter. The second (vss 22-66) is inserted within the first and constitutes an extensive digression which combines the theme of the 'two ways' with the 'categories of monks'. With a criticism of sarabaites-gyrovagues as its point of departure, it exalts by contrast the obedience of the cenobites and closes with an evocation of the 'martyr' of obedience, whose recompense is the celestial 'refreshment'.

This digression, from vs 38 on, follows a course parallel to the chapter on humility, using the same citations to criticize the 'self-will' of bad monks, to define the obedience of cenobites, and lastly to describe their martyrdom (RM 10:30-58). These two parallel pericopes may be considered two redactions of the same orally preached theme. And yet RM Seven does manifest signs of anteriority to RM Ten. In it the spontaneity of an initial draft is more perceptible, whereas the redaction of the chapter on humility reveals a process of reflection and classification required by the framework of the 'twelve rungs'. Moreover, while the text looks like a digression in RM Seven, its insertion in RM Ten has something artificial about it too, as an examination of the structure of the 'first rung' in particular discloses. A third redaction of this discourse on obedience, generally more faithful to RM Seven than to RM Ten, comes at the end of the rule in the form of an admonition to the postulant (RM 90:3-43).

The dissertation on the 'two ways' therefore presents a manifest connection with the first four rungs of RM Ten. The treatise on the qualities of obedience within which it is intercalated cannot be so clearly connected to the chapter on humility. The sole common *testimonia* are Lk 10:16 and Ps 18:45, two texts which figure both at the beginning and at the end of RM Seven and at the third rung of humility. But the treatise on humility does not direct its attention to the 'qualities' of obedience, that is, its outward promptness and the inward 'good will' which ought to accompany it.

The treatise on obedience sees in this virtue, however, the 'first rung of humility'. The Master seems to be referring by these words to the ladder of humility as he had originally conceived it, modeled that is, on Cassian's marks, a series beginning not with 'fear of the Lord' but with obedience to an elder. Here again, RM Seven seems to have been conceived before RM Ten came to be written.

An evaluation of Chapter Seven must still, to be complete, make mention of two important parentheses. The first of these (RM 7:16-19) takes advantage of the repetition of commands (*praeceptiones*) to justify in a parallel manner the repetition of interrogations; these lines do not tie in with the treatise on obedience except very tenuously. They are a pure *excursus* which would be much better situated in the next chapter. The other parenthesis (RM 7:53-56) interrupts the dissertation on the narrow way but, unlike the preceding parenthesis, has an immediate bearing upon the doctrine of obedience and enriches it with some very significant considerations: he who is obedient enjoys the most complete security, both temporal and spiritual, because he has transferred his personal responsibility which will henceforth be borne by his superior.

A schematic table will help the reader find his bearings in the midst of this forest:

Qualities of obedience:	*Parentheses:*	*Necessity of obedience (the two ways):*
1-9: at the first sound (the perfect). 10-21: at the second command (the weak). The command has to be repeated.	16-19: repeated interrogations	
		22-38: criticism of false monks (description). 39-46: criticism of false monks (Scripture). 47-52: encomium of the cenobites (narrow way).
	53-56: security of him who obeys; transfer of responsibility.	
		57-66: the narrow way is a martyrdom; it leads to heaven.
67-74: wholeheartedly, beneath the gaze of God.		

As we see, the dissertation on the Two Ways is wholly and entirely one long digression and is itself interrupted by the parenthesis of vss 47-56. Moreover, the text on the qualities of immediate obedience requires a parenthesis (vss 16-19).

As to the sources of these various paragraphs, we have isolated the probable influence of Cassian and Sulpitius Severus upon the description of immediate obedience (1-9). Cassian's influence is more generally perceptible, either directly or through the medium of anterior texts of RM, such as Chapter One, upon a full set of ideas which form the groundwork of this chapter: obedience comes 'first' in this life of humility which is the monk's. Obedience characterizes cenobites in distinction to sarabaites. It is inspired by the example of Christ (Jn 6:38). It is rendered to God himself. Thanks to it, one may be sure of being undeceived. It is abnegation of self, patience to the point of martyrdom, the narrow way.[59]

Yet even in such developments, in which he is following or siding with Cassian, the Master evinces some originality in the choice of *testimonia* to illustrate these themes. Those brought in to criticize sarabaites are almost all his own,[60] as also are those which refer to the 'martyrdom' of obedience. His terse application of Mt 16:24 to obedience is not lifted from Cassian either. He also made specific and organized the 'narrow way' theme to which Cassian had only quickly and rather vaguely alluded.[61] But the most salient novelty of RM Seven's scriptural illustration is surely the use of Lk 10:16, a text Cassian never employed.

Besides the originality (relative to Cassian at least) of the scriptural citations, some new elements on the plane of ideas merit our attention. First of all, the curious theory of the two forms of obedience, *sine mora* or *cum mora*, attested to neither in Cassian nor in the rest of tradition, seem to have issued entirely from the mind of that teacher and casuist, a mind minute to the point of puerility. We noted too how the parenthesis on transfer of responsibility carried to its ultimate consequences the traditional idea of direction and of the 'security' thereby procured for the obedient monk—consequences never conceived of by Cassian. Finally, by stressing the interior qualities of obedience, the Master became engaged in a distinction between outward and inward, something which had never occurred in the matter of obedience to the author of the *Institutes*.

These are the results to which our personal examination of RM

Seven-Ten has led us, an examination conducted independently of the studies by Vanderhoven and Weber on the same texts. We must now compare our conclusions with theirs.[62]

Hubert Vanderhoven isolates one case of interpolation in RM Seven: the dissertation on the Two Ways interrupts the exposition on the manner of obeying. The exposition flows beautifully if vs 67 is made to follow immediately upon vs 21. Having described the auditory phase of imperfect obedience, the Master passes to the executing phase, according to a plan which had already guided him in the description of perfect obedience. As for the dissertation on the Two Ways, its interpolative nature is discernible not only by the fact that it does not correspond to the title of the chapter and, as we just remarked, disrupts the continuity of the text on the manner of obeying, but also by the fact that it is put together with excerpts from other RM passages (Prologue, Chapter One, Ten, Ninety). The rule would have had to have been composed before this dissertation was written and then intercalated in Chapter Seven. Finally, Vanderhoven proposes that the first sentence be understood in this sense: obedience *sine mora* is the 'highest pinnacle' of humility. *Gradus* here would mean 'grade', post of honor, as in RM Ninety-Two through Ninety-Four. No allusion to the 'rungs of humility' in RM Ten would be intended and the problem of conciliating the first sentence of RM Seven with the theory of RM Ten would be completely dispelled.

This last suggestion certainly has the merit of putting the first sentence of the chapter in perfect accord with what immediately follows. As Vanderhoven emphasizes, there is no evocation of the mystical ladder in this opening part of the treatise on obedience. Obedience *sine mora* is hailed as a mark of perfection, and it is difficult to imagine it as a virtuous activity of beginners or of those advancing.

Vanderhoven's interpretation runs aground, however, on several solid objections. First, it would be extraordinary that, with no proof of different authorship, two adjacent texts should employ the same expression (*primus humilitatis gradus*) in two diametrically opposed senses: the height of humility, the first step of humility. RM Seven and RM Ten ought really to agree on the meaning of these words, and there is little likelihood that the two chapters do not envisage one and the same 'ladder of humility', whose arrangement alone varies from place to place. Besides, if the 'lowest' step of the ladder is in fact at issue in RM Seven and RM Ten, such an interpretation would imply no contradiction with the 'perfection' imputed to those who obey *sine mora.* In RM Seven, the fact that obedience is set at the 'first rung' does not imply that this virtue is in anyway inferior. The idea is not that obedience should be the ABC of humility, an elementary manifestation of humility, within reach of the less perfect, but rather that it imposes itself from the outset on anyone who wants to be humble and that it constitutes the 'primordial' step of *ascesis.*

Gradus, then, does indeed have the sense of 'rung' (and not of 'grade'), but *primus* signifies both 'first in time'[63] and 'fundamental' from a pedagogical standpoint.[64] This concept of the 'primacy' of obedience in cenobitic formation is proper to the whole tradition, as we saw earlier.[65] This is what the Master was thinking of here, not of a distinction between the obedience *sine mora* of the perfect and the tardy obedience of the negligent. In other words, the Master's exordium serves two clearly distinct purposes: an affirmation of traditional character on the initial place and primordial role of obedience in the monk's education (according to the tradition, such obedience can only be *sine mora*), and then an entirely personal remark on the small number of those capable of it, a remark which augurs the indulgent considerations of vss 10-21. The study of the sources is a solid guarantee for us in this matter. While the description of immediate obedience is a commonplace, the Master finds himself alone in devising a theory of obedience 'for the weak'.

The two themes should therefore receive separate consideration. After the general affirmation setting forth the classical doctrine, the author advances an observation born of personal experience (*sed haec forma paucis conuenit et perfectis*) before resuming the conventional encomium of immediate obedience. The *sed* introducing this observation shows clearly enough that the author is not following the line of thought he had just been pursuing. The declaration of the 'first rung of humility' which immediate obedience constitutes ought not therefore to be seen in relationship to the idea that this form of obedience is inaccessible save to a small number. Each of these assertions has its own individual worth and demands being understood in its own right. Had the Master wanted to prolong the first by the second, he would not have set them in opposition with a *sed,* but would rather have joined them with an *enim.*[66]

Let us proceed to another assertion of Vanderhoven. The final part of the chapter, he says, ties in perfectly, except for the dissertation on the Two Ways with its description of imperfect obedience. In other words, the Master in vss 10-21 is describing the phase of hearing the order, and he follows up in vss 67-74 with a description of the executing phase. We fully agree with this analysis insofar as it marks the continuity of the two parts interrupted by the digression on the Two Ways. But, for our part, we have not been able to discover so rigorous a sequence between 10-21 and 67-74. The distinction between the two phases of the act—perception and execution—cannot serve as a transition between the two paragraphs, for in 10-21 the order has not simply been heard but has been put into execution, although with a delay.

Then too, the final paragraph is not content with merely demanding promptness in the execution of the act (*non tarde*), nor even with proscribing certain visible failings which correspond to the executor's imperfection, but introduces a new consideration, the gaze of God and the joyous good will which the obedient person should cultivate to the very depths of his heart. Here we have a development that may have been occasioned by an anxiety for the 'imperfect', but which renews the whole mass of previously expounded doctrine, including the initial description of obedience *sine mora*. The interpretation of Vanderhoven would need to be qualified since, according to him, this last paragraph did not at all envisage the 'perfect' spoken of at the beginning of the chapter. The truth is (granting that mention of them does pertain to the first redaction itself), the 'perfect' are not excluded from this exhortation to obey not only punctually, *in uelocitate timoris Dei,* but with a full and generous heart, *cum bono animo,* and without the slightest interior murmuring.

Although the sequence of ideas in these texts on the qualities of obedience appears to us a little less clear than it did to Vanderhoven, however, our results diverge from his especially over the digression on the Two Ways. For him, this dissertation is no more than a restatement of preceding or subsequent material; it could not therefore have been written until after the whole of RM had been completed. For us, on the contrary, a comparison with RM Ten suggests the anteriority of RM Seven.

We are glad to have discovered in a study by Robert Weber, subsequent to Vanderhoven's, a confirmation of our views on the relationship between RM Seven and Ten.[67] Weber bases himself not only on Qo 18:30, as we have done, but also on the citation of the *Acta S. Sebastiani,* which is notably more faithful and more complete in RM Seven, arguing the anteriority of this chapter to that on humility. Weber's remark is all the more interesting in that it obliges him to conclude that RB, which possesses this series of citations only in its later form (RB Seven = RM Ten), reveals itself in this respect as a document more recent than RM. In any case, Weber's arguments, allied with ours, solidly establish that the 'interpolation' of RM 7:22-66 contains the series of citations common to it and to RM Ten in their first state, the authorship of which cannot possibly be attributed to a later interpolator.

Vanderhoven also thinks that the series constituted by Ps 44:22 + Ps 66:10-12 is, in the 'interpolation' of RM Seven, a restatement of RM 90:33-43. Earlier we pointed out in passing the parallel between RM Seven and RM Ninety, without at that time examining the relationship between the two texts. Vanderhoven's assertion of the posterior nature of RM Seven has obliged us to conduct this examination. We have in fact arrived at the contrary conclusion: RM Ninety must have been written after RM Seven. Distinctly more developed, careful to relate the *testimonia* to one another and to cite them with elegance in an uninterrupted paraphrase which avoids excessively obvious sutures or reduces them to a minimum, the discourse of RM Ninety turns out at the same time to be less well-ordered than RM Seven. The disorder clearly appears in just the Ps 44:22 + Ps 66:10-12 series. Traces of the chronological arrangement to which we devoted attention in RM Seven are in fact present again in RM Ninety:

RM 90	RM 7
29: *In schola monasterii*	60: *in monasterio*
30: *Judicio*	61: *in iudicio*
41: *In illo iam saeculo*	62: *in illo iam saeculo*

But the present tense in Ps 44:22 (*morti adficimur*) is infelicitously placed in the mouths of the judged, whereas RM Seven attributes it, not unreasonably, to those suffering here below. Furthermore, RM Ninety follows up the Ps 44:22 citation with two earlier verses of the same psalm (Ps 44:18-19), all the verbs of which are in the same tense. The author is obviously no longer conscious of the precise connection of the texts cited with the three phases of human destiny which they had served to illustrate in RM Seven. The chronological indications themselves lack distinctness (*iudicio,* without a preposition, does not stand in clear parallel with the other two terms preceded by *in; in scola monasterii* does not present the assonance common in *o*). Above all, the last two are separated by an immense interval which causes their relationship to be forgotten.[68]

There seems no doubt then that RM Seven represents the original form of the common text. The 'interpolation' of RM Seven thus reveals itself for a second time as more primitive than a text thought to be its source.

It is surprising that neither Vanderhoven nor Weber pursued to its end the confrontation of RM Seven with RM Ten and Ninety. Parallelism between RM Seven and Ten is not limited in effect to the series of *testimonia* of the 'first rung', as their comparative tables would lead one to believe, but is extended throughout the second and fourth rungs, as we indicated. Then, too, RM Ninety does not reproduce only Vanderhoven's series B (Ps 44:22 + Ps 66:10-12), but also presents texts cited in the remainder of RM Seven and Ten:

RM 90:7 : Prov 16:25	(RM 7:40; 10:32, 46)
RM 90:10 : Mt 16:24	(RM 7:52)
RM 90:13 : Rom 8:18	(RM 10:92)
RM 90:49 : Mt 6:10	(RM 10:31)

This cluster of parallels permits us to affirm that RM 90:3-59 is entirely an echo of Chapters Seven and Ten. More precisely, the same basic outline underlies the three texts: criticism of self-will and praise of obedience conceived as martyrdom. From the standpoint of composition, Seven and Ten pursue more strictly parallel tracks, while Ninety lacks rigor and mixes different parts, besides inserting an extensive and highly imaginative development comparing the sufferings of martyrdom to eternal delights (90:13-28). From the literal standpoint, Seven and Ninety share more points of contact between themselves than they do with Ten. Finally, each of the three texts has a framework of its own: a description of two categories of monks, combined with the two ways, in Chapter Seven; the first four rungs of humility in Ten; the discourse of an abbot to a postulant in Ninety.

As for interdependence among the three texts, there is no doubt that Seven cannot be considered a 'crude restatement' or a 'plagiarism' of the other two. On the contrary, everything suggests that the chapter on obedience contains the original redaction, the first setting-to-paper. We would be inclined to regard RM Seven as the common source for Ten and Ninety, because these two chapters present two common citations (Rom 8:18 and Mt 6:10) not found in Seven.

Rather than speak in terms of dependence, would we not be more correct to regard these three passages as successive states of the same orally preached theme? There is no need for recourse to the hypothesis of several authors composing from written documents. Chains of *testimonia,* today as much as in antiquity, repeat themselves every time a speaker returns to a favourite subject. We have here three redactions of the same discourse, diversified by the literary framework within which they are inserted. In all likelihood the same person composed all three of them, taking his start from the general outline of the same homily or conference. As happens with anyone who is repeating himself, certain variants entered from one redaction to the next. In particular, the chronological arrangement of Pss 44 and 66, vividly present to the mind of the conference speaker as he wrote the treatise on obedience, lost much of its sharpness in Ninety and was totally effaced in Ten. In the hypothesis we are advancing, an attempt at 'dating' any of these diverse redactions by relation to the others would be futile. All we can affirm is that the arrangement of Pss 44 and 66 is presented in Seven in its original and perfect form, while Ten and Ninety constitute less perfect reiterations or degradations of it, whatever the time of their respective redactions. In the same way, the author possessed a keener recollection of the *Acta Sebastiani* text when he composed Seven than when he wrote Ten. As for Qo 18:30, this verse in Seven has preserved its rough tenor, whereas Ten subjected it to an accomodation which put it out of joint.

In conclusion, not without some hesitation would we acknowledge the term 'interpolation', used by Vanderhoven to characterize the dissertation on the Two Ways. There is no doubt that this pericope was inserted at a later date into the text on the qualities of obedience, which alone conforms to the chapter title. But we see no decisive reason—not even the argument based on vocabulary[69]—to compel us to attribute this 'interpolation' to a writer distinct from the author of the text within which it stands. A reworking by this same author is not improbable inasmuch as the issue is a homiletic theme which reappears in RM Ninety, and is also introduced (not without difficulty) in RM Ten.[70] The digression of vss 16-19, missing in E, is more suspect of interpolation. The parenthesis on the 'security' of obedience should also be classed among the interpolations or reworkings. These three digressions nevertheless offer so many points of contact with other RM passages that only a study of the whole of the various strata of the texts of the rule would permit us to make a pronouncement on their true nature. We believe such an inquiry would swiftly disclose that many of the suspect texts bear too close an affinity with 'primitive' texts to necessitate ascribing them to different authors. Then too, one would have to reckon with the stylistic habits which the most certainly authentic passages betray. Repetitions, reworkings and digressions all play a part in the author's characteristic style, and these traits of his literary personality may indeed explain the anomalies which led to the charge of 'interpolations' in RM.

Turning our attention now to what RB has done with this treatise on obedience, we note first of all that it retains RM elements pertaining both to the dissertation on the Two Ways and to the exposition *De oboedientia qualis debeat esse*. The plan of RB Five, in relation to RM, is this:

RB 5:1-9:   description of immediate obedience (RM 7:1-9).
RB 5:10-13: cenobites on the narrow way (RM 7:47-51).
RB 5:14-19: the obedience which is pleasing to God, that which
             is performed wholeheartedly (RM 7:67-74).

The RB redactor, then, had certainly read the digression on the Two Ways in his source. But this revision left no trace of the theory of a kind of obedience for the 'weak' (RM 7:10-21) presented by the Master in his second sentence (RM 7:2). It is impossible to affirm whether this theory did not yet figure in RM or whether the RB writer knew and deliberately omitted it. In the second alternative, we would have to credit him with a very steady perspicacity, for the deleted passage is original to the Master, without any parallel in the tradition. Our reviser was perhaps guided in his selection of pericopes to be suppressed by such instinct for tradition, at any rate, in the same way he deleted analogous considerations based on the same distinction between 'the perfect' and 'the imperfect' in RM 9:46-50.

But RB 6:3 seems surely to bear a trace of such a distinction: *perfectis discipulis* is, to all appearances, a reference to it (cf. RM 8:33). Judging by this indication, one would be inclined to believe that the theory distinguishing two modes of practising obedience and silence already existed in the rule of the Master when these RB chapters were composed and that RB purposely abolished the distinction, retaining the traditional 'thesis' and rejecting the 'hypothesis' born of the personal pedagogical experience of the Master.

We attach no great importance to the slight addition of RB
5:11b,[71] nor to the two phrases which appear more simply expressed than in RM.[72] However this last fact is interpreted, the
more concise redaction of RB certainly retains the essence of the
Master's thought in both instances. Neither need we bemoan the
loss of Ps 18:45 in RB 5:15. Inseparable companion of Lk 10:16 in
RM,[73] this *obauditu auris oboediuit mihi* has fortunately been
preserved at the beginning of the chapter (RB 5:5).

Of greater significance is the RB 5:19 addition which serves to
conclude the new redaction: *immo poenam murmurantium in-
currit si non cum satisfactione emendauerit.* This formula *si non
emendauerit* is repeated no less than seven times in parts peculiar
to RB.[74] *Satisfactio* and *satisfacere* are also very frequent in this
rule,[75] which multiplied cases of 'satisfaction' theretofore rather
rare in RM.[76] Considering the vocabulary of both rules, this addition indubitably constitutes a juridical 'final sanction' such as one
often finds at the end of legislative prescripts.

This tone, taken over from the style of penitential codes, sounds
odd in a chapter of pure spirituality. The RB writer was certainly
thinking here of the disciplinary measure of smiting 'murmurers'[77]
and not of the judgment God levies on this sort of fault.[78] He let
himself get so carried away that he introduced a disciplinary
remark where the issue had been uniquely the qualities of obedience envisaged from a spiritual standpoint. By doing so he imitated, without perhaps realizing it, the Master's inclination for
inserting penal threats into his treatise on spirituality.[79] This
disparate note need cause no dismay, but it comes very inopportunely at the end of a paragraph which had just been striving to
emphasize the interior aspect of the virtue of obedience, the
qualities it ought to present not only to the eyes of men, but in the
eyes of God himself, who sees in secret. The drift towards interiorization is unfortunately reversed by this final note, which
redirects attention to the visible act and its social consequences.

Apart from this last phrase, the RB revision was quite skillfully
executed. Only a few lines describing the obedience of the
cenobite have been retained from the dissertation on the Two
Ways. This passage is well joined with the first development on
immediate obedience. As regards its conjunction with the final
pericope on wholehearted obedience, it comes off as less *gauche*
than the corresponding RM 7:67 juncture. Thus, from beginning to end in RB Five, the only issue is the obedience of the
cenobite—presented without any concessions as an exigent ideal.

What remains of the dissertation on the Two Ways retains its fundamental theme. Several omitted elements will reappear in the chapter on humility: condemnation of self-will at the first rung, the martyr theme (minus the term itself, which is a pity) at the fourth rung. Possibly the writer was prompted to skip over these passages because he foresaw that Chapter Seven (RM Ten) would furnish him their equivalent.

Lost for good, however, is the important parenthesis on the security enjoyed by the obedient, the result of the transfer of his responsibility to the abbot (RM 7:53-56). This suppression might well be due to the same fixed purpose which had caused the suppression of vs 35 of the Master's abbatial treatise in both E and RB. In both these suppressed passages, the Master propounds the same doctrine: the abbot alone is responsible for everything done at his command; the brethren unload on him all responsibility. Our redactor must have recoiled in the face of such ruthless logic, which draws extreme consequences from the principle of spiritual direction. To condemn self-will is one thing, to preach a veritable substitution of the will and the responsibility of the Master for that of the disciple is another. As we stated previously, RM is here more in Columban's company than in Cassian's. The RB redactor might have felt himself in harmony with the better tradition by laying aside such corollaries of the classic doctrine. Here as in the suppression of the verses on imperfect obedience, the abridger's 'blue pencil' caused the more personal views of the Master to be deleted.

Given the close ties linking the treatise on obedience to that on humility, we would lack a complete idea of the obedience theme in this RM overture if we failed to trace a rapid history of the RM Ten (= RB Seven) process of composition, starting from Cassian. The task will be easy since a comparative table of 'marks' and 'rungs' has already been devised.[80] We need only revert to that table and draw new conclusions. At the same time, we must keep before our eyes the following table[81] in which we have listed the passages from Cassian and RM Seven-Nine which correspond to the sequence of 'rungs'. Everything we have to say about the ladder of humility is already contained in those two schemata.

The first indication, in *Inst* 4.39, emerges as the Master's second rung already anticipated by the last paragraphs of the first rung:

Primo si mortificatas in sese omnes habeat uoluntates	*Secundum... si propriam non amans uoluntatem desideria sua non delectetur implere....*

The Master enlarges upon the lesson of Cassian. *Propria uoluntas* is hardly typical of Cassian's vocabulary, but was current among ascetic authors, notably in the *Regula Basilii.*[82] *Desideria* forms a couplet with *uoluntas* even in Cassian.[83] So the second rung is no more than a slightly more developed rendering of the first mark. Scriptural illustration is gleaned from the 'encomium of cenobites' in RM Seven (Jn 6:38), and rounded off by a citation from the *Passio Anastasiae* 17.[84]

The second mark has suffered important modifications, however. Note first how it has been wrested from its primitive position and inserted after the fourth rung. Its tenor, too, has undergone a significant change:

Secundo si non solum suorum actuum, uerum etiam *cogitationum nihil suum celauerit* seniorem.	Quintum... si omnes *cogitationes* malas cordi suo aduenientes uel mala a se absconse conmissa per humilem linguae confessionem abbatem *non celauerit suum....*

Whereas Cassian had stressed the all-encompassing scope of the confession, which should embrace 'not only actions, but also thoughts', the Master suppressed this gradation. He goes at once to 'thoughts' and only afterwards mentions actions (*conmissa*). This inversion suppresses the effect sought by Cassian, who had wanted to focus attention on the depth of the avowal by proceding from the exterior to the intimate. But the Master introduced an altogether new note: it is *evil* thoughts which are to be confessed, and likewise the *evil* actions committed in secret.[85]

The addition *per humilem linguae confessionem* evidently corresponds to the insistence on the word *mala(s)*. In this addition the chief word is the adjective; this rung pertains to humility by a special right which the Master wanted to emphasize and which had not yet been indicated in Cassian. Cassian had made his second mark a preparation for the third: after the manifestation of the disciple's conscience follows the direction of conscience by the elder. Having revealed his thoughts, the one being directed would take to heart, with total docility, the judgment passed upon them by his director. So the second mark described just one phase of spiritual direction. It concerns one aspect of the renunciation of

self-will. One keeps the perspective of obedience which is opened
by the first indication and extends to the sixth. The Master, on the
contrary, wanted to make confession an act specially stamped by
'humility'. This explains why he presents it as an avowal of *evil*
thoughts and *evil* actions. This is also the reason why this rung
does not figure in its original place. Instead of falling, as in Cassian, into line within a series of acts relevant to the virtue of *obe-*
dience, and through the medium of that virtue to the virtue of
humility, the confession is set within a different series which
causes humility itself to be raised into direct and immediate relief.
Two more rungs then follow which even in Cassian are presented
as manifestations *par excellence* of *humility:* to reckon oneself an
evil laborer, to proclaim and to believe oneself least of all.... Thus
the Master withdrew the second mark from the 'obedience' series
in order to set it in the 'humility' series.

Two verbal ties underline the relationship he wanted to
establish between the fifth and seventh rungs: the 'tongue', spoken
of at the fifth rung, together with thoughts and actions not only
forms a triad familiar to the Master,[86] it prepares as well the
gradation for the seventh rung: *non solum sua lingua pronuntiet*
sed etiam intimo cordis credat affectu, a text in which our author
no doubt purposely substituted the word *lingua* for the
corresponding expression in Cassian (*superficie labiorum*). In that
way, the fifth rung heralds the seventh. For already at the fifth
rung, 'confession with the tongue' is a proclmation of one's 'in-
feriority to everyone', since it bears especially upon evil actions
and evil thoughts. That is not enough: to the avowal of the tongue
should be joined conviction of the heart.

The other characteristic term is *humilem,* used again in
humilians se, which patently underscores the purpose of the RM
composer. He conceives these fifth and seventh rungs as special
steps of humility. Cassian had carefully avoided pronouncing this
word in his marks, and for good reason: to speak of humility in
order to define the marks of humility would verge upon tautology.
The Master did not notice this awkwardness because his
methodical mind had engineered a classification of the marks
based on a new division all his own: the first four were to be rungs
of obedience, the next three rungs of humility.

But this arrangement itself could well have had its origin in the
necessity the Master found for assigning a new place and meaning
to this 'second mark' which, remember, did not play a part in the

outline of the obedience discourse our author followed for the first four rungs. In fact, nothing in the two parallel redactions of that discourse (RM Seven and RM Ninety) corresponds to the second mark of Cassian. The Master was therefore obliged to relegate it to a position after the conclusion of the discourse (fourth rung) and come up with a new meaning for it.

As a result of such accommodation, RM has deprived us of a capital element of the doctrine on obedience as Cassian had developed it. Instead of a 'second mark' on the manifestations of conscience preliminary to direction, we have a 'fifth rung' related to the humble confession of mistakes and evil thoughts. Cassian's intention has been subjected to major alteration. To refer back to *Inst* 4.9 is enough to realize the extent of the loss caused by the Master's recension: such manifestation had formed for Cassian a unity with the direction given by an elder. Of this capital doctrine, the Master has kept for us only an impoverished and disfigured reflection, an exercise of humility which consists in testifying to one's own wickedness. Where is the judgment of the elder declaring this particular thought to be good or that one bad, exposing the snare of the devil and by such judgment granting liberation to the disciple's tempted conscience? The picture of the relationship between director and directed depicted so carefully by Cassian in *Inst* 4.9, reproduced in miniature in marks 2 and 3, and representative of the fundamental monk-abbot relationship, has by the Master been sundered and smeared with new colors until it is unrecognizable.

When he speaks again of the manifestation of conscience in Chapter Fifteen, his perspective is still so narrow that it restricts considerably Cassian's teaching. There, also, only 'evil thoughts' are at issue. The tempted brother is supposed to perceive them by himself and to expose them to his superiors only to obtain healing from them. Useful as that may be, such therapy through prayer and Scripture reading is something less extensive than the direction of conscience described by Cassian in *Inst* 4.9 and in marks 2 and 3.

We can trace to the third rung the alteration performed by the Master on his source. We shall not probe in detail the problems posed by this difficult text.[87] Limiting ourselves to the probably overworked form which it dons in P, we may at least note in the first part of the sentence the words *si nihil suo iudicio,* which could be a carry-over from the third mark:

Tertio *si nihil suae* discretioni sed *iudicio* eius uniuersa committat, ac monita eius sitiens ac libenter auscultet.	Tertium... *si* postquam *nihil suo iudicio* praesumens eligat... omni oboedientia se subdat maiori.

Apart from the extreme awkwardness of *postquam,* which transforms a simple negative explanatory element into a preliminary introductory clause, we should note the deletion of *discretioni,* a term highly characteristic of Cassian's vocabulary of direction.[88] The Master kept on effacing traces of that doctrine. Nothing more in his writing calls to mind the examination made by the director to discern good from bad in the thoughts his disciple submits to him. Emphasis falls instead on 'submission' and 'obedience'. Noteworthy, too, is the disappearance of the final colon of Cassian's sentence, where the cenobite's spontaneity in seeking the elder's counsel had been stressed. Instead of calling for a colloquy between master and disciple, RM limits itself to noting dryly the 'two moments' of perfect obedience: to decide nothing by oneself, and to submit oneself completely to a superior.

The same characteristic word, 'to obey', punctuates the series of citations which illustrate the rung: *oboediens* (vs. 49)... *oboedientia... abaudiuit... obaudire... audit.* In Cassian the issue was indeed one of obedience, but the word itself was not yet pronounced, and stress was laid instead on the intimate and confidential relationship between the brother and his 'elder' in the act of direction: complete opening of soul, full surrender (*uniuersa committat*) of conscience into the hands of the director who would 'discern' and judge, and the earnest reception of his advice. This picture of spiritual direction does not survive in RM. The Master preferred to revert once again to his favorite doctrine of renunciation of personal judgment and obedience to 'our teachers', as in Chapters One and Seven, based on the decisive Lk 10:16 text.

Yet he enriched his collection of *testimonia* on obedience by citing this time in first place Phil 2:8, a quotation he found already used by Basil and Cassian for this purpose.[89] This is indeed the text found at the heart of the third rung, just as was Jn 6:38 in the preceding rung. Both these verses are prefixed by an introduction which exhorts the disciple 'to imitate the Lord'. Both seem to have influenced the redaction of the corresponding rung. Starting probably from these two 'examples of the Lord', the Master fabricated the second and third rungs in the precise form usual with him, unlike that of Cassian's marks 1 and 3. Note that Phil

2:8 and Jn 6:38, thus drawn into association by RM, were previously united in one of the great texts of Cassian on cenobitic obedience.[90]

The fourth rung combines Cassian's fourth and fifth marks. This amalgamation deserves more attention as the Master's general tendency in this chapter is to lengthen rather than to shorten the enumeration of his sources; there are twelve rungs in place of ten marks. Moreover, the fourth rung has a length disproportionate to the others, except the first. This is no doubt because the Master had brought together in a single rung two originally distinct developments, each of which had its origin in one of Cassian's marks. In fact, if we examine the RM text attentively, we are led to believe that it is composed of two developments on the fourth and fifth marks; between them is inserted the scriptural series on the martyrdom of obedience (Ps 44:22 + Ps 66:10-12) taken from the great discourse of RM Seven and Ninety.

Quarto *si in* omnibus seruet *oboedientiae* mansuetudinem *patientiaeque constantiam.*	1) vss. 52-53: Quartum... *si in* ipsa *oboedientia* duris et contrariis rebus uel etiam quibuslibet *inrogatis iniuriis* tacite *patientiae constantiam* amplectatur et sustinens non lassescat uel discedat dicente scriptura... (Mt 24:13; Ps 26:14).
	2) vss. 54-58: (Ps 44:22; Ps 66:10-12).
Quinto si non solum *iniuriam* inferat nulli sed ne ab alio quidem sibimet *inrogatam* doleat atque tristetur.	3) vss. 59-60: Sed et praeceptum Domini in aduersis et *iniuriis* per *patientiam* adinplentes... (Mt 5:39-41; 2 Cor 11:26; 1 Cor 4:12).

This table at first sight occasions the objection that expressions typical of the fifth mark of Cassian already exist in the

Master's first paragraph (*inrogatis iniuriis*), and in a form more complete than the simple *iniuriis* of the third paragraph. Then, too, *patientia,* deriving from the fourth mark, recurs in the final paragraph of RM. These facts surely compel us to acknowledge that some interference occurred between the two developments at some point in the redaction. Note nevertheless that the scriptural illustration of the first development (Mt 24:13; Ps 26:14) is strongly oriented towards the idea of 'constancy',[91] whereas that of the second develops the theme of non-resistance to 'injuries'.[92] So the choice of *testimonia* in these two passages does not seem to have been inspired by the corresponding marks in Cassian. In addition, observe that the Master's second development like the fifth mark to which it is related, cannot be envisaging the relationship between the monk and his superior. Only the fourth mark and the Master's development on it match the situation of an obedient monk, as is underscored, moreover, by the word *oboedientia* in both Cassian and the Master. In the series of *testimonia* of the second development, on the contrary, the issue is one of 'false brethren' and 'maledictions', which can hardly be understood as applying to the superior. The situation is evidently that of the just man unjustly persecuted, so this text could not originally have been meant to represent a cenobite suffering tests of obedience. And yet the word obedience is not even uttered.

Thus the fourth rung is an amalgam of the two marks of Cassian, one concerning 'constancy' in obedience, the other endurance of 'injuries', no matter who may inflict them. In other words, the fourth mark regards the relations of the monk with his superiors, the more general fifth mark, his relations with all the brethren. The concept of long-suffering common to both of them prompted the Master to amalgamate them, but by so doing he put everything under the standard of obedience, even his development on the fifth mark. In that way he managed to incorporate the series of 'rungs of obedience' within the ladder of humility; these rungs 1-4 are immediately followed by the series of 'rungs of humility' (5-7).

Painstaking realization of this arrangement could have influenced the fusion of marks 4 and 5. With its predecessor mark five formed an intermediate group on long-suffering, but this grouping was at the same time connected to the first four marks by the *oboedientiae* reference on the fourth mark. The Master chose to capitalize upon this latter possibility and made his fourth rung the conclusion and diadem of the 'obedience' series through the assimilation of Cassian's fifth mark within this encomium of long-suffering.

Another factor which may have contributed to such a fusion is the scant interest the Master had in fraternal relationships. The disappearance of the fifth mark corresponds to the infrequency of RM testimony on this subject.[93]

Finally, we must reckon with the necessity of arriving at the number twelve, despite the addition of two rungs unknown to Cassian (the first and twelfth) and the bifurcation of the ninth mark.

The final obstacle yet to be smoothed over in our road is the Master's treatment of Cassian's sixth mark. This indication, which had preceded the two special marks of humility (*omnia uilitate... cunctis inferiorem*) is now relocated after them as rung eight, immediately before the rungs of silence. It has moreover undergone significant modification at the Master's hand.

Displacement of the sixth mark can be explained by the fact that indication 2, excised from the 'obedience' series, was still left out. The Master wanted to reinstate it as soon as possible and did so by transforming this mark of obedience into a rung of humility, as we saw above, making it first in the series formed by rungs 5-8. But the insertion of mark 2 as the fifth rung forced mark 6 out of its primitive place. So the Master simply transferred 6 to the end of the 'humility' series, which happened to be the first vacant spot.

Let us now examine its tenor:

Sexto *si nihil agat,* nihil praesumat, quod non uel *communis regula uel maiorum cohortantur exempla.*

Octauum... *si nihil agat* nisi *quod communis* monasterii (om. E) *regula uel maiorum cohortantur exempla,* dicens cum scriptura quia lex tua meditatio mea est (Ps 119:77),et cum interrogat patrem suum adnuntiabit ei, seniores suos et dicent ei (Deut 32:7), id est per suam doctrinam abbas.

The first striking fact is the *monasterii* addition, at least in P and followed by RB. We are dealing for sure with a modification of Cassian's thought. Cassian was not in fact thinking just about 'the rule of the monastery', but more generally of 'the accepted usage among monks', as the parallel passage of *Inst* 11.19 shows: *Quid-*

quid etiam in conuersatione fratrum minime communis usus recipit uel exercet, omni studio ut iactantiae deditum declinemus. This *usus communis* is the exact equivalent of *regula communis* in the sixth mark. Elsewhere Cassian speaks of a *catholica regula* or *monasteriorum regula,* that is, a traditional discipline observed in all the *coenobia* of Egypt which ought to be imposed in like fashion on all occidental monasteries. To swerve from that traditional norm—by attracting notoriety for some peculiarity of clothing such as the hairshirt, for example—would be to expose oneself to *elationis uanitas,*[94] a term synonymous to the *iactantia* spoken of in *Inst* 11.19.

We see then Cassian's thought in this sixth indication. He was thinking of respect for the tradition and usages accepted in *all* monasteries. This conformist attitude seems also to him a proof of humility. One does not wish to make a show of oneself, therefore ostentatious singularity is shunned. The sixth mark is thus a 'mark of humility' for a special reason: it is opposed to vainglory or vanity. Note finally that in this traditionalist context the *maiores* are the 'elders' of past generations, the great forefathers, as well as the 'superiors' of the present, to the extent that the two senses tend to meet.[95]

By adding the word *monasterii,* RM has specified and restricted Cassian's teaching. This time *the* rule of *the* monastery, that is, of RM itself, is at issue. As for the *maiores,* the further addition *per suam doctrinam abbas* shows that the abbot is meant. This precision tends, like the preceding, to limit Cassian's teaching, to confine it to the particular horizons of the community for which RM was composed. We pass from the general notion of monastic tradition to the authority of *one particular* rule prevailing in *one particular* monastery governed by *one particular* abbot. In the words *suam doctrinam* we have little difficulty recognizing the theory of the abbot-teacher.

By limiting the sixth mark in this fashion, the Master compromised to some extent the arrangement originally binding it to the marks or rungs 'of humility'. Whereas Cassian's sixth mark is especially a matter of humility because especially opposed to vainglory (hence its place ahead of marks 7 and 8), the eighth rung of the Master maintains a tighter bond with the rungs of obedience (1-4) which it irresistably evokes when it speaks of the rule of the monastery and the doctrine of the abbot. E has perhaps preserved for us a primitive state of the text in which *monasterii* had not yet been inserted and in which, consequently, the physiognomy of Cassian's mark, impressed especially by 'humility', was better preserved. Yet the possibility that this word was suppressed by the E copyist cannot be excluded. He might have emended his text in order to make it consistent with that of Cassian which he knew well.[96]

Be that as it may, the eighth rung of the Master singularly recalls the definition of cenobitism given by RM One, *monasteriale, militans sub regula uel abbate.*

The scriptural illustration in its turn underscores this 'rule and abbot' couplet. The Ps 119:77 citation likens the rule to the law of God, while Deut 32:7 introduces the addition on the abbot-teacher. This last text merits special attention. Cassian had previously cited it (*Conf* 2.15), but the commentary he gave it accents *seniores* and not *patrem: doctrinam seniorum uel instituta,* he wrote. The Master comments upon the text in almost identical terms, but it is the abbot, evoked by *patrem suum* in the singular, which holds his attention: *per suam doctrinam abbas.* This comparison confirms the theory we advanced above on the alteration of meaning effected by RM at this rung.[97]

By reassembling the observations made in the course of our comparative analysis of RM Ten and *Inst* 4.39, we arrive at the following summary:

The marks of Cassian can be organized into three chief groups:

— marks 1-4: obedience (mark 5, in appendix fashion, being grouped with mark 4 under the rubric 'long-suffering').
— marks 6-8 effacement, abasement (one dares not say humility).
— marks 9-10: speech and laughter.

These three series recur in the Master:

— rungs 2-4: obedience (mark 5 is absorbed into the fourth rung).
— rungs 5-8: humility (the word itself is used).
— rungs 9-11: speech and laughter.

Such fundamental correspondence ought not to blind us to several important modifications, however.

— mark 2 (obedience) becomes rung 5 (humility).
— mark 6, which had with good reason[98] opened the 'humility' series, becomes rung 8, and presents a still more marked affinity with the 'obedience' series.

— marks 1 and 12, at both extremities, are created in their entirety, although the first issues from the preliminaries posed by Cassian in *Inst* 4.39. The 'obedience' series begins, at the end of this first rung, with the indented lines condemning self-will and the desires of the flesh. Rungs 1-4 thus form a unit parallel to RM Seven, and from that fact their recension adheres much less closely to Cassian's text than does the text of the subsequent rungs.[99]

An examination of the rungs concerning humility (6-7) does not enter within our present purpose, nor of the 'speech and laughter' series (9-12). We would note just one interesting fact for understanding the doctrine on obedience with which we are here occupied. At the ninth rung, developing the ninth mark, the Master introduced a reference to the RM Eight-Nine theory of 'taciturnity': *et taciturnitatem habens usque ad interrogationem non loquatur* (RM 10:75). These words evoke the whole system of regulations covering the relationship between a brother and his abbot which were set out in the treatise on silence. They lend precise determination to Cassian's rather vague counsel, *si linguam cohibeat.* Here, as at the eighth rung, we pass from a general principle to a restrictive application, and it is the monk-abbot relationship which engrosses all our attention. As RM 8:37 stated the matter, to speak and instruct pertains to the master, to be silent and listen befits the disciple.[100] This severe discipline, wholly unknown to Cassian, ultimately gives the Master's ladder its unique aspect. From the marks of humility he has drawn some unforeseen consequences on behalf of his cherished theory of the abbot-teacher. Each in its own way, rungs 3, 8, and 9 testify to this preoccupation with shoring up abbatial authority and with interpreting the doctrine on humility within the precise framework of regular observances. Obedience, respect for tradition, silence — all these monastic virtues materialize in well-defined institutions whose firm axes are the abbot and the rule.[101]

Alongside this general orientation, the most important fact among those we have highlighted is surely the alteration of the second mark and its separation from the third. For in specifying the practice of humility in terms of the conventual life he intended to implement in his monastery, the Master at the same time lost sight of certain aspects of Cassian's thought. The authority of the abbot as a teacher accredited by God rises into sharper relief, but the spontaneous *élan* which moves the disciple to submit his thoughts to the elder's judgment, confide himself to his discretion, and take his counsel to heart—this whole movement from lower to higher which is the motivating force beneath such direction—becomes somewhat lost from sight.

Finally, there is no doubt that the presentation of the first four rungs constitutes an effort at giving the doctrine on obedience a more systematic and reasoned demeanor. The Master on his own initiative took the 'fear of the Lord' from among Cassian's preliminaries and made it the foundation of obedience. Suppressing all mention of *contemptus rerum,* he attached this 'fear' to the first rungs of the spiritual ladder. He saw in it the source from which springs renunciation of self-will and subjection to one who represents God. By it he grounded and reinforced his demand for submission to the abbot.[102]

After this study of RM 10, we have only to point out one or two things which especially concern RB Seven.

Omission of three paragraphs of the first rung concerning tongue, hands, and feet (RM 10:20-29), although it has the unfortunate result of leaving a gaping cavity, does contribute nonetheless to setting in relief the two paragraphs concerning self-will and desires of the flesh, and thereby stresses the meaning of the first rung as the base for the others.

At the third rung, the RB redaction seems to yield to the same preoccupation for lightening which we have observed twice previously in the simplification of the redundant phrases of RM 7:47-50, 71-74. This set purpose renders all the more remarkable the slight addition *pro Dei amore* (RB 7:34). One may ask whether this mention of divine love is well placed at so intermediate a point in a ladder whose summit alone is believed to touch upon charity. But the RB writer here reveals a rather characteristic tendency of his, his insistence on love. We shall meet it again when commenting on the rule's final chapters.

Scriptural illustration for this third rung, moreover, is reduced to a minimum. Only Phil 2:8 has been retained, and this sobriety sets off well a new and important text which had been somewhat eclipsed in the Master by the proliferation of *testimonia* taken over from RM Seven and from the first rung. Allusion to the abbot-teacher has disappeared, however, and along with it the relationship between the treatises on obedience and humility.

Ever since the study of Bernard Capelle appeared,[103] it has been a commonplace in the polemic over RM-RB relations to note the greater conformity of RM with Cassian's text which evidently served as source for this chapter. We shall insist no further on that universally-recognized fact, the most obvious interpretation of which is that RB amended the text bequeathed it by RM, which remained more faithful to Cassian.

Of these modifications, the only one of interest to us here is the change of *praebentur* to *iniunguntur* at the sixth rung. The reading of Cassian and of the Master makes no allusion to obedience. These things 'presented' to the brother, of which he considers himself 'unworthy[104] as an evil laborer', are probably the indispensable material objects of life: food, clothing, and footgear (which constitute both the minimal remuneration for all work and the condition for its pursuit), perhaps also the work tools and humble objects which each had 'for personal use'.[105] An accident in the transcription of RM rendering the sentence less clear[106] led the RB writer to make a correction introducing the idea of obedience into the text, without for all that elucidating the grammatical construction. The monk considers himself evil and unworthy to work, *ad omnia quae sibi iniunguntur,* at anything enjoined on him. This then is how the theme of obedience insinuated itself into this rung of abasement.

At the eighth rung, the scriptural illustration is completely missing, a loss which puts this rung in an unusual situation. Those who defend the anteriority of RM could base their argument on this anomaly. For us, the most important thing to be noted once again is the disappearance of an allusion to the abbot-teacher. We may well marvel that at least RB 5:6 preserved a reference to this doctrine. A little more, and we could ask ourselves whether the RB composer even knew of it, or whether, knowing of it, he systematically deleted it. The omissions noted lead one to think that this theme, at least, did not seem particularly worthy of his attention. This is the single induction of any significance which we might make from the rare modifications to which RB subjected the texts on obedience in this chapter.

DOCTRINE

Literary criticism has permitted us to perceive in RM Seven two quite distinct pericopes, the essential part of which has been preserved in RB Five. St Benedict retained in particular the two scriptural texts of major importance which in these pericopes relate monastic obedience either to the person or to the example of Christ: 'Anyone who listens to you listens to me' (Lk 10:16); '...I have not come to do my own will, but to do the will of the one who sent me' (Jn 6:38). Our reflection on the doctrine of obedience can choose no better guides than these two texts.

The first presents Christ as *he to whom* obedience is rendered. In this perspective, the abbot appears as the representative of Christ. His mission is to transmit the divine word, to speak in the name of Christ who has sent him. We re-encounter here the abbacy conceived as 'vicarious' power, as 'doctoral' charism, as hierarchic authority likened to episcopacy, according to the doctrine propounded at length by the Master at the end of Chapter One and in those passages of Chapters Two, Eleven and Fourteen which are its natural commentary.[107]

The second text presents Christ as *he whom one imitates* in obeying. In this perspective, Christ is no longer he who commands, but he who obeys. Not the word of command but the example of obedience is sought from him. What, then, is the role of the abbot in this case? It is much less easy to define than it was in the preceding perspective, and the Master himself avoided analyzing it. We shall imitate that prudence, limiting ourselves to remarking that Christ obeyed his Father and was obedient also to his executioners, to the authorities of this world, to his parents. The obedience of Christ to a design of his Father who subjected him to the will of men is revealed above all in his passion. 'Not my will, but yours'.[108]

In line with Lk 10:16, the objective content of the order received is of paramount importance, as also is the quality of him who commands. I obey that man because he is speaking to me in the name of God. What he commands me to do is infinitely precious to me. It is the message of Christ for my salvation which he communicates to me.

In line with Jn 6:38, the divine will again requires my obedience, but by a different claim. No longer is it a case of God telling me through the intermediary agency of a qualified 'teacher' what his commandments are and by what actions I shall be pleasing to him. Rather, he invites me to realize, existentially in the particular circumstances in which he has placed me, his crucifying and redemptive will. I ought to imitate Christ by preferring God's will to my own. And his will is that I let my life be taken from me through the mediation of other men, that I renounce my own desires and let them do with me as they wish. It matters little whether their will is good or evil, their intention just or perverse, their actions laudable or sinful. Little does it matter whether they are vicars who speak in the name of Christ or only authorities constituted by God in the world, or even simple casual agents of his Providence. It is enough for me to recognize in them the ministers of the salvific design for the sake of which I must be crucified. What they command of me interests me only in so far as that design is furthered. I learn from their mouth neither the truths of salvation nor the manner in which I ought to realize these truths in my life, but I receive from their hands the cross of my sacrifice and my salvation. Thanks to them, I shall be able to say with Christ, 'Not my will, but yours'.

It was not fortuitously that the first pericope of RM Seven describes the qualities of obedience, while the second bold-stroked its painful passage along the narrow way. If it is Christ who commands through the abbot, obedience ought to be immediate, with no murmuring of lips or heart. If, moreover, this is a matter of following Christ, the path will necessarily lead to Calvary.

Monastic obedience owes its complexity to this double perspective. From either standpoint it is abandonment of one's own will and submission to the divine will.[109] In either the superior figures as the representative of God.[110] Yet these traits, fundamental and common to both perspectives appear in each under a different light.

One becomes keenly aware of this by re-reading the two chapters in which Cassian successively describes each of these aspects of obedience.[111] The first duty of the *praepositus,* he tells us, is to teach the young monk to overcome self-will; to that end he shall unceasingly command him to do whatever runs counter to his likings. Then Cassian notes another kind of exercise: the monk is instructed to make known to his elder all his thoughts and to relinquish them entirely to the judgment of that director. The director will discern the good from the bad, frustrating the contrivances of the devil which plunge the inexperienced ascetic into delusion.

Cassian therefore represents the exercise of authority in the *coenobium* under two aspects: the role of the superior consists both in methodically mortifying the will of his subject and in 'discerning' divine inspiration from diabolical suggestion in the thoughts laid open to him. In this we recognize the two perspectives distinguished in the Master, though Cassian lists them inversely and describes them in different and much more precise terms.[112] The superior procures for his disciple a double benefit: he directs him by counseling in response to the confession he receives, and he educates him to self-conquest by imposing on him what he dislikes. In the first role, the elder speaks in the name of the ascetic tradition of which he is the retainer. He is master, director, teacher. In the second role, he does not judge but trains. What he gives is not an oracle of discretion but a testing command.

We shall see the similarity of the exposition of Cassian and the Master still better by inquiring into the scriptural *testimonia* with which the author of the *Conferences* illustrates these two aspects of obedience. It is true he never uses Lk 10:16 to reinforce the authority of the director. But *Conference Two* cites as an example the child Samuel whom God enlightened through the aged Eli, and the apostle Paul whom divine vocation sent to Ananias.[113] God, says Cassian, did not want to instruct those two chosen souls directly, but obliged them to have recourse to human interpreters of his will. There is a hierarchic order from which no private illumination dispenses. The Lord enlightens us through elders. With this theory, we are not far from the principle which the Master propounds while citing Lk 10:16: 'Whoever listens to you listens to me'.

Then, too, in *Conference Nineteen* Cassian bases the value of cenobitic obedience on the example of Christ. When the hermit John returned to the *coenobium* after twenty years of solitary contemplation, he did so because loss of the 'purity' of the desert seemed to him amply compensated by certain privileges of cenobitism: no worries for the morrow, imitation of Christ in his obedience *usque ad finem*. John then cites Phil 2:8 and Jn 6:38.[114] A little further on, Cassian resumes praising the cenobites, especially their obedience. He sees it from a negative point of view as a man's renunciation of his own will, and cites Is 58:13.[115] This text will again flow from the pen of Cassian, along with Jn 6:38 and Mt 26:39, in a final portrait of cenobites which for all practical purposes closes the whole series of *Conferences*.[116]

Thus, in his last *Conference,* Cassian strove to provide a scriptural justification for cenobitic obedience. Negatively, it appeared to him as a man's abandonment of 'his will' and 'his ways', in conformity with Is 58:13, Jn 6:38, and Mt 26:39, but these last two texts present Christ as the model to be followed in such renunciation, and Phil 2:8 makes the Lord an example of obedience 'even unto death', through humility. This series of *testimonia* largely coincides with the Master's. The three texts on Christ, model of obedience, figure in RM, and Jn 6:38 is cited in it with partiality.[117]

We are therefore justified in paralleling Cassian's description of the two aspects of obedience (*Inst* 4.8-9) with the double perspective, detectable with the aid of the scriptural texts invoked, by which the Master envisages obedience in the course of the two pericopes which make up his treatise. Each author in his own way presents the cenobitic superior in a double role: on the one hand, as a master of the spiritual life who instructs, discerns, judges, with an authority coming from above; and on the other hand, as a conductor testing the person he is leading along the narrow way, mortifying his will, restraining his desires.

Of course these two roles constantly interweave to such an extent that they can often be distinguished only with difficulty and often come to be confused. So Cassian and the Master were far from opposing the two modalities of obedience or even from formally distinguishing them in the greater number of texts in which they dealt with it. Yet this duality persists at the base of their joint conception of obedience. According as one envisages the monk's subjection as the attitude of the disciple who receives the divine word or as the martyr who receives his cross, one is led to consider Christ either as the master who is obeyed or as the exemplar of obedience to the Father, and the superior figures respectively as either the 'teacher' transmitting the word of God or as the providential agent for the consummation of the sacrifice.

Against this background of common ideas, the doctrine of the Master stands out by certain peculiar traits. First of all, he defined much more precisely the nature and basis of the magisterial authority of the superior. Cassian had been satisfied to establish in *Conf* 2.14-15, with the aid of two scriptural examples, the providential law by which God always makes use of 'elders' to instruct men here below. Samuel and Paul illustrate in the Old and New Testaments this rule of obligatory recourse to the earthly representatives of God. Elsewhere Cassian limits himself to noting, without scriptural justification, that he who obeys accomplishes the orders received *tanquam si ex Deo sint caelitus edita,*[118] so

great is the 'reverence' which the 'elder' inspires,[119] and so ardent
the 'faith' which sees him as one who speaks in the place of God.[120]

We do not know from a reading of the texts on what such faith
and respect are grounded. But it is probable that Cassian has in
mind his theory of the apostolic origin of cenobitism. The elders
are thus the organ of an uninterrupted tradition which goes back
to the primitive Church and the apostles in person.[121] The providential law of having recourse to elders is thus confirmed by the
authentic titles which can set off the superiors of *coenobia*. As successors of the apostles, they transmit apostolic teaching in its most
pure form, and their voice is that of speakers authorized by God.

One can divine this theory behind the texts in which Cassian
presents obedience to elders as obedience to God himself. Yet we
admit that it is not especially in connection with obedience that he
mentions it; conversely, the descriptions of obedience make no
definite allusion to it. Cassian considers that the elders' authority
goes without question; the principle that they are to be obeyed as
if the order were proffered by the Lord in person is indisputable.

The Master's thought revolves around just this given of 'faith'.
He felt a more solid grounding of abbatial authority was
necessary, a demonstration from Scripture that Christ really is the
one who commands through the abbot. This is why he repeatedly
cites Lk 10:16, a text Cassian never employed, 'Anyone who listens
to you listens to me'. To obey the superior is to obey Christ. What
had almost always been just a simple postulate in Cassian becomes
here a meditated conviction and theological argument. Like Basil
and Jerome,[122] the Master held that, in addressing these solemn
words to the seventy-two disciples sent on mission, Christ was committed not only to the apostles and their successors, but also to the
superiors of monastic communities. In such superiors, in such
'fathers', Christ himself is obeyed or scorned.

This doctrine goes further than all Cassian's efforts in justifying
the authority of the elders or heads of *coenobia*. Eli instructing
Samuel and Ananias enlightening Paul were no more than *types*
of the teaching mission of the elders. With the Master, the scriptural argument becomes more precise. A general law, which
would apply (how, is unspecified) to the case of monastic
authorities, is no longer the issue. These authorities precisely
receive their mandate from the Lord. From typology we penetrate
to the intrinsic justification of the superior's powers, linked to
Christ himself, defined by the same texts which ground hierarchic
authority in the church.

The progress registered by the Master's doctrine seems no less important when compared with the theory of cenobitic apostolicity, whether or not this theory in Cassian has a direct relationship to obedience. The myth of Cassian spotlights the authority of the heads of *coenobia* as depositaries of a tradition reaching back to the apostles. Application of Lk 10:16 to abbots, on the other hand, makes Christ appear present here and now in them. Further recourse to a risky historical proof to demonstrate the uninterrupted succession of the fathers of cenobitism from the apostolic age onwards becomes unnecessary. For Christ's promise to his emissaries to be fully realized in the person of the abbot, it is enough for him to be an authentic 'teacher', that is, one of the pastors who in our day rule the christian communities, whether they are called churches or monasteries.

Another of the Master's distinctive traits in relation to Cassian is the confusion he introduces in describing the master-disciple relationship. As justification for abbatial authority acquired strength and clarity in his rule, the skein of living relations between abbot and brethren became proportionately impoverished. We refer here to the alterations which the 'ladder of humility' imposed on the 'marks' of *Inst* 4.39.

Taking up again the sequence of material he had propounded in *Inst* 4.8-9, Cassian offers as the first mark mortification of self-will (cf. *Inst* 4.8); as second and third marks the diptych on spiritual direction (confession of actions and thoughts to an elder, reception of his judgment and advice [cf. *Inst* 4.9]). Now, by transposing the second mark to the fifth rung and insisting on the *humiliating* nature of the avowal and on the *evil* thoughts and actions underlying them, the Master has profoundly modified the physiognomy of this mark. Dissociated from its natural complement, isolated, and considered a rung of 'humility' rather than of 'obedience', it has lost its original sense of being a manifestation of thoughts aimed at obtaining the elder's reply.

Correlatively, the third mark, become the third rung, no longer suggests the movement of confidence of the disciple submitting his personal judgment to his master's 'discretion' and avidly awaiting the word of salvation from him. The Master is interested exclusively in two moments of obedience: renunciation of one's own will, and accomplishment of the superior's will. Beyond that, he retains nothing of the relationship of spiritual direction suggested by marks 2 and 3. One could say that for him obedience is chiefly important as execution of an order given. It is better suited within

a social and communitarian context than within that of a
disciple's quest for salvation, a personal search for the will of God,
and an intimate and confident relationship with a spiritual father
whose counsel is sought with eager spontaneity in order to obtain
light from him.

These modifications made in marks 2 and 3 are all the more
significant and consequence-laden in that nothing in the treatise
on obedience compensates for the loss of the elements sacrificed.
RM Seven says nothing about spiritual direction, not even in the
pericope on the qualities of obedience in which Lk 10:16 is cited
twice. This verse is quoted by the Master, both here and at the
third rung, only to establish the abbot's authority within a
perspective of command, of orders given and immediately implemented, and not at all in a perspective of spiritual direction
solicited by the opening of conscience and received as a liberating
instruction.

So the Master's doctrine on obedience, compared with
Cassian's, evinces this paradox: on the one hand it lifts into much
sharper relief the authority of the master as one who speaks for the
Lord, but on the other hand it effaces his role as a spiritual director. Perhaps the two facts result jointly from an evolution of the
concept of superior in the hierarchic sense, as the abbot pro-
gressively comes to figure more as the head of a community and
less as a spiritual master. This might explain the insistent recourse
to the great text which grounds the mission of the hierarchic
pastors of the Church, as well as the diminished interest shown for
the education of consciences and the accent placed on the execution of orders and on the correct accomplishment both interior
and exterior, of prescribed acts. Let it not be forgotten, moreover,
that RM speaks of the abbot where Cassian meant the *praepositus*
or head of a group of ten.

Now that we have acknowledged the fundamental convergence
of the Master and Cassian, and at the same time their distinctive
characteristics, we must resume our analysis of the two aspects of
obedience found in their writings.

In the perspective of Lk 10:16, the superior appears before all
else as a master of evangelical doctrine. The benefit expected
from him is instruction in the divine law. He teaches how to avoid
sin and how to know and fulfill the will of God. Those to whom
this message is directed are sinful men, by themselves incapable of

understanding the word of God and putting it into practice. They need a master to communicate it to them, someone who knows how to interpret it for them, to apply it to their life and urge its accomplishment without slackening.

This need for a 'teacher' is the most basic reason for monastic obedience. One obeys above all because such obedience to a man is practically the sole sure means of obeying God: the obedience of the disciple, the obedience of one who is ignorant to one of greater experience than himself, the obedience of the sinner to the man of God who can save him. Such an attitude does not differ essentially from that in which all Christians find themselves before their pastors. Only by its further-reaching exigencies does the monk's obedience distinguish itself from the obedience of the ordinary faithful. Because the divine word is taken more seriously, the direction sought from the master leaves not the least facet of life untouched. The ascendancy accorded the 'teacher' is total.

Obedience imposes itself first of all, then, as a pedagogical necessity. Anyone who wants to learn an art must enroll in a good school. The spiritual art is no exception to this rule.[123]

In such a perspective, the quality of the superior is of supreme importance. In reality, one turns to him in his capacity as master. Should he fail to provide effectively what is expected of him, the enterprise miscarries. And what is expected of him is authentic teaching, direction, which conforms to the divine law, and knowledge of the spiritual art he is believed to possess. He ought therefore to show by what right he teaches divine law and to present himself as a duly authorized 'teacher' (Lk 10:16). In addition, he must effectively prove himself 'learned in divine law', capable both of setting the example and of preaching, adroit at eluding the devil's stratagems, and indefatigably vigilant. The successful outcome of this educational undertaking depends completely on the worth of the master. Seen from this viewpoint, then, obedience rests on the conviction that the person obeyed is a qualified master, authentically transmitting the word of God.

By the same stroke, the essential objective character of such obedience looms into sight. This virtue by its very nature does not recommend itself as a good for the subject regardless of the act it causes to be accomplished, but commends itself rather as a means towards realizing conformity of the acts of him who is obeying with divine law. What counts here is not the subjective value of obedience as an exercise of renunciation or of humility, but its indispensable mediation in the quest for God's will. One obeys the superior in the hope of accomplishing what God commands. This means that the accent falls on the conformity of the superior's orders with the message of Christ. The concrete expression of the divine teaching is seen in those orders adapted to circumstances and persons. The person who obeys will feel himself possessed, through the medium of his master's word, by the commandment of God, the literary formulation of which he has read in the sacred books without understanding it. The objective reality is the same, it is the same word of God, but expressed for his sake and placed within his reach *hic et nunc*. Through the mediation of the superior's command, obedience adheres to the divine truth itself.

The chapter on the abbot previously gave us occasion to underscore how familiar this theme of hierarchic mediation between creatures and God was to the thinking of antiquity.[124] Here we may point out another series of references, also highly significant. Among the Fathers, the idea was quite common that servitude is a good thing for the simple-minded.[125] Providence itself has arranged in that way for the governance of those incapable of governing themselves. When someone is so devoid of senses as not to be master of his own acts, he does better to serve under the yoke of someone wiser. 'Thus directed by the reasoning of the master, one is like a vehicle controlled by its driver, like a ship whose captain stands at the helm'.[126] Esau become the servant of his brother is the type of such feeble minded persons, for whom slavery is advantageous.[127] This theme finds an echo in ascetical literature, where it influences the master-disciple relationship.[128] Has RM itself not in this manner presented the need for placing oneself under the orders of an abbot? *Ideoque omnes quibus adhuc insipientia mater est, expedit sub unius esse potestate maioris* (RM 1:87).

One can see, however, that such a way of conceiving obedience has its limits. If the motive for obedience is the subject's incapacity to conduct himself according to God, what will happen after he has benefited from the master's direction to the extent of being henceforth capable of doing without it? In short, subjugation to a 'teacher' ought to result sooner or later in rendering the disciple apt to direct himself at least, if not others as well. A master's direction is not intended solely to make him perform actions good and pleasing to God; it creates virtuous habits in him, it is meant to form a spiritual man who spontaneously obeys the law of the Spirit. Consequently, it is normal that obedience, in the measure to which it appears an educational necessity, comes little by little to lose its meaning.

Cassian explicitly envisages the eventuality. The monk who has successfully completed his cenobitic education 'takes into his own hands the weighing of issues in the light of discretion, being henceforth strong enough not to fall while relying upon his own judgment'.[129] The time has come to pass to anchoritism. Instead of blindly following a single master, as he had done in the *coenobium,* the monk seeks virtuous example everywhere, benefitting from the best he perceives in everyone. He continues to be inspired by others and by traditional norms, to be sure, and in the difficult cases he will still have recourse to the direction of elders. But the time for obedience in the precise sense of the term has passed. Seen as an educational method, as a condition of salvation for the man who is a sinner, obedience is but a necessary means. Once the end is attained, the means cease to be indispensable.

Obedience seen as an imitation of Christ, on the contrary, never ceases to invite the monk. The same Cassian who describes for us the emancipation of the cenobite passing to anchoritism is also the author of *Conference Nineteen,* in which John the Hermit justifies his return to the *coenobium* after twenty years of contemplative perfection. Now, according to John, the irreplaceable benefit of cenobitism is, along with the absence of temporal anxieties, the imitation of Christ obedient 'even to death' (Jn 6:38; Phil 2:8). So there is an aspect of obedience whereby this virtue not only recommends itself, as previously, to imperfect souls but attracts even the perfect. Then it appears as a good in itself and no longer simply as a means. Faustus of Riez admirably expressed this permanent value of obedience: *oboedientia in iunioribus necessitas, in senioribus uero dignitas.*[130] What was a necessity for the imperfect man has become for the elder a glory, a good cultivated for itself. And this 'dignity' of obedience appeals to the example of Christ: *oboedientia quae Deum decuit!* One might further invoke the pachomian texts which present cenobitic obedience as the supreme value of monasticism.[131]

This exaltation of obedience preferred to everything else, even solitude, re-echoes even in the apophthegmata. The supreme class of saints is the *ordo oboedientium!*[132]

That is why, we remark in passing, cenobitic literature can recommend perseverence *usque ad mortem* in the *coenobium* while at the same time maintaining in principle the superiority of anchoritism and its necessity for anyone who would attain perfection. The theme of perseverence is opposed not only to flight — I mean the defection to which sarabaites have yielded and which is no more than failure and cowardice — it tends also, as *Conference Nineteen* shows, to weigh the particular advantages of *coenobium* and desert. In this comparison, the value of obedience in the imitation of Christ appears weighty enough to offset the benefits of solitude. Considered as an indispensable means, obedience detains in the *coenobium* only the imperfect; considered as a good in itself, ranked in the highest order of values, it makes even the perfect man hesitate at the moment of crossing the threshold and heading into the desert.[133]

What then, really, is this 'good of obedience'? The first answer to this question is given by St Paul in the famous text in which he proclaims the greatness of Christ's obedience (Phil 2:8): *humiliauit semetipsum factus oboediens.* Obedience after the example of Christ therefore owes its worth before all else to the virtue of humility. Now humility, since it stands opposed to the deadly sin of pride, holds uncontested primacy among Christian virtues. Jerome and Cassian, both speaking as monks, expressed themselves with all desirable clarity on this subject.[134] RM and RB do no more than prolong that classic doctrine when they center their whole exposition of *ascesis* on humility.

It is therefore enough to recognize in obedience the surest mark of humility in order to transfer to it immediately all the privileges of this primordial virtue. Such was Jerome's achievement. He expounded that obedience is the highest of virtues. Virtues can foment pride, which God hates more than anything. In obedience there is something directly opposed to pride. To adopt another's advice is to acknowledge the superiority of the other and of his counsel, thereby reckoning oneself inferior to one's neighbor.[135]

Cassian in turn, followed by RM and RB classed obedience among the marks of humility, indeed, as its very first indication. As an antidote to pride, obedience attacks the root of all sin. Consequently it ranks as the 'first' virtue for the same reason humility does. When the fathers of cenobitism laud its 'primacy', they are thinking not only of its necessity as a means of ascetical formation within the pedagogical perspective surveyed above, but also of its significance as an apprenticeship in humility, as a remedy especially appropriate for the radical vice of pride.

Yet to set obedience in the forefront on account of its relationship to humility and opposition to pride is still not enough. We must regard it from another standpoint as well, if we are to estimate its grandeur accurately. When monastic authors refer obedience to such texts as Jn 6:38 or Mt 26:39, they invite us to look upon the obedience of Christ not only as an example of humility, but as the very substance of the redemptive act: 'not my will, but yours'! Self-will—'my will'— is the spontaneous movement of the human appetite for created goods, the desire which carries man towards all that is not God himself. In the gospel text, there is no question of a sick or deranged will, but of the most legitimate and deep-seated desire of a sinless nature: not to die, not to suffer. This very desire is what must be sacrificed. Redemption consists in disengaging the human will from itself, from its own spontaneous movement towards created goods, in order to make it coincide with God's mortifying will, loved for itself. The will of Christ was not evil, but he preferred the Father's will to his own. That was his sacrifice, his redemptive act in which every Christian participates. In this consisted his obedience on its deepest level.

We understand, then, why the ancients saw in obedience the sum of all perfection. In their eyes it encompassed all the renunciations to which a disciple of Christ should consent. 'To renounce one's own will' is, in their language, to crucify one's flesh after the example of Christ, to deliver up to God the most deep-seated appetites of one's nature. Thus understood in its full extent, abandonment of self-will or 'obedience' comprehends all the renunciations of monastic life minted in the various details of observance. The monk is one who, together with Christ, has determined to obey the salvific will of the Father, and that will is mortifying. This obedience to God's redemptive and crucifying design finds its concrete expression in the life of renunciation led in the monastery, whose rule and superior are its organizers and guardians.

In this relationship of obedience to the Father, which defines the life of the monk, the abbot, then, intervenes primarily as the regulator of common observance. For a cenobite to obey God means to accept the program of abnegation which the rule imposes and the abbot implements. In this respect, it would be vain to opppose obedience to mortification, as has been done in recent times, as if the former were some sort of substitute for the latter, or even a loftier and more spiritual form of it. A little further on we shall say what ought to be kept of that idea. But the fundamental meaning of obedience to a superior certainly does not imply a dispensing from other renunciations, nor even standing it alongside them as one particular form of abnegation. On the contrary, it implies all of them; it is their sum and their safeguard. If obedience is required before all other *asceses* of the young monk, it is because future combats are virtually won from the fact that obedience is carried to a good end. The one who has committed himself unreservedly to obedience shall be led by obedience to every victory for he has resolved to fulfill in everything the superior's will which unfailingly shall lead him to strip off all his sins completely.[136] In that way, obedience to the superior is the efficacious sign of obedience to God, embracing all the sacrifices God asks of the monk in order to conform him to his crucified son.[137]

Nevertheless, 'to obey' and 'to renounce one's own will' are expressions that ought not always to be understood in the very comprehensive sense we have just indicated. For we need to take account of a subtle form of self-love which delights even in ascetical practices on the condition that they are self-chosen and not imposed by the will of the superior. This refined but not fanciful form of 'self-will' must in turn be expelled. Thus our authors often envisage under this title the desire for independence, the refusal given to obedience in the precise sense of the word. We then rejoin the theme of obedience as an antidote for pride: what good would there be in renouncing the satisfaction of lesser desires if one refuses to sacrifice the will? As long as consent is withheld from that supreme sacrifice, pride reigns in the will, the better part of one's nature has not been handed over to God, and the root of all sins remains alive. At the same time, we skirt once again the theme of hierarchic obedience: outside of subjugation to the representatives of God there is no salvation! From them alone one may expect a sure direction on the road of *ascesis*.

Whatever may be said of the reciprocal implications of these various aspects of obedience, there is no doubt that under the name 'self-will' the writers of cenobitism hound out expressly the refusal to obey superiors in any domain whatever. Whereas obedience to the superior appeared previously as the key to *all* renunciations, the complete assurance of an obedience without reserve to the mortifying will of God is revealed in the present instance as *one* of those renunciations, the most decisive and costly of all, the one by which the higher faculties are specially mortified in a sur--render to God of the will itself, the *arbitrium proprium*, the last stronghold of pride.[138]

Our analyses, then, bring us back continually to a reality which seemed excluded by the point of departure we chose: the reality of vice and sin. We took our start from the example of Christ who delivers a will perfectly whole and pure to his Father, and now a reminder of humanity's sinful condition presses upon us. In reality why should there be any cause for surprise, since the sacrifice of Christ, the sinless victim, can only be explained by men's sin, for which he had to atone? But we do need to underscore the difference between Christ's obedience and our own, even when ours is meticulously envisaged as imitation of Christ.

Our obedience, unlike that of Jesus, is always the obedience of sinners. The sacrifice demanded of us is at once reparation of the disorder reigning within us, and remedy for the evils from which we are suffering. Our will finds its healing in the act of love by which it renounces self and clings to the will of the Father. If we imitate Christ's obedience, if we participate in his redemptive act—'not my will, but yours'—the salvific effect of liberation is produced first of all within ourselves. In this participation in Christ's obedience, we are the beneficiaries as much as the cooperators. Hence one may never isolate absolutely what we have called 'the obedience of the perfect', as though it were no more than a gratuitous and disinterested imitation of the pure love of Jesus for the Father and for men. Consideration of an infirmity to be healed, of a possible return of the evil to be warded off, will forever be mingled in the attraction of the *bonum oboedientiae*.

One may understand from this why our authors usually take so few pains to distinguish expressly the different aspects of obedience illustrated by their descriptions. From the viewpoint of concrete man, which theirs is, such distinctions matter little; obedience is ultimately recommended at every instant and from every point of view. Only exceptionally and, as it were, in passing does it occur to them to suggest openly a comparison between one form of obedience and another, as we saw Faustus of Riez do above.[139] The rest of the time we are compelled to reflect at our own risk and peril on the information which they tender us with no attempt at systematizing it.

Having said that, let us now bring to a close our analysis of obedience in the steps of Christ. Within such a perspective, we will pay less attention to conformity to the commandments of God than to the realization of the salvific plan through the cross. Whereas Lk 10:16 sets off handsomely the transmission of divine law by means of 'teachers', the texts on imitating Christ emphasize instead the sacrificial aspect of obedience: renunciation of one's own will in order to accomplish that of the Father. At certain times the accent strikes an objective element. The divine will is revealed as the law which ought to dominate our actions in this life; one takes to heart this teaching coming from Christ through the intervention of his representatives and strives to put it into practice. At other times the value of obedience as a subjective attitude is set in relief. The divine will is manifested as a crucifying ordeal; one receives this cross and bears it with patience, in abnegation of one's own will.

It matters little, then, whether the order to be executed is in itself more or less connected with what Christ in his Gospel ordered to be done. It matters little, objectively speaking, what act is commanded by the superior. The fruit of my obedience is not to be my conformity to one or another prescript of the divine law which I would not have been capable of following by myself, but rendering me obedient, procuring for me the good of obedience. There is at issue no longer the utility of this virtue as a means to something else, but its intrinsic meaning as a characteristic attitude of Christ and of his disciples. Obedience in itself is a good because it is renunciation, egress from self, adherence to the Other.

This sacrificial perspective does not abrogate the value previously attributed to obedience viewed as a functional means for the accomplishment of divine commands. Quite the opposite: through a more subjective consideration it completes and deepens the role given to obedience in the objective order of conforming to the law of God. Is the law of Christ not summarized, moreover, in the commandment of abnegation and of love? Obedience is thus not only the means by which we accomplish that law, but the very accomplishment of its most profound demands.

One understands, in consequence, why the first through fourth marks of Cassian, as well as the great discourse on obedience, inserted on three occasions in RM in forms that hardly vary,[140] finish with an evocation of the martyr's patience. One understands too why our authors are reticent in displaying before us a sort of systematic mortification of the subject's wishes by the superior. Cassian speaks of orders which are 'superfluous', 'impossible', 'unreasonable', epithets which take us far from the perspective of Lk 10:16! A superior who is conscious of speaking in the name of Christ—'Anyone who listens to you listens to me'—is certainly not inclined to toss out such orders. But Christ is not only the one who

speaks through his mouth; Christ is also the obedient monk stand
ing before him, delivering up his will to the Father's. In
commanding nothing which deviates from the divine precepts,
can the superior dispense himself from imposing the cross on his
disciples? Speaking in the name of Incarnate Wisdom, how can
his orders fail to look like foolishness?[141]

Moreover, the quality of the one commanding is not important
here to the same extent or in the same manner as it was in the first
perspective. He is not considered as 'teacher' and spokesman of
Christ. Instruction from on high, which he alone knows and can
dispense, is not required of him. His role now concerns puting the
precept of abnegation into practice. A brother will thus be obeyed
just as much as a superior: in both instances the *bonum oboedien-*
tiae is the same.[142] No matter who gives the command, 'one is sure
that the path of obedience leads to God'.[143] Such is the conclusion
drawn very logically by RB from the considerations we have
developed. If the Master on his part has not done so, it is because
the abbot's role as 'teacher' absorbed too much of his attention to
permit him to discern clearly the other aspect of the function,
which is nevertheless implied in the description he gives us. In the
Master's monastery, in line with Lk 10:16, only the abbot and his
delegates, the provosts, exercise command.[144]

To terminate this analysis of the doctrine of obedience in the
Master and St Benedict, it is interesting to compare it with certain
contemporary theories on the nature and the foundation of
religious obedience. 'Authority and obedience', it has been said,
'have as their common fundamental rule the common good of
society'. Commands are issued only in its name. Ultimately, one
obeys only its demands. Obedience is then that eminent activity of
the virtue of social justice whereby the individual pays his debt of
justice to the community. Only by supererogation does it concern
the subject's personal life. One does not obey in order to submit
oneself to a superior, but, thanks to his order, to serve the common good of which he has charge. Ascetical or mystical considerations, such as the care to mortify self or to imitate the obedient
Christ, appear quite accidental.[145]

We leave to Thomists the task of examining whether such
affirmations agree with the doctrine of religious obedience proposed in the *Summa*.[146] They offer, in any event, an arresting con-

trast to the concept developed by ancient monastic literature. In the latter, the issue is never anything but the good of the subject in an ascetical and mystical perspective. If RM happens to point to the common good as one of the factors to be considered when an order is given,[147] it never enters the author's mind to ascribe to obedience any motive other than 'Anyone who listens to you listens to me'.

The same remark applies *a fortiori* to certain commentaries on the rule of St Benedict which claim to uncover in the chapter on which we are commenting a concept of obedience based on the community welfare. St Benedict, we are told, did not want to make holy monks, but a holy monastery, a holy community. Now, a community cannot exist unless it is composed of a head and members and grounded on authority and service, command and obedience. Obedience appears as the principle which binds all the members into a body, then, and as the necessary consequence of stability.[148] It is the vital nerve of the community and also its supreme law.

This interpretation of RB, in our opinion, puts the cart before the horse. What comes first in the ancient perspective is not *stabilitas in congregatione,* understood as an end in itself and as a common good to which the interests of the individuals are subordinated, but the education of persons in quest of personal perfection. Obedience is conceived as an indispensable educational means and also as the pre-eminent expression of self-denial and love. No considerations of the social order intervene, even on the mystical plane, in such motivation for obedience. The cenobitic society in the first place results from a sum of individual relationships between the monks and their abbot.[149] As for stability, it is nothing but perseverance in this same obedience.

NOTES

1. The study which follows was conducted independently of the researches of Hubert Vanderhoven and Robert Weber on these same chapters. We give it as such, and in conclusion place our results over against those of these two critics, whose works were not accessible to us until ours was almost finished.

2. Butler, Regula, p 39, produces no parallels to marks 1, 3, or 4. Leander Bopp, in *Benediktus der Vater des Abendlandes* (Munich: Schnell, 1947) p 243, saw clearly that rungs 2, 3, and 4 corresponded more or less to those marks, but like Butler he failed to note the connection between the first rung and the 'fear of the

Lord' which Cassian places 'at the beginning' of the ascent. The same lacuna exists in Bernard Capelle, 'Les oeuvres de Jean Cassien et la Règle Bénédictine', *Rev. Liturg. et Monast.* 14 (1929) 311-314.

3. Thus *uoluntas* (mark 1) and *uoluntatem* (rung 2); *iudicio* (rung 3 in RM 10:45, resuming the second rung) and *iudicio* (mark 3); *patientiae constantiam* (mark 4, and rung 4 in RM 10:52; cf. *patientiam* in RB 7:35).

4. Cf. RM 2:51-52, which heralds only the *ars sancta.* When RM 10:123 speaks of the *actus militiae cordis,* and RM 11:1 of the *actus iustitiae,* these words may be understood equally of RM 3-6 and RM 7-10.

5. Compare RM 10:34-39 with 3:65 (desires of the flesh); 10:30-33 with 3:66 (self-will); 10:45-51 with 3:67 (obedience to the abbot). These parallels are all the more significant inasmuch as the texts on either side are brought closer together. Cf. also 10:10-13 and 3:51-55 (fear of hell, desire for eternal life; guard over oneself; presence of God); 10:59-60 and 3:34-38 (patience); 10:61-65 and 3:56 (evil thoughts); 10:78-79 and 3:60 (laughter); 10:75-77 and 3:58 (silence); 10:80-81 and 3:59 (manner of speaking).

6. Compare RM 3:84-94 with 10:93-117 (cf. 90:19-27).

7. In this sense humility, in RM 10, precedes and encompasses the other two virtues. Nevertheless, we shall see that rungs 5-8 may be considered rungs 'of humility' in a special manner. But those rungs come after the rungs 'of obedience' (1-4) and before those of 'taciturnity' (9-11), just as the corresponding marks of Cassian do.

8. Bopp, *Benediktus der Vater,* p 225.

9. Bopp seems to have glimpsed this in his second attempt at an explanation. The fear of God, he says, is only a general attitude of soul as yet having no essential tie with humility, so that the treatise on humility does not begin until the second rung, which deals with obedience. This judicious remark needs only to be corroborated by a comparison with Cassian's text.

10. See Gregory Penco, 'Un tema dell' ascesi monastica: la scala di Giacobbe', *Vita Monastica* 14 (1960) 99-113. To the texts cited in that study may be added Cassiodorus, *Inst., Praef.*; and R Fruc II 10. The expression *humilitate ascendere* recalls VP 5.15.49 and 77. As for the comparison of body and soul to the sides of the ladder (*latera*), the same sort of image is found in Gregory of Nyssa, *De perfectione* (Jaeger, 193, 9-19): body and soul are like the two walls which Christ, as cornerstone (Eph 2:20), joins. Therefore virtue of soul should go hand in hand with decorum of body.

11. Besides *Conf* 14.2 (cited by Butler) which concerns degrees of contemplation and of action, see *Conf* 9.16 and 10.8 (degrees of prayer), and the six bases of true friendship in *Conf* 16.6.

12. *Inst* 11.10: *ut qui [Ezechias] de tam excelso meritorum fastigio elatione impellente deciderat, non nisi per eosdem rursum humilitatis gradus ad amissum culmen ascenderet.* Cf. *Inst* 12.8.

13. These formulas resemble less the long introductory phrase repeated before each rung by RM than the simplified RB formula. RB reads *gradus est si* in every case (a vestige of RM or reminiscence of Cassian?) save at the third rung where the reading is *gradus est ut.* Did this *ut* derive from the *et* which, in RM 10:49, immediately precedes *omni oboedientia?*

14. Jerome, Lr 22.35.

15. *Dial.* 1.10-11.

16. *Dial.* 1.19.

17. R Fer 1. Two chapters follow on reverence and charity. This trilogy of virtues at the head of the rule *propter numerum Trinitatis* (RM 1.82) cannot fail to recall the obedience-taciturnity-humility trilogy in our two rules. Obedience also comes

at the head of the R Col M and is followed by a chapter on *taciturnitas*. This sequence constitutes a remarkable parallel with RM 7-9. And this is not the only sign of Columban's dependence upon RM or RB (cf. below, n. 58).

18. Cassian, moreover, describes promptness in obeying the orders of an elder in the same terms. Cf. *Inst* 4.26: *confestim;* 4.27.4: *confestim celeri cursu.*

19. Cf. RM 9:48-50 (silence); 61 (the fast for those who are traveling).

20. The same word (*monachus*) figures in vs 30, evoking Chapter 1. It is found nowhere else in RM, except in RM 81:16, which Vanderhoven considers a gloss. See 'Les plus anciens manuscrits de la Règle du Maître transmettent un texte déjà interpolé', *Scriptorium* (Brussels: Editions 'Erasme', 1946) vol. 1, p 203, n. 23.

21. Cf. RM 8:7-10: *cor, oculus, lingua;* 8:17: *anima, oculi, os, aures;* 8:26: *cogitatio, eloquium, aspectus;* 8:27-30: *cogitatio, eloquium.* The interior principle (heart, soul, or thoughts) is always mentioned before the senses or external actions, in conformity with the psycho-physiological theory set forth in RM 8:6ff (cf. 14: 83-85).

22. RM 10:14, 19, 23, 24.

23. RM 10:30. For the *desideria carnis*, on the contrary, the Master had the good fortune to hit on a text evocative of the divine presence (Ps 38:10). With the aid of that discovery, he was able to take up once again the introductory formula of the first four paragraphs (RM 10:34). Weber came up against the difficulty we are pointing out here (the absence of the divine presence theme concerning self-will) and remarked that since self-will is always evil, the author could be satisfied with a condemnation of it at the outset. See 'Interpolation ou omission? A propos de la Règle de S. Benoît et de celle du Maître', REL 23 (1945) p 132. But why did he not do the same in the subsequent paragraph? Are *desideria carnis* not by definition just as evil as self-will? If our remarks on the adventitious nature of the development on self-will and desires of the flesh is accepted, it is less difficult to explain the fact Weber spotlighted in the same study: the paragraphs on the tongue, hands, and feet, all three of these paragraphs peculiar to the Master, are devoid of the 'warning to observe custody' which we read in the other paragraphs; the presence of God alone is evoked. Because the last two developments (will and desires) do not belong to the primitive redaction, that redaction therefore included only a single development, that on thoughts, in which the warning followed the evocation of the divine presence. Absence of the warning to observe custody in the three subsequent paragraphs consequently appears less abnormal than it does in the present redaction, where the warning recurs in the final paragraphs. These, far from testifying against the authenticity of the developments in which the warning is missing should be considered additions modeled (quite poorly as far as 'volitions' go!) on the development related to 'thoughts'.

Note that the verses announcing the theme (RM 10:12-13 = RB 7:12-13) place the presence of God after the warning to keep custody and not before, as in the paragraph on thoughts. The plan is therefore less 'rigorously identical' than Weber claimed.

24. *Inst* 4.32-35. Cf. *Conf* 4.11; 7.6; 24.26; *Inst* 12.29.3 (*desideria et uoluntates*). Rarely, however, does the expression *uoluntas propria* occur in Cassian, and still more rarely does it carry a pejorative meaning, as in *Conf* 16.3.4; 24.23. By this term Cassian ordinarily means free choice, in distinction to necessity of nature (*Inst* 3.5 and 3.12; in *Conf* 7.26 the pejorative meaning results from the context rather than from the expression itself). To designate what the Master calls *uoluntas propria*, Cassian most often says *mea, tua, sua uoluntas* (*Inst* 4.8 and 5.28; *Conf* 16.6 and 16.23). Should one wish to trace the probable origin of *uoluntas propria* in the Master, therefore, one must seek it elsewhere than in Cassian. We would mention Basil (R Bas 12, 81, 88, 176, 181), Faustus of Riez, *Hom.* 3 (Eus. 37, PL 50:839), and HM 31. The Master had previously said *uoluntas propria* in the treatise on obedience (RM 7:7).

25. Compare RM 10:12 (*custodiens se... a peccatis et uitiis... uel uoluntatis pro-*

priae sed et desideria carnis) with RM 10:42 (*si propriam non amans uoluntatem desideria sua non delectetur implere*). The redundancy is obvious. Note too how in RM 10:12 *uoluntas propriae et desideria carnis* link with the preceding lines by means of *uel* and of *sed et*, whereas the four preceding terms succeed one another without any conjunction. Would this not indicate a later interpolation of these two elements, at the time when the Master completed his first rung?

26. The Ps 44:22-Ps 66:10-12 sequence reappears in RM 90:33-43. This time the redaction is, on the whole, nearer RM 7 than RM 10. The three phases depicted by RM 7 are re-encountered: *in scola monasterii* (90:29); *iudicio* (90:30); *in illo iam saeculo* (90:41). The Ps 66 citation extends to vs 12b, which gives rise to a commentary which repeats RM 7:65b-66 word for word. Note also *amaricatio* and *amaricare* in the two texts (7:59, 66; 90:29, 32, 37). We shall give closer attention to these two redactions in the course of our investigation. Though nearer RM 7, RM 90 does nevertheless display some points of specific contact with RM 10, such as the Rom 8:18 citation (10:92 and 90:13); Mt 6:10 (10:31 and 90:49, 54); the commentary on Ps 66:12a (10:58 and 90:39).

27. The Master regains it in Chapter 90, where he is set at his ease by a freer literary genre (cf. n. 26). It may seem as if we have admitted contradictory principles in the interpretation of the first and fourth rungs. At the first rung, RM 7 is the less complex, at the fourth, RM 10 is. Would it not be logical to consider the simpler text in each case the more ancient, and vice-versa?

The two cases are not really parallel: at the first rung, the themes of RM 7 are *rearranged* by RM 10; at the fourth rung, on the contrary, both observe *the same order*, and this order, identical in both texts, is what occasions the ingenious commentary of RM 7.

28. *Conf* 20.9.5: *sunt uiae quae uidentur apud homines rectae, nouissima autem earum uenient in profundum inferni. Conf* 1.20.8: *sunt uiae quae uidentur rectae esse uiro*, etc. This oscillation between the plural *apud homines* and the singular *uiro* may spring from the LXX text, which gives *para anthrôpois* in Prov 4:12 and *andri* in Prov 16;25. As for *demergit* in RM and RB, one can see in it the influence of Mt 18:6: *demergatur in profundum maris*. The *Vita Ambrosii* 41 speaks of the yoke of avarice *quod demergit ad profundum inferni*. See also Cassian, *Inst* 7.11: *usque ad profundum inferni deuoluti* (referring to some monks affected by avarice) seems to allude to 1 Tim 6:9: *desideria... quae mergunt homines in interitum et perditionem*. The original form in which RM cites this text has been studied by Hubert Vanderhoven, 'S. Benoît a-t-il connu la Règle du Maître?' RHE 40 (1944-45) 185-186. See the remarks of Bernard Capelle, 'Le Maître antérieur à S. Benoît?' RHE 31 (1946) p 73.

29. It regards the recollection of past sins: when brought back to mind under pious pretexts, they are the occasion of new temptations.

30. *Hom* 3 (Eus. 37); PL 50:838B. The text is for all purposes that of Cassian: *sunt uiae quae rectae esse uidentur hominibus*, etc.

31. R Bas 12 (*descendi de coelo*), 80 (*non ueni*), 181, 184. Cassian, *Conf* 16.6.4; 19.6.6; 24.26.14. Faustus, *Hom* 3 (Eus. 37); PL 50:839D. HM 31:458c. R 4 Pat 30.

32. This *non ueni*, which seems foreign to the authentic Jn 6:38 text, derives very likely from Heb 10:9, another great text on the obedience of Christ: *ecce uenio ut faciam Deus uoluntatem tuam*. Jn 7:28: *a meipso non ueni* also comes to mind. In any case, the constancy with which monastic authors cite the text in this form seems to indicate that they take it from the same literary tradition, which perhaps goes back to Basil.

33. For example, in *Conf* 24.26.

34. *Conf* 24.2.5.

35. The text reappears, cited this time in explicit terms, in RM 90:10. There also the context is one of obedience. The application is very general in RM 3:10:

abnegare semetipsum ut sequatur Christum. This expression *sequi Christum* agrees with several other instances in which the word *sequi* appears concerning obedience in this chapter and in the treatise on the abbot: RM 7:4 (*in sequendo*, which RB 5:4 amends to *in faciendo*), 7:8, 38; 2:29, 47; cf. Prol. 12, 23. The Mt 16:24 + Jn 6:38 sequence had already figured in a context regarding obedience in HM 31.

36. *Conf* 19.6-8.

37. *Inst* 4.9; *Conf* 2.10 and 13.

38. RM 7:56 ought to read: *rationem reddere qui imperauit, non qui imperata perfecit.* Agreement of E and A here against P is decisive (compare an analogous case in RM 1:83: *regerentur* EA, *regenerentur* P). And besides, the EA reading alone makes plausible sense. In the next verse (7:57) we again find E and A in agreement on the correct reading, against P: *minime* EA, *anime* P.

39. *Conf* 18.3.

40. *Inst* 4.27. Cf. Sulpitius Severus, *Dial.* 1.18; VP 5.14.18.

41. R Bas 13 (= SR 114). On this question see Irénée Hausherr, *Direction spirituelle en Orient autrefois* (Rome: Pontifical Institute of Oriental Studies, 1955) 197-200. R Caes V 64 prescribes staging resistance to an unworthy abbess. See also the *Pactum* of Fructuosus.

42. The Rule of St Francis: *Regula Prima*, Chapter 5; *Reg. Secunda*, Chapter 10; (cf. *Admon.* 3.9; *Ep* 1.41). St Thomas, *Summa Theologica*, II^a II^{ae}, qu. 104, art. 5, ad 3.

43. VP 5.14.11. Hausherr (*Direction Spirituelle*, pp 194-195) reproduces an analogous opinion of Barsanuphius.

44. R Col M 9 (Walker, 138, 9-24).

45. RM 2:36 (exc E).

46. RM 1:90-92; 2:6, 50; 89:12-16; 90:45, 47-58.

47. Cf. Jerome, *De persecutione Christianorum*, ed. by Germain Morin, *Anecdota Maredsolana* (Maredsous, 1895) III/2, pp 402-405; *Vita Honorati* 37-38; Gregory the Great, *Dial.* 3.26 (ed. H. Moricca [Rome: Instituto Storico Italiano, 1924] 198, 9-12 and 3.28, 199, 17-200, 10).

48. VP 5.14.17; Sulpitius Severus, *Dial.* 1.18; R Col M 9 (Walker, 140, 8).

49. *Conf* 18.7. Cf. *Inst* 12.33.1; *Conf* 9.14. It is significant that the first of these texts is the precise source of the 'criticism of the sarabaites' developed by the Master earlier in this same chapter.

50. *Inst* 5.2.3.

51. *Inst* 4.9. Cf. *Inst* 4.23-31.

52. Sulp. Sev., *Dial.* 1.16-18; VP 5.14.18.

53. *Non tarde* (7:67) recalls obedience *sine mora.* Cf. *tarda natura* (7:11) and *tardi aut negligentes* (7:20).

54. In 7:5, *auris-audit* seems to be the key word: one obeys as soon as one hears. In 7:68-69, the accent perhaps falls more on the delegation of authority given the superior by God. The order of the two citations is reversed: Ps 18:45 seems occasioned by the proximity of Lk 10:16, with which it forms a couplet.

55. Cassian notes solely (*Inst* 4.24.1) that the obedience of John of Lyco aroused the suspicion of his master. The master feared it might have been *adfectaticia et quodammodo coacticia atque ad imperantis faciem praebita.* So, wishing to ascertain 'whether it derived from genuine faith and profound humility of heart', he imposed some extravagant obediences on his disciple. The theme, one can see, is close but still rather different.

56. To judge from the Index of Petschenig (CSEL 17). Note, however, *Conf* 23.7: *serenitatem nostrae hilaritatis obnubilat avara cunctatio* (apropos of almsgiving, as in St Paul).

57. R Bas 71; OM 5.23-24; R Caes V 17; R Fruc II 5; R Col M 1; R Mac 11, etc.

58. R Col M 1 (Walker, 124, 12-13); R Cui 29 (cited by *Concordia* 8.3 and 6). Cf. R 4 Pat 21: *cum omni subjectione et laetitia.*

59. For this last theme, see *Inst* 4.38 citing Mt 7:14.

60. Reciprocally, a text which Cassian was quick to use for stigmatizing self-will, Is 58:13-14, is not found in RM. Cf. *Conf* 19.8.3; 24.26.13-14.

61. See above, note 1. The theme of the two ways does appear clearly within a context of obedience in Caesarius, *Serm.* 223 (Morin, 884, 1-22).

62. Vanderhoven, 'Les plus anciens manuscrits', pp 197-201; Weber, 'Deux séries parallèles de citations dans la Règle du Maître', RMAL 4 (1948) 129-136.

63. Cf. RM 1:82: the *primus gradus doctrinae* is that of the Old Testament prophets, that is, 'the most ancient'. Cassian speaks of the *eruditio principalis* in the same sense concerning obedience, though the viewpoint of pedagogical method likewise intervenes.

64. Thus in R Fer 1.

65. See p 187.

66. We confess that the theory of the two forms of obedience seemed to us, as it had to Penco (Regula, p 232), likely to be 'a digression rather than an original section'. One may ask whether vss 10-21 are not attributable to a hand other than the one which wrote vss 1-9, and that the little phrase *sed haec forma paucis conuenit et perfectis* (vs. 2) had been adapted to introduce vss 10-21. RB would then be giving us the untampered text. However, we shall see below that *perfectis discipulis* (RB 6:3) suggests that St Benedict read in RM the distinction between 'the perfect' and 'the imperfect' as it is propounded in RM 90:46-50. If Benedict found this theory in RM 8-9 and set it aside (save for the RB 6:3 allusion), nothing allows us to suppose he had not in the same way come across it in RM 7 and left it out.

67. See n. 62. Summing up this study in his *Regula* (pp 234-235), Penco seems to confuse Prov 16:25 with Qo 18:30. This second text, and not Prov 16:25, served as the basis for Weber's argument.

68. Note also the explication of the words *tota die* of Ps 44:22 by *cottidie* (7:59). This explication, which reveals the meditative attention of the first redaction, is missing in RM 90.

69. *Monachus* (7:30), *cenobiis* (7:50), *sarabaitarum* and *girouagorum* (7:24). All these terms are peculiar to RM 1 and 7 (the sole exception being the recurrence of *monachus* in 81:6. Cf. n. 20). But the writer is evidently tributary to Cassian, *Conf* 18, and this fact may explain why he uses here a terminology which he neglects or shuns elsewhere. The reason for such abstention remains in other respects to be explained. François Masai touched rather fleetingly on this problem in a paper delivered at the congress of Spoleto and published in *Il Monachesimo nell' alto medioevo e la formazione della civiltà occidentale* (Spoleto: Centro Italiano di Studi, 1957) 458-459.

70. Let us remember that the developments on 'volitions' and 'desires' are not in their normal place at the end of the first rung. What is more, they belong not to RM 8-9, as do the considerations which precede them, but, like the subsequent rungs, to RM 7. Lastly, the text on 'volitions' presents some unusual peculiarities. In this respect, the outline by Robert Weber as given in his article 'Deux séries parallèles', p 133, ought to be corrected. The text on the will does not in fact include the paragraph on the 'presence of God' found in all the others. Weber, moreover, had noted this absence and tried to explain it in a previous article, 'Interpolation or omission?', p 132 (see above, n. 23).

71. *Unde Dominus dicit: angusta uia est quae ducit ad uitam* (a parenthetical explanation which remedies the deletion of the Master's development on the Two Ways).

72. See Penco, *Regula,* pp 235-236, where he reproduces Weber's synoptic tables while rejecting his interpretation. For Jacques Froger, the RB simplification of the first of these two phrases (RB 5:12; cf. RM 7:48-50) results from two skips from *and* to the same word (*homoeoteleuton,* a kind of mistake often made by a copyist, whereby the eye skips from a syllable or word to another identical syllable or word in close proximity, and the intervening text is omitted).

73. RM 7:5; 10:50. Cf. above, n. 54.

74. RB Chs 23; 28; 32; 43; 48; 62; 65.

75. They recur nine and eight times respectively.

76. RM 13:57-75 (general theory); 17:8 (negligence in looking after tools); 19:17 (tardiness in table service); 73:4 (tardiness in comming to office). RB does not mention tardiness in table service, but does add the following cases: lateness in ringing bells (Chapter 11); faults in reciting the office (45); all shortcomings (46); corrections by an elder (71); delay in coming to table (43). See also the 'regular discipline' stipulated for reprimanding the deans (21), priests (62), provost (65), and those who 'excuse' or correct inopportunely (70).

77. Cf. RB 23:1-3: *si... murmurans... non emendauerit.*

78. As is the case in OM 5: *nemo cum murmurio aliquid faciat, ut non simili iudicio murmuratorum pereat.*

79. RM 7:21: *culpa contumaciae reatui deputetur* (cf. 7:17: *non reatui... deputatur*); 9:44: *mox a praepositis suis eis imperetur silentium.*

80. See above, p 181.

81. Above p 182.

82. See n. 24.

83. Ibid.

84. For the scriptural illustration of these rungs, see our table on p 191.

85. As for these words: *cogitationes malas cordi suo aduenientes,* cf. RM 3:56. The order adopted in the enumeration (thought-actions) corresponds to that found in RM 8 and in the first four paragraphs of the first rung (see above, n. 21).

86. Cf. RM 7.

87. Penco (*Regula,* p 249, n. 3) glides over this rung, which the critics do not seem to have exploited. Yet the first member of the phrase presents an evident reworking: Prov 16:25 and Ps 14:1 separate 1 Cor 6:12 from its introduction. The two incriminated citations are omitted by E, but that mss has conserved *item dicit apostolus* (vs 48), which seems to indicate that the E copyist had these quotations in their place and deliberately omitted them, awkwardly preserving the subsequent words, now deprived of meaning. It is likely, then, that Prov 16:25 and Ps 14:1 have not been worked-in, but that 1 Cor 6:12 and its foreshadowing in vs 45 (*quae non expediant*) have; its relationship to the context is much less clear. Moreover, the entire first member (vss 45-48) appears suspect. The heavy armature: *postquam... ergo non solum cauens haec sed et...* is particularly awkward both in style and thought. All the same, the Master's style does offer other examples of such unskilfulness. As for the content: if we are right to be surprised that renunciation of personal judgment and 'submission in all obedience' are presented to us as two *successive* moments, we must bear in mind that Cassian is wont to present things in the same way. For him, as for the Master, a vice is eliminated *before* the corresponding virtue is attained. Cf. *Conf* 9.2-3. So there is no reason to jump to the conclusion that there has been an interpolation here. Subject matter and form may both derive from the Master, and the re-working mentioned above could be his.

88. See the passage parallel to this last in *Inst* 4.9, where this word recurs twice (Petschenig, p 53, 11, 12 and 17).

89. R Bas 65, 69, 83, 126, 131. Cassian, *Inst* 12.28; *Conf* 19.6.6. Cf. VP 5.14.11.

90. *Conf* 19.6.6.

91. *Qui perseuerauerit usque in finem...* (cf. Cassian, *Inst* 4.36); *sustine Dominum.*

92. This is true above all for Mt 5:39-41 and for 1 Cor 4:12b.

93. Nevertheless, we ought to point out the literal parallel in RM 3:34-38: *Malum pro malo non reddere, iniurias non facere, sed et factas patienter sufferre, inimicos plus quam amicos diligere, maledicentes se non solum non remaledicere, sed magis benedicere, persecutionem pro iustitia sustinere.*

94. *Inst* 1.2.2-3. Cf. Preface to the *Inst*, 8, and *Inst* 2.2-6.

95. See *Inst* 1.2.2, which associates the *ueteres sancti* of the past and the *patres nostri temporis*. The best commentary on this rung is found in *Conf* 2.10 (*seniorum traditione, maiorum exemplo*) and 2.13 (*traditione maiorum*).

96. The tendency of E to correct is pointed out by Augustin Genestout, 'Le plus ancien témoin manuscrit de la Règle du Maître: Le *Parisinus Latin 12634*,' *Scriptorium* 1 (1946-1947) 136. In this respect see a fact we brought to light in RM 1:82 (Chapter Two, n. 71).

97. Deut 32:7 likewise figures in *Apophthegmata patrum* Alphabetic series: Antony 37 (PG 65:88b); R Bas Prol. (PL 103:487a); R Col M 9 (Walker, 138, 8); R Wal 2.

98. There is probably a crescendo in marks 6-8: mark 6 aims at inculcating effacement—one shuns making oneself singular; mark 7 goes a step further: *omni uilitate contentus... uelut operarium malum;* mark 8 advances further still: *cunctis inferiorem... intimo cordis affectu.* Carrying mark 6 over to the eighth rung obliterates this gradation.

99. The remark has already been made by Capelle, 'Les oeuvres de Jean Cassien et la Règle bénédictine', 311-314. One sees how much light the comparative study of RM 7 and 10 sheds on this information.

100. RB 6:6. RB has again utilized this sentence, completely changing the meaning, in treating the council of the brethren (RB 3:6). See above, Chapter Three, n. 26.

101. In this respect, note the substitution of *abbatem* for *seniorem* at the fifth rung. For Cassian, the director to whom this word of advice is addressed is the *praepositus* or the captain of a deanry (*Inst* 4.7-9. Cf. RM 15:12). This is the person designated here by the word *senior*. The Master prefers *abbas* because in his eyes the provosts are simply executive agents of the abbot, who alone is the artisan of the monastery's spiritual life. This dependency of the provost on the abbot is not stated precisely by Cassian. At the third rung, similarly, *maior* replaces the *senior* of the third mark, and the Master does not fail to specify subsequently that the abbot is meant (RM 10:51). See below, Chapter Five.

102. Bernard Capelle formulates some useful remarks on this point in his article 'Les oeuvres de Jean Cassien et la Règle bénédictine', pp 311-314.

103. 'Cassien, le Maître et S. Benoît', RTAM 11 (1939) 110-118.

104. Cf. Cassian: *ad omnia se... iudicarit indignum.* The Master adds an *et* in front of the *indignum*, which unfortunately makes it an epithet of *operarium* instead of an attribute of *se: ad omnia uelut operarium malum se iudicet et indignum.* This *et* is probably a reduplication of the final letters of *iudicet*.

105. Cf. Cassian, *Inst* 4.13-14. In a narrative of Gregory (*Dial.* 4.57; Moricca, 319, 2), *estrema quaeque et uilia* = the least objects the monks had for their use.

106. See n. 104. The three mss of RM have this reading which must have been introduced early.

107. This notion of the abbot-'vicar' of Christ penetrated the second pericope of the Master (*uice Dei*, RM 7:64).

108. Mt 26:39-42. Cf. RM Thp 35-39; this word of Christ in agony casts light on Jn 6:38, cited so often by RM, as well as on Mt 6:10. The obedience of Christ in his passion is evoked again with the aid of Phil 2:8. Cf. RM 10:49.

109. In the first pericope: *uoluntatem propriam deserentes* (7:7); in the second: *a uoluntatibus tuis auertere* (7:46, citing Qo 18:30, and summarizing the entire criticism of self-will: 7:38-46).

110. 7:5, 68 (Lk 10:16), 64 (*uice Dei*).

111. *Inst* 4.8-9.

112. These two aspects of obedience described by *Inst* 4.8-9 are arranged in the same order by *Inst* 4.39. The first mark (*si mortificatas in sese omnes habeat uoluntates*) corresponds to *Inst* 4.8; marks 2-3 describe direction (the avowal of the brother and the judgment of the elder) and pick up *Inst* 4.9.

In *Inst* 12.29 the two themes betray themselves once again in the final 'marks of pride', but in that text they are, on the contrary, blended together without any well-defined plan.

113. *Conf* 2.14-15.

114. *Conf* 19.6.6. Phil 2:8 is likewise cited by *Inst* 12.28 in the same context. Cassian interprets *usque ad mortem* in a temporal sense. 'Unto death' does not mean for him the ultimate abasement of Christ, as it does in the pauline text, but the last moment of human life, which is the end towards which obedience should reach. *Usque ad mortem* is thus opposed to *pro tempore*, and becomes a byword for the 'stability' of the monk.

115. *Conf* 19.8.3.

116. *Conf* 24.26.13-14.

117. See above, n. 108.

118. *Inst* 4.10. Cf. 4.27.4: *uelut a Domino sibi esset praeceptum*.

119. *Inst* 4.24.3 (*ueneratione solita*); 4.26 (*pro reuerentia senis*); 4.10 (*pro senioris reuerentia*).

120. *Inst* 4.10 (*fides ac deuotio*); 4.24 (*feruore fidei et oboedientiae*); 4.28 (*fides atque deuotio*).

121. Preface to the *Inst*, 8; *Inst* 1.2; 2.2-6; 7.17-18; *Conf* 18.5; 21.29-30.

122. See above, Chapter Two, Appendix, n. 187. The text of Jerome is particularly significant: *Hoc totum quare dico? Ut oboedientiam exhibeamus in patres nostros. Qui patribus non obsequitur, Deo non obsequitur. Dicit enim Deus: qui uos contemnit, me contemnit. Qui ergo contemnit apostolos, contemnit Christum: qui contemnit patres, contemnit Christum, qui in patribus est (De oboedientia*, Morin, *Anecd. Mareds.* III/2, p 398). The *patres* of whom Jerome is speaking here are, according to his monastic terminology, the superiors of *coenobia*. He explicitly assimilates them to the 'apostles' whom Christ addressed in Lk 10:16. In fact, these words of Christ are addressed to the seventy-two disciples, but it did not occur to Jerome, any more than it had to the Master, to capitalize upon this fact, which could diminish the parallel between apostles and abbots. He evinces no difficulty over the legitimacy of applying this text to monastic superiors who are not by right, and often not in fact, members of the hierarchy and successors to the apostles.

123. Cf. St Thomas, *Summa Theol.* II^a II^{ae}, qu. 86, art. 5.

124. Above, Chapter Two, p 106.

125. The theme seems to go back to Philo, *De nobilitate* 3-4. From him it passed to Clement of Alexandria (*Stromates* 2.19.99), Basil (*De Spiritu Sancto*, Ch. 20), Ambrose (*Ep* 37.8), and Theodoret (*Discourses on Providence* 7 and 8).

126. Basil, *De Spiritu Sancto,* 20 (trans, by R.J. Deferrari).

127. This exegesis of the Esau story is at the root of all the texts cited in note 125, except that of Theodoret.

128. So too the catechesis of Pachomius (CSCO 160, p 6, 1.17-22): 'If you cannot manage alone, attach yourself to someone who is laboring according to the Gospel of Christ, and you will progress with him. Either be a good listener, *or else submit yourself to someone who is.* Either be so strong as to be called an Elijah, or *else obey those who are strong,* so that you be called an Elisha: for having obeyed Elijah, he received a double share of the Spirit of God'.

129. *Inst* 5.4.1.

130. Faustus, *Serm.* (Eus. 37; PL 50:839C-840A.

131. *Vies Coptes,* p 267ff. (S 5, n. 120-121), and pp 176-178 (Boharic 105).

132. VP 5.14.19.

133. In this sense complete our commentary on RB One, p 51.

134. Cassian, *Inst* 12. Jerome, *De oboed.* (*Anecd. Mareds.* III/2, pp 398-401).

135. *De oboed.* (*Anecd.* p 399, 1-10 and 400, 1-6).

136. Such is at least one of the plausible interpretations of *Inst* 4.8.

137. Compare the terminology of Cassian in *Inst* 4.8 and 4.38. Both texts speak of 'mortifying self-will', but the first particularly envisages obedience, the second describes the whole monastic life generally. The second is fully summarized in the first. The Master also talks in the same terms ('not to do one's own will') either about christian life in general (Thp 24-53) or about monastic obedience in particular (RM 10, second rung).

138. This sort of 'self-will' — independence in spiritual matters — is hounded out by Basil (R Bas 88, 89, 181, 184 etc.); Cassian (*Conf* 18.3-8); RM (74 and 22:5-8) RB (43:19; 49:8-10).

139. See above, n. 133.

140. RM 7; 10; 90.

141. Cf. Cassian, *Inst* 4.24: *superflua, minusque necessaria uel inpossibilia; Inst* 4.25: *ineptia praecepti... inpossibilitate praecepti... in cassum ac sine ratione.* Concerning the obedient disciple, Cassian also speaks of 'foolhardiness' (*Inst* 4.41.3 — cf. 1 Cor 3:18). The observation has been made that St Benedict, in the case of 'impossibility', speaks altogether differently: instead of flinging himself into the performance of the order, the inferior is invited to 'suggest' the reasons for his inability to the superior (RB 68; cf. Capelle, 'Les oeuvres de Jean Cassien et la Règle bénédictine', pp 316-319). It is surely true that St Benedict, treading in the footsteps of Basil, here introduced something not mentioned by Cassian which endows his doctrine of obedience with a new depth (see below, Chapter Nine). But, granted this, can one say he tacitly disapproves of the former practice, the 'over-naive heroism' demanded by Cassian? Actually, Cassian is describing here the ideal type realized in faraway Egypt, and Benedict is legislating for the monks of his own monastery. This alone could account for the difference in tone, even if there were not also a sure reference to R Bas 69. The 'rare and discerning independence' of St Benedict, therefore, is instead dependence on a different source. Moreover, in taking over RM 7 and 10, the RB writer demonstrated the case he was making for Cassian's theories.

142. The expression *bonum oboedientiae,* previously utilized by Cassian (*Inst* 4.30 and 12.31), figures in RB just where it recommends mutual obedience (RB 71:1 — see the commentary on RB 63-72). Cassian, furthermore, also recommends mutual obedience, basing himself on the same texts which, for him, ground obedience to the superior (Jn 6:38; Mt 26:39. Cf. *Conf* 16.6.4).

143. RB 71:2.

144. See below, Chapter Nine.

145. Cf. H.M. Féret OP, *Sur la terre comme au ciel* (Paris: Cerf, 1953) 44-72 and 88-91.

146. A response to Féret has been made by Henri Holstein SJ, 'Le mystère de l'obéissance', in *Etudes* 278 (1953/III) 145-156.

147. Cf. RM 58:14-16: the refusal of a brother to make a trip *pro actibus monasterii* is reprimanded with the aid of Lk 10:16.

148. Herwegen, *Sinn und Geist*, pp 108-109. This altogether modern mystique of the community, as opposed to individualism, should not be confused with the accent which Basil and Gregory of Nyssa tended to put on serving the 'brotherhood' as a whole. Cf. *De Instituto Christiano*, pp 67-68: the brother ought to consider himself 'a slave of Christ bought for the common good of the brotherhood' (cf. Cassian, *Inst* 4.14 and 19).

149. Nevertheless, RB developed a theory of 'horizontal' relationships in its last chapters. See below, Chapter Nine.

ABBREVIATIONS

Whenever possible, reference is made to the *Clavis Patrum Latinorum* (*Sacris Erudiri* 3. Steenbrugge, 1951), in which reference to the text may be found.

I. MONASTIC RULES

RB
: *Sancti Benedicti Regula Monachorum,* ed. Cuthbert Butler. Third edition, Freiburg im Breisgau, 1935.

RM
: *La Règle du Maître, édition diplomatique des manuscrits latins 12205 et 12634 de Paris,* ed. H. Vanderhoven and F. Masai. Brussels-Paris, 1953. The following symbols designate manuscripts of RM:
: A   Monacensis latinus 28118.
: E   Parisinus latinus 12634.
: P   Parisinus latinus 12205.

R Aug
: *Regula Augustini,* ed. De Bruyne in *Revue Bénédictine* 1930, pp 320-326. (*Clavis* 1839). The *Ordo monasterii* (*Rev Ben* 1930, pp 318-319) is indicated by OM.

R Aur M
: *Regula Aureliani ad monachos.* PL 68, 385-398 (*Clavis* 1844).

R Aur V
: *Regula Aureliani ad virgines.* PL 68, 399-406 (*Clavis* 1845).

R Bas
: *Regula Basilii.* PL 103, 487-554. Special symbols designate:
: LR (Long Rule) *Regulae fusius tractatae.* PG 31, 889-1052
: SR (Short Rule) *Regulae brevius tractatae.* PG 31, 1051-1306.

R Caes M
: *Regula Caesarii ad monachos.* PL 67. 1099-1103 (*Clavis* 1012)

R Caes V
: *Regula Caesarii ad virgines,* ed. G. Morin in *Sancti Carsarii Arelatensis Opera Omnia,* 2 (1942) (*Clavis* 1009).

R Col C   *Regula Columbani coenobialis,* ed. G.S.M.
                 Walker, in *Sancti Columbani opera.* Dublin,
                 1957, pp 142-168 (*Clavis* 1109).
R Col M   *Regula Columbani monachorum,* ed. Walker,
                 pp 122-142 (*Clavis* 1108).
R Cui   *Regula cuiusdam.* PL 66, 987-994 (*Clavis* 1862).
R Fer   *Regula Ferreoli.* PL 66, 959-976 (*Clavis* 1849).
R Fruc I   *Regula Fructuosi Complutensis.* PL 86, 1099-1110
                 (*Clavis* 1869).
R Fruc II   *Regula Fructuosi communis.* PL 87, 1111-1127
                 (*Clavis* 1870).
R Is   *Regula Isidori.* PL 83, 867-894 (*Clavis* 1868).
R Mac   *Regula Macarii.* PL 103, 447-454 (*Clavis* 1842[1]).
R Or   *Regula Orientalis.* PL 103, 477-484 (*Clavis*
                 1840[2]).
R Pat 2   *Regula Patrum.* PL 103, 441-444.
R Pat 3   *Regula Patrum.* PL 103, 443-446.
R 4 Pat   *Regula Serapionis, Macarii, Paphnutii, et alterius
                 Macarii,* ed. D. Vanderhoven, *La Règle du
                 Maître* (Brussels-Paris, 1953) pp 125-132. (*Clavis*
                 1859).
R Pac   *Regula Pachomii.* A. Boon, *Pachomiana Latina,*
                 Louvain, 1932:
                 Pr   *Praecepta.*
                 Inst   *Praecepta et Instituta.*
                 Iud   *Praecepta atque Iudicia.*
                 Leg   *Praecepta ac Leges.*
R Tar   *Regula Tarnatensis.* PL 66, 977-986 (*Clavis*
                 1851).
R Wal   *Regula Waldeberti.* PL 88, 1053-1070 (*Clavis*
                 1863).
Conc.   *Concordia Regularum Patrum* of Benedict of
                 Aniane. PL 103, 713-1380.

Notes to abbreviations I

1. On the similarities between this Rule and R Pat 2, R Pat 4, and R 4 Pat, see A.
Mundó, "Les anciens synodes abbatiaux et les 'Regulae SS. Patrum' ", *Regula
Magistri-Regula S. Benedicti.* Studia Anselmiana 44 (Rome, 1959) 107-125.

2. In large part, this rule is a cento of R Pac. See C. de Clercq, 'L'influence de la
Règle de saint Pachôme en Occident', *Mélanges Louis Halphen* (Paris, 1951)
169-176. de Clercq includes tables of the correspondence between the two texts.

II. LIVES

Vita Antonii	Antony the Egyptian. PG 26, 835-976.
Vita Caesarii	Caesarius of Arles. PL 67, 1001-1042 (*Clavis* 1018).
Vita Fulgentii	Fulgence of Ruspe. PL 65, 117-150 (*Clavis* 847).
Vita Honorati	Honoratus, the founder of Lérins. PL 50, 1249-1272 (*Clavis* 501).
Vita Hilarii	Hilary of Arles. PL 50, 1219-1246 (*Clavis* 506).
Vita Martini	Martin of Tours. PL 20, 159-176 (*Clavis* 475).
Vies Coptes	*Les Vies Coptes de saint Pachôme et de ses premiers successeurs*, tr. L. Th. Lefort (Louvain, 1943).
VP	*Vitae Patrum.* PL 73-74.
Greg Tur VP	Gregory of Tours, *Vitae Patrum.* PL 71, 1009-1097.
HL	Palladius, *Histoire Lausiaque*, ed. Lucot (Paris, 1912) ET by Robert T. Meyer, *Palladius, The Lausiac History* Ancient Christian Writers 34 (1965).
HM	*Historia Monachorum.* PL 21, 387-462 (*Clavis* 198).
HR	Theodoret, *Historia Religiosa.* PG 82, 1284-1496.

III. ASCETICAL WORKS

Conf	Cassian, *Conferences (Conlationes)*, ed. E. Pichery. Sources chrétiennes 42, 54, 64 (Paris, 1955-1959) (*Clavis* 512).
Inst.	Cassian, *De Institutis coenobiorum*, ed. M. Petschenig. CSEL 17 (Vienna, 1888) (*Clavis* 513).
Cassiod. Inst.	Cassiodorus, *Institutiones.* PL 70, 1105-1150 (*Clavis* 906).
Caes Serm	Caesarius of Arles, *Sermons*, ed. G. Morin. CC 103-104 (Turnhout, 1953). N.B. *Sermons* 233-237 in particular were addressed to monks.
Dial.	Gregory the Great, *Dialogues*, ed. Moricca (Rome, 1924)
Faustus	Faustus of Riez, *Sermones ad monachos:* Serm. 35-44. PL 50, 833-859 (*Clavis* 966). In parenthesis we indicate the number of the sermon in the collection of Pseudo-Eusebius. For *Sermon 43*, given by Maximus of Riez, see Schott, *Bibliotheca Maxima Patrum* (Lyon 1677) Vol. 6, pp 654-656.
Greg Letters	Gregory the Great, *Letters*, PL 77 (*Clavis* 1714).

Greg Nys. De Inst Christ.	*Gregorii Nysseni opera,* Vol. 8, *pars* I: *De Instituto Christiano,* ed. Werner Jaeger (Leiden, 1952).
Lib Ors	*Liber Oriesii,* in *Pachomiana Latina,* ed. A. Boon (Louvain, 1932) 109-147.

IV. SERIES AND PERIODICALS

AS	*Acta Sanctorum* (Bollandists).
AS OSB	*Acta Sanctorum Ordinis S. Benedicti,* edd. L. d'Achery and J. Mabillon, 9 vols. Paris, 1668-1701.
CC	*Corpus Christianorum.* Turnhout, Belgium.
Coll OCR	*Collectanea Ordinis Cistercium Reformatorum.* Westmalle, Belgium.
CS	*Cistercian Studies Series.* Spencer-Kalamazoo. 1969-.
CSCO	*Corpus Scriptorum Christianorum Orientalium.* Louvain-Washington D.C.
CSEL	*Corpus Scriptorum Ecclesiasticorum Latinorum.* Vienna.
DACL	*Dictionnaire d'Archéologie chrétienne et de Liturgie.* Paris.
DHGE	*Dictionnaire d'Histoire et de Géographie ecclésiastiques.* Paris.
Dict. Spir.	*Dictionnaire de Spiritualité.* Paris
DThC	*Dictionnaire de Théologie Catholique.* Paris.
PG	Migne, *Patrologia Graeca.* Paris 1855-
PL	Migne, *Patrologia Latina.* Paris 1855-
PO	Graffin-Nau, *Patrologia Orientalis.*
RAM	*Revue d'Ascétique et de Mystique.* Toulouse.
Rev Ben	*Revue Bénédictine.* Maredsous.
REL	*Revue des Etudes Latines.* Paris.
RHE	*Revue d'Histoire ecclésiastique.* Louvain.
RLM	*Revue liturgique et monastique.* Maredsous.
RMAL	*Revue du Moyen-âge latin.* Paris.
RTAM	*Recherches de Théologie ancienne et médiévale.* Louvain.
SCh	*Sources chrétiennes.* Paris: Cerf. 1941-.
Stud. Patr.	*Studia Patristica,* edd. K. Aland and F.L. Cross, 2 vols. Berlin, 1957.

Scriptural citations have been made acording to the enumeration and nomenclature of the *Jerusalem Bible.*

CISTERCIAN PUBLICATIONS INC.

Titles Listing

THE CISTERCIAN FATHERS SERIES

THE WORKS OF BERNARD OF CLAIRVAUX

THE WORKS OF WILLIAM OF SAINT THIERRY

THE WORKS OF AELRED OF RIEVAULX

THE WORKS OF GILBERT OF HOYLAND

OTHER EARLY CISTERCIAN WRITERS

THE CISTERCIAN STUDIES SERIES

EARLY MONASTIC TEXTS

CHRISTIAN SPIRITUALITY

MONASTIC STUDIES

CISTERCIAN STUDIES

STUDIES BY DOM JEAN LECLERCQ

THOMAS MERTON

FAIRACRES PRESS, OXFORD

PROJECTED FOR 1979—1980

*   out of print
t   tentative